Seedbeds of Virtue

Seedbeds of Virtue

Sources of Competence, Character, and Citizenship in American Society

EDITED BY

Mary Ann Glendon

AND

David Blankenhorn

MADISON BOOKS
Lanham • New York • London

Published by Madison Books
4720 Boston Way
Lanham, Maryland 20706

3 Henrietta Street
London WC2E 8LU England

Distributed by National Book Network

The paper used in this publication meets the minimum
requirements of American National Standard for
Information Sciences—Permanence of Paper for
Printed Library Materials, ANSI Z39.48–1984. ∞™

Manufactured in the United States of America

Library of Congress Cataloging-in-Publication Data

Seedbeds of virtue : sources of competence, character, and citizenship
/ edited by Mary Ann Glendon and David Blankenhorn.
p.   cm.
Includes bibliographical references and index.
1. Citizenship—United States.   2. Civil society—United States.
3. United States—Moral conditions.   4. Family—United States.
I. Glendon, Mary Ann   II. Blankenhorn, David.
JK1759.S44   1995   303.3'72—dc20   95-32344   CIP

ISBN 1–56833–046–4 (cloth: alk. paper)

Contents

Acknowledgments

The editors wish to thank the Board of Directors and financial supporters of the Institute for American Values for sponsoring the "Seedbeds of Virtue" project of which this book is a result. In particular, we wish to thank the Carthage Foundation for its generous financial support. We are also grateful to Harvard University for hosting the project's original conference in Cambridge in December of 1992.

In addition to the authors whose essays appear in this book, we are grateful to Amitai Etzioni, Nathan Glazer, Heather Richardson Higgins, Lawrence Mead, Vesna Neskow, Father Richard John Neuhaus, David Riesman, James Skillen, Christina Hoff Sommers, Sara Baumgartner Thurow, and Barbara Dafoe Whitehead for their important participation in our discussions and for their valuable comments on these essays.

For editorial help and guidance, we are deeply grateful to Vesna Neskow and Deborah Strubel as well as to Jon Sisk and his colleagues at Madison Books.

This book is part of a larger conference and publication series sponsored by the Institute for American Values on the topics of family well-being, family policy, and civil society. For a publication list or for more information, contact the Institute for American Values at 1841 Broadway, Suite 211, New York, New York 10023. Phone: (212) 246-3942. Fax: (212) 541-6665.

Forgotten Questions

Mary Ann Glendon

Families, Virtue, and Citizenship

Seedbeds of Virtue represents the joint efforts of a group of observers of American family life to initiate the development of more
comprehensive, coherent, and useful ways of thinking, speaking,
and acting on family issues. It is widely recognized that the deteriorating circumstances of child-raising households in the United
States amount to a major national crisis, and that the country as a
whole cannot remain unaffected by the fact that record proportions
of children are being raised in fatherless homes under conditions of
social and material deprivation. But what, precisely, is the nature
of that crisis? The standard responses to that question, across the
political spectrum, are that many of the nation's children will never
have a chance to develop their full potential as human beings, that
the quality of the nation's work force will suffer (with adverse consequences for our social security system and our competitive position in the world economy), and that crime and delinquency will
spiral ever more wildly out of control. Those responses are accurate, but incomplete. For the state of the nation's child-raising families is also importantly linked to the fate of the American
experiment in liberal democracy.

Americans, though, have tended to forget that their version of
democracy *is* an experiment, one that requires (as the authors of
The Federalist Papers put it) a higher degree of virtue in its citizens
than any other form of government.[1] As a result, we have neglected

a basic problem of politics—how to foster in the nation's citizens the skills and virtues that are essential to the maintenance of our democratic regime. *Seedbeds of Virtue* aims to place that forgotten problem at the front and center of American public deliberation.

If history teaches us anything, it is that liberal democracy cannot be taken for granted. There are conditions that are more, or less, favorable to liberty, equality, and self-government; and those conditions involve the character and competence of citizens and public servants. But character and competence, too, have conditions, residing in nurture and education. The American version of the democratic experiment leaves it primarily up to families, local governments, schools, religious and workplace associations, and a host of other voluntary groups to teach and transmit republican virtues and skills from one generation to the next. First and foremost among these "seedbeds of virtue" is the family. Thus, impairment of the family's capacity to develop in its members the qualities of self-restraint, respect for others, and sturdy independence of mind cannot help but impair the prospects for a regime of ordered liberty.

The stakes are high, for as Alexis de Tocqueville pointed out, if democratic nations should fail in "imparting to all citizens those ideas and sentiments which first prepare them for freedom and then allow them to enjoy it, there will be no independence left for anybody." Tocqueville took for granted that, in America, many of the requisite habits and beliefs would be taught and transmitted within families—chiefly by women, who were the main teachers of children and the "keepers of orderly peaceful homes." Like many of his contemporaries, he regarded the family as one of the few remaining institutions that could effectively moderate individual greed, selfishness, and ambition. James Madison, though, had already cautioned in *The Federalist Papers* that no one could foresee what changes might take place in the "political character" of Americans with the passage of years and with increases in the size and diversity of the population.[2]

Madison's prudence was justified. Enormous strains were placed on families and their surrounding networks of small-scale institutions by geographic mobility, the rise and decay of great cities, the atrophy of local government, and the dependence of most of the population on wage work and governmental largesse. Family life has been transformed in ways that neither the Founders nor Tocqueville could have anticipated. The family farms and businesses where parents and children once cooperated in common enterprises have been almost totally replaced by wage-work outside the home. Beginning in the 1960s, divorce rates, births outside marriage, and the labor force participation of mothers of young children rose steeply. At about the same time that demographic indicators began to give warnings of acute trouble in family life, there were similar signs of disturbance in schools, neighborhoods, churches, local governments, and workplace associations—institutions that have traditionally depended on families for their support, and that in turn have served as important resources for families—especially in times of stress.

The authors of *Seedbeds of Virtue* are in accord that the simultaneous weakening of child-raising families and their surrounding and supporting institutions constitutes our culture's most serious long-term problem. They are united, too, in the belief that the country's social resources, like its natural resources, can no longer be taken for granted. As in the case of natural resources, America in its early years was blessed with abundance. Now, as a mature nation, we are beginning to realize that we cannot indefinitely consume our social capital without replenishing it. What lends particular poignancy to the present situation, though, is that—as with the natural environment—many threats to the social environment are the by-products of genuine improvements in the general standard of living—technological advances, social welfare programs, and increased opportunities for individual self-determination. The crucial question is: How can we preserve and pursue the social, economic, and political goods of a liberal regime without eroding or destroying its cultural foundations?

What Skills? Which Virtues?

The American framers believed that republican governments, more than any other form, required certain kinds of excellence in their citizens and leaders. In the first place, a regime of self-government must have an adequate supply of citizens who are skilled in the arts of self-government—deliberation, compromise, consensus-building, civility, reason-giving. Of equal importance, a regime of ordered liberty demands certain character traits in its citizens. If liberty is not to degenerate into license, citizens have to learn to exercise their own freedoms responsibly and to respect the liberties of their neighbors. As if those skills and virtues were not enough to master, the ante was raised when subsequent generations of Americans made even more audacious commitments than the Founders. With the Civil War Amendments, the United States set out on the path toward a more inclusive society, making tolerance a more important civic virtue than ever. With the social legislation of the 1930s, we undertook a collective responsibility for the welfare of the poorest and most vulnerable among us—a commitment which asks citizens, on the one hand, to accept a certain responsibility for others in need and, on the other, to assume as much responsibility as possible for their own needs and the needs of their immediate dependents.

For a time, it seemed as though Americans could have it all—ever-enlarging spheres of liberty and equality, individual freedom, plus freedom from want sustained by habits and beliefs that held human appetites in check. But as James Q. Wilson points out in this volume's opening essay, the convictions that undergird those habits have seriously eroded. The hermeneutics of suspicion have trickled down from the coffee-houses and the academy to the kitchen table and the playground. We are all post-modernists now. While expressing confidence in "the capacity of a free society to sustain what is truly human and to correct its own errors," Wilson does not underrate the gravity of the cultural challenges currently facing the United States.

Politically, what is at stake is nothing less than the great question of whether a self-governing republic can exist in an extended territory with a heterogeneous population. The classical political philosophers doubted it. The framers of the American Constitution wagered it could be done. Today we struggle to vindicate the faith of the founders under immensely more difficult conditions than they could have imagined. Meanwhile, notes Wilson, "Abroad, our critics watch and wait." As do our friends.

The prospects will improve, Wilson claims, if "all of us, but especially the intellectuals, recognize that the exercise of freedom presupposes the maintenance of . . . an order that arises from the familial seedbeds of virtue." But how to raise the notion of "seedbeds" in an electronic public square from which complexity and a sense of the long-term are virtually absent? And how to deliberate "virtue" in the postmodern academy?

Words like "virtue" and "character" have nearly disappeared from the lexicon of the modern human sciences. Thus an important contribution of William Galston has been to explain why (contrary to what many of his fellow political theorists have claimed) liberalism cannot do without virtue. With his differentiated analysis of the various types of virtues, Galston also helps to clarify which virtues, in particular, are needed to support and sustain the American version of the democratic experiment. A liberal regime like ours, he points out, needs the general virtues required by every political community (courage, law-abidingness, loyalty), but in addition requires certain virtues specific to itself. Because our regime emphasizes individual liberty, we need citizens who are independent, moderate in their demands, and able to discern and respect the rights of others. Our great diversity places a premium on tolerance. Our economic system relies on the work ethic and the ability to postpone gratification.

Having argued that "the health of liberal polities is intertwined in complex ways with the practice of . . . the liberal virtues," Galston poses the key question: "By what means are they to be engendered?" He identifies three positions, each with significant grounding in the literature: life in the liberal polity itself is sufficient to habituate the citizens to the liberal virtues; the liberal virtues must be actively fostered by the institutions of liberal society; liberal culture may actually tend to undermine the very virtues it requires. Galston refrains from accepting or rejecting any of these hypotheses in its entirety, observing, wisely, that the question is an empirical one and that the available evidence is mixed. He concludes, however, with two empirically grounded observations: families play an especially important role in the formation of American citizens, and the breakdown of the family in recent decades has jeopardized the well-being of the entire nation.

While Galston approaches the question of civic virtue from the lofty vantage point of political theory, Judith Martin (also known as Miss Manners) examines the matter from the ground up. Her illuminating discussion of "the oldest virtue" suggests that "ordinary" civility may be the indispensable precondition to the acquisition of civic skills and virtues. Etiquette, she argues eloquently, is not a frill, but the very prototype of the art of communal living. Though her starting point is distant from Galston's, they meet in the same place: the family home. "No one," she writes, "has yet come up with a satisfactory substitute for family etiquette training in the earliest years of life to foster the development of the child in such manners principles as consideration, cooperation, loyalty, respect, and to teach the child such etiquette techniques as settling disputes through face-saving compromise."

Like Galston, Martin discerns troubling implications in the social changes of the past few decades. The decline in socially cooperative behavior, she warns, cannot be compensated for by an increase in legal commands and prohibitions. The increasing attempt to "legalize" areas once regulated by social norm systems is not only ineffective to restoring civility, but is itself a symptom of disorder in the body social. Whether by the high road of political theory or through the everyday path of good manners, we come, therefore, to the institutions where men and women learn—or fail to learn—to control their basic impulses and to cooperate in orderly, peaceful living: the seedbeds of virtue.

The Seedbeds

In the early years of the republic, the sources of character, competence, and citizenship must have seemed to be self-sustaining, or nearly so. Four-fifths of the non-slave population was self-employed in family farms or businesses, and the township form of government, plus a host of other small-scale associations, afforded numerous opportunities for cooperative, participatory activity. As urbanization and industrialization proceeded, the family and its traditional surrounding institutions—schools, neighborhoods, religious organizations—showed considerable resilience and ability to adapt to new circumstances. New institutions like political parties and workers' associations took rise and flourished for a time. Over the past thirty years, though, all of these groups have shown signs of distress.

David Popenoe points to the irony that just as we have begun to know more than ever about the childrearing conditions that foster competence and character, those conditions are "being eroded before our very eyes." It has long been recognized that a strong, interactive family life is the optimal environment for children's flourishing, and it is now well-understood that our society is experiencing a serious decline in family stability. What is less well-understood, as Popenoe points out, is the fact that "to be strong, a family requires a supportive environment of its own." In a bravura demonstration of the utility of a more "ecological" approach to family studies, Popenoe relates the decline in family life to the decline of neighborhoods and communities. He not only shows how these developments are mutually conditioning, but points to the frequent failures of planners and social engineers to consider the potentially harmful side-effects of their decisions and actions. He concludes that "to improve the conditions for childrearing in America today, nothing may be more important than trying to protect and cultivate those natural, tribal- or village-like communities that still remain—communities which have families as their basic building blocks, and in which a mix of people through free association and sets of relational networks maintain a common life." That proposal, Popenoe recognizes, is radical and controversial. Yet, as he points out, "There is no evidence that realistic social alternatives exist for the traditional 'tribal' structures of family and community."

Support for Popenoe's analysis and for the feasibility of his proposal is provided by Don Browning's account of the role of the Apostolic Church of God in Chicago's Woodlawn neighborhood, one of that city's worst urban slums. The vitality of that church and the remarkable efforts of its pastor to restore family life, control teenage gangs, improve public education, and restore economic health to the community merit further study. What factors have made the Apostolic Church "Woodlawn's most powerful force for social reconstruction"? Could its successes be replicated? How could similar reconstructions be fostered elsewhere?

At the same time that the seedbeds of civic virtue have been eroding, the nation also has lost many of the arenas where citizens traditionally have acquired and practiced the skills of self-government. The township form of government, so admired by Tocqueville, has long been reduced to relative ineffectiveness. The voluntary organizations that dot the American landscape subsist increasingly on money contributions, rather than on the time and effort, of their members. Political parties and labor organizations, which once afforded many Americans opportunities to develop civic skills, have lost much of their former vitality.

Though workplace associations have declined, Thomas Kohler points out that the workplace has become the primary social arena for most Americans. It is where men and women spend most of their waking hours when they are not with their families. And it is at work that many citizens now form their opinions and engage in deliberation concerning the issues of the day. The decline of unions and collective bargaining, therefore, cannot be analyzed in purely economic terms. Nor can it be mere coincidence, Kohler argues, that the art of associating began to decline in the workplace at the same time that it was deteriorating elsewhere in the society. Like Popenoe, Kohler effectively deploys an ecological approach to connect the state of workers' organizations to the condition of neighborhoods and family life and to declines in church membership and attendance. Americans are not only losing the arts of associating but are abandoning the habits that sustain the conditions for acquiring those arts.

America's varied seedbeds of character, competence, and citizenship—families, schools, communities, religious organizations, the workplace, and hosts of other small-scale associations—thus seem to be in precarious condition. Contrary to what earlier generations may have thought, these social institutions are not like gravity—ever present and the same, keeping us grounded, steady, and attached to our surroundings. They are, as the seedbed metaphor suggests, more like topsoil—of varying richness and subject to erosion. Statesmen and public philosophers, therefore, need to think more "ecologically" about character and competence and the institutions that foster the skills and virtues required by liberal welfare democracies.

Social Ecology

The problem is that ecology is in its tentative and experimental stages, and we know even less about the dynamics of social environments than we do about natural environments. Still, a tentative approach is better than a bankrupt one. Alan Wolfe has called attention to the serious weakness in currently dominant models of social thought and policy analysis. Standard economic and political analysis, by concentrating on the individual, the market, and the state, tends to block out the seedbeds of civic virtue. By ignoring the institutions that compose the fine texture of civil society, prevailing modes of analysis not only impede the development of creative responses to America's most pressing problems, they tend to obscure the relationships among those problems that have been usefully identified by many of the writers in *Seedbeds of Virtue*. A number of the contributors in this monograph, including Wolfe, have been engaged in developing more holistic approaches—both to the understanding and to the management of contemporary social and political problems. Those converging efforts seem to be on the right track. For if democratic states need individual citizens with an array of qualities that—so far as we know—can best be nurtured within interactive and reasonably stable families; if families, in order to function effectively, need to be composed of individuals capable of commitment and supported by communities of various sorts; and if the health of communities in turn depends on certain kinds of individuals and families; then, an ecological perspective is essential.

A shared assumption of the writers of *Seedbeds of Virtue* is that what is valuable in human societies is not likely to endure unless it is tended and nurtured.[3] Their common dilemma is that, though we know a good deal about what nurtures human beings in infancy and childhood, we know much less about what promotes or impairs the health of the nurturing institutions themselves—the family and other seedbeds. The strength of the ecological approaches is thus also their weakness—their reach exceeds their grasp.

That weakness is not fatal, but it does have certain methodological implications for both research and policy making. A "Seedbeds Guide for the Perplexed Gardener" would counsel the need for new types of research—directed less toward investigating the pathology of individuals and groups and more toward the discovery of what it is that helps certain individuals and groups (like the Assembly of God Church described by Browning) to flourish against all odds and expectations.[4] Researchers and policy makers alike must learn to be attentive to indirect and unintended effects, and to the problem of what the new science of complexity calls sensitive dependence on initial conditions.

Recognizing how little we know about social environments, an ecological approach to policy would proceed modestly, preferring limited, local experiments and small-scale pilots to broad, standardized top-down programs. Regulatory techniques need to be reimagined, for ham-fisted regulation is not the only alternative to hands-off laissez-faire. Regulatory intervention can take the form of promoting self-organization and private-ordering (as under the American labor laws of the 1930s) or protecting pockets of social diversity (unpopular religious groups, single sex schools) or helping parents to regain control over the education of their children (as in school choice plans). In many cases, abstinence from regulation will be the best environmental policy. Where social services like health care, education, and child care are concerned, it will often be the case that smaller seedbed institutions (religious groups, workplace associations) can deliver them better, more economically, and more humanely than state bureaucracies. Reawakened interest in federalism and in the principle of subsidiarity (assigning social tasks to the smallest social unit that can perform them adequately) are encouraging signs of a shift toward more creative use of the mediating structures of civil society.

Renewing the Seedbeds

As in the case of natural ecological systems, the possibility exists that certain processes of social decline have progressed beyond repair. The contributors to this book have varying degrees of optimism on this point. They all acknowledge that circumstances impose constraints on the possibilities of renewing the seedbeds of virtue. Given that substantial uncertainty surrounds the nature and extent of those constraints, however, no one in the group regards the efforts to shift probabilities in a more favorable direction as useless.

To revitalize the fragile structures of civil society, however, would involve nothing less ambitious than reshaping the large economic and political structures that impose constraints on, and offer possibilities to, families and their surrounding institutions. At least, that is the position of William Sullivan, who nevertheless suggests that we may be living in a historical "moment" when those large structures are in such a state of flux that opportunities do exist to shift conditions in a direction more favorable to the development of the social environments that human flourishing requires. With the end of the cold war, the world economy and regional political structures are changing rapidly. In this new atmosphere, Sullivan speculates, civic virtue "may be finding its voice and a constituency."

In support of that view, he points to several developments. The difficulty of establishing liberal democratic regimes in many regions of the world testifies to liberalism's dependence on certain cultural conditions. Democracy, it seems, does not simply "take root" wherever it is planted. Liberals and friends of liberalism are beginning to realize that not only are "good institutions . . . the crucial matrix of any effective virtues," but that seedbeds of good habits and attitudes are essential for the maintenance of good institutions. As awareness of the necessary cultural foundations of liberalism sinks in, social thinkers in liberal regimes are beginning to reevaluate the relationship of the state to civil society. Sullivan finds encouragement in the way that social and political theorists increasingly resort to ecological metaphors and in the remarkable revival of widespread concern for the family.

Even if these scattered developments could somehow coalesce into a general recognition of the need to reshape institutions for the sake of revitalizing civil society, Sullivan acknowledges that still greater problems would lie ahead. One challenge would be to develop, in our increasingly heterogeneous society, a public philosophy that provides "a convincing and coherent vision of not only how but why such institutional reconstruction should be undertaken." Another would be to encourage, among our highly mobile population, a taste for stable communities in which the social environment can be continuously cultivated. Both Popenoe and Sullivan place great emphasis on the importance of "settled life," yet the American story to a great extent is one of cashing out, packing up, and moving on.

Another recurring concern in *Seedbeds of Virtue* is whether, by some cruel paradox, liberalism is intrinsically inimical to some or all of the very qualities and institutions that it needs in order to survive. Certainly, as Stanley Hauerwas points out, the specifically liberal virtues described by Galston are not identical to classical virtues, Biblical virtues, or aristocratic virtues. Christian courage, to use Hauerwas's example, is not only different from civic courage, but may on occasion be positively subversive of the aims of the polity. Conversely, liberal tolerance (as distinct from religiously grounded tolerance) could be lethal to many seedbeds. Not only is liberal tolerance intolerant of its rivals, but it slides all too easily into the sort of mandatory value neutrality that rules all talk of character and virtue out of bounds.

The solution to the conundrum may lie in another pair of paradoxes. First, liberalism, in order to survive, may need to refrain from imposing its own image on all the institutions of civil society. Democratic experiments may depend, as Tocqueville suspected, on preserving here and there within the liberal polity certain institutions, like the family, that are not necessarily democratic, egalitarian, or liberal, and whose highest loyalty is not to the state. Second, the best hope for unpopular, non-liberal seedbeds of virtue may be the tolerant liberal polity whose ultimate values are at odds with theirs.

What, though, could hold together a polity composed of small institutions that thrive on different virtues from those that animate the regime itself? And what would assure that the seedbeds, liberal or non-liberal, would be conducive to the flowering of virtue rather than the growth of weeds of vice? And how would one know the flowers from the weeds? The answers to such questions—or at least the path to better rather than worse judgments—must ultimately be sought, not in the seedbed, but in the seed: the human person, uniquely individual yet inescapably social; a creature of unruly passions who nevertheless possesses a certain ability to transcend and even to transform the passions; a knower and a chooser who constitutes himself, for better or worse, through his knowing and his choosing. As Thomas Kohler puts it, we have been losing, along with our social environments, any kind of deep understanding of what humans are and what they need in order to flourish.

What is it that causes individual men and women to keep their promises, to limit consumption, to stick with a spouse in sickness and health, to care for their children, to answer their country's call for service, to reach out to the poor, to respect the rights of others, and to moderate their own demands on loved ones, neighbors, and the body politic? More particularly, how do children first learn to empathize with others and to acquire self-restraint along with self-confidence? It is remarkable, in a country where law and ethics have become highly sophisticated areas of study, that little systematic attention has been given to the ethics of everyday life. Yet Brian Benestad points out that, under modern circumstances, it requires something close to heroism to practice the "ordinary" virtues like marital fidelity, filial piety, and parental responsibility.

The family, all contributors seem to agree, is the principal setting for learning ordinary, decent behavior. Judith Martin emphasizes the importance of early acquisition within the home of habits that enable one to develop further skills of communal living in other sites such as schools and workplaces. But families, now more than ever, need help in transmitting those habits and skills. And that kind of knowledge cannot be improvised or invented anew by each family. Thus Benestad rightly insists on the importance of storytelling as a means of conserving, handing on, and making vivid the hard-won insights of succeeding generations. With the decline of reading, Americans are losing a rich and varied moral heritage.

One of the main reasons why families are excellent schools of virtue is that, even under the best of circumstances, they are places of testing and trial. Sentimentalism about family life tends to obscure the fact that the ordinary virtues are difficult to practice on a day-to-day basis. Dickens's Mrs. Jellyby—who labored night and day on behalf of the natives of Borioboola-Ga while her own neglected children were wailing, soiling themselves, and falling downstairs—is a very contemporary figure. As Jean Elshtain suggests in her fiendishly clever "Newtape Letters," the main lapses from virtue for most of us are not spectacular bad acts, but ordinary bad habits—often affecting our nearest and dearest. Like Mrs. Jellyby, we often can summon great energy for the easy virtues of distant causes, while showing little heart for the hard virtues of kindness to and forbearance with friends and family.

Thus the starting point and the terminus of the *Seedbeds of Virtue* is the human person in all his imperfection and with all his potential. The various virtues are neither contrary to human nature nor inherent in human nature. They arise, if at all, through the capacity of men and women to reflect upon their existence and to make judgments concerning the good life and how to live it. Those judgments can be powerfully influenced by the settings in which we find ourselves, and those settings in turn can be affected to some degree by norms and institutions of human design. Human beings, having shown themselves capable of creating norms and institutions, can be supposed to be capable of reshaping norms and institutions. Now, as in ancient times, all depends on how we employ those qualities for which Sophocles praised the human race in the famous chorus in *Antigone*: "mastery of the art of speech, and of wind-swift thought, and the skill of living together in neighborliness." It cannot be an accident that the Greek word he chose to describe our species in that Ode to Man carries two meanings: "wonderful" and "terrible."

Notes

1. *Federalist No. 55* (Madison).
2. Ibid.
3. Wolfe citing Arendt.
4. The prototype and model for this sort of research is the series of pioneering studies by Dr. Emmy Werner and her colleagues on the "protective factors" that enable high-risk children to survive and thrive

despite seemingly insurmountable obstacles. The most recent report on their studies of the children of Kauai from birth to adulthood is Emmy E. Werner and Ruth S. Smith, *Overcoming the Odds* (Ithaca, NY: Cornell University Press, 1992).

CHAPTER 1

Liberalism, Modernism, and the Good Life

James Q. Wilson

A central problem of contemporary political philosophy is whether a liberal democratic society can sustain the culture necessary for the good life. It is a problem raised in this volume explicitly by Mary Ann Glendon, William Galston, and David Blankenhorn and implicitly by Judith Martin, David Popenoe, and others. The issue may be put somewhat technically as follows: can liberalism rest on a theory of rights that is not subordinate to some theory of the good? Or it may be stated a bit more melodramatically this way: can liberal democratic regimes foster a shared culture that will restrain human appetites without relying on oppressive political force?

Rights and Virtue within Liberal Democracy

Men and women throughout much of the industrialized West look about themselves and find high and rising levels of property crime, high and rising levels of out-of-wedlock births, and high levels of both divorce and drug abuse. Many adults worry that young people are inordinately drawn to idleness and self-indulgence; many young people worry that their parents are so preoccupied with success and status as to neglect the needs of their children. In the United States especially, but increasingly in other

Earlier versions of this chapter were presented as the Tocqueville Lecture at St. John's College in Sante Fe, New Mexico, and as the James Lecture at the University of Illinois.

nations as well, people find evidence of what they take to be moral decay.

As democracy has spread, prosperity grown, and freedom expanded, public morality has apparently declined. So common are these trends that they cannot be explained by particular differences in national policies or economic conditions. When both Sweden and the United States are becoming more alike with respect to everything save violence, we are witnessing something more fundamental than the consequences of alternative versions of the welfare state. We are seeing the consequences of a common culture.

That common culture is liberal democracy. By liberalism I do not mean left-wing politics; Sweden and the United States are quite different in the degree to which they have embraced the welfare state. By liberalism I mean those political arrangements based on popular consent and the protection of individual rights that aim at accommodating several conflicting and incommensurable conceptions of the good life. Liberalism, so defined, represents a radical break with the classical view of politics. In the older view, the purpose of politics—the reason why man lived in the *polis*—was to foster virtue. In the modern view, the purpose of politics is to balance the competing demands of public order and personal liberty. The decisive change ushered in by liberalism was to elevate rights over virtues.

There is, of course, a spirited debate among contemporary supporters of the liberal state as to what those rights are. To some, they are, chiefly, liberty, whether in personal life, the economic order, or both. To others they are equality, defined as either a right to some socially determined share of the social product or a right to equal respect and dignity. John Stuart Mill and Robert Nozick have elevated liberty to the first rank; John Rawls and Ronald Dworkin have emphasized equality.

The ideas that in time made liberalism the dominant Western view of the legitimate state began, of course, with John Locke but took full shape during the Enlightenment, when thinkers such as David Hume, Adam Smith, and Immanuel Kant sought to emancipate mankind from what Kant called its "self-imposed tutelage." In practice this meant defending reason against religion, tradition, or authority as a way of understanding the human condition. The enlightened man was not to be governed by revealed religion, ancient custom, or inherited power. This meant, of course, that he was not to be governed by an externally imposed moral order; morality would be a matter of personal commitment, not political or religious indoctrination.

For two centuries the emancipation of skeptical reason and the weakening of external authority seemed to produce enormous gains at little or no cost. The West acquired the benefits of modern science unfettered by superstition, free trade unconstrained by mercantilist policies, free speech uninhibited by royal censors, and free conscience unburdened by an established church. Slavery was ended, democracy established, and economic progress unleashed.

There were, of course, some costs: excesses of language and drink, the grim beginnings of wage labor, a weakening of aristocratic virtues, and a growing indifference to the claims of high culture. But throughout the 19th century, what is most evident is a general improvement in the habits and virtues of most people: generally rising standards of living, low and declining rates of illegitimacy, and stable or falling rates of crime and intemperance despite industrialization, urbanization, and immigration. The modest costs were far exceeded by the gains.

The costs were small because the West was living on the basis of an accumulated moral capital. The Enlightenment took for granted that families and villages would produce decent folk. The Declaration of Independence proclaimed American rights but assumed a natural human morality. The Constitution created a national regime with no authority to mold character but assumed a village life in which character would automatically emerge. Thomas Jefferson worried that big cities and a commercial republic would corrupt the people, but it was hard to take this worry too seriously when the biggest city, Philadelphia, was quite small by modern standards. It seemed more important, even to Jefferson, to keep the national government from controlling the conscience of the people than to make it capable of imposing an austere virtue. The American Revolution, as Gordon Wood has shown, transformed a society held together by the "secret bonds" of aristocratic blood, royal patronage, and personal influence into the first democratic society held together by the natural sociability of free men. Ancient virtue may

have been produced by man's participation in politics, but modern
virtue would arise from his participation in society. Free society
was naturally good, free government was a necessary evil. "Society," Thomas Paine wrote, "is produced by our wants and government by our wickedness."[1]

Early in the 19th century Americans and Englishmen alike
began to worry that man's natural sociability and instinctive benevolence might not be enough to sustain a virtuous life. The combined impact of urbanization, strong drink, and economic
dislocations led many people to believe that morality had to be
inculcated by sterner measures than what had sufficed in small,
independent villages. Crime and intemperance became issues, the
police were invented, and moral reform efforts were mounted. To
an astonishing degree they succeeded, and succeeded without much
expansion of state authority. Crime declined, temperance spread,
and illegitimacy remained low. The moral capital that the Enlightenment took for granted was successfully replenished by the energies of temperance societies, religious revivalists, philanthropic
endeavors, and a professional police force.

By the late 19th and early 20th century, however, that capital
began to exhaust itself. We seem to have spent it faster than we
replaced it. The core ideas of the liberal Enlightenment that had
for so long coexisted comfortably with traditional morality began
to change in ways that made that coexistence problematic. Both
reason and history—that is, both arguments and events—
combined to alter the content, extend the range, and deepen the
impact of Enlightenment principles that had already extended their
sway over much of the Western world.

Reason in the Service of the Individual

As intellectuals came to grips with the assumptions of the Enlightenment, they radicalized those assumptions by doing what intellectuals inevitably and necessarily do: follow an idea to its logical
end. Let me sketch this change with respect to four ideas: the status
of reason, the nature of liberty, the scope of equality, and the meaning of culture.

Skeptical Reason

Originally this meant only that man could know his own condition without revelation or dogma. As thinkers examined its implications, however, it came to mean much more. Reason acquired a distinctive, scientific meaning, a meaning that excluded from its purview the possibility of moral philosophy. In 1740 David Hume published his famous statement that in all "vulgar systems" of philosophy there was a confusion of factual and value statements.[2] By the early 20th century, that had been interpreted to mean that in *all* systems of philosophy "is" and "ought" statements must be kept rigorously separate. Hume, indeed, had argued that morality rests on sentiments; for saying that, and for denying that they rested on divine commands, he was thought to be impious. Of course, Hume never dismissed the sentiments on which morality rests as trivial or subject to arbitrary choice. But with the advent of logical positivism as formulated by the Vienna Circle in the 1920s, ethical statements were held to be meaningless because they were not empirically verifiable according to the canons of modern science. Hume, I think, would have been astonished to be told that sentiments generally, and moral sentiments in particular, were "meaningless." No matter: the word "sentiment" had been transformed into the phrase "mere sentiment."

Individual Rights

Originally this phrase meant that men were naturally endowed with a right to life, liberty, and property and that no political order was legitimate that did not respect these rights. In time the idea of liberty was enlarged to mean not simply freedom from arbitrary political power but freedom from conventional opinion. That transformation was chiefly achieved by John Stuart Mill. In *On Liberty*, he argued that liberty meant not simply freedom from arbitrary arrest or unjust taxation but freedom from any government restriction not designed to prevent a direct and palpable harm to another person and from social pressure or conventional opinion that sought to constrain people beyond what was necessary to avoid those palpable harms.

In his words, "the sole end for which mankind is warranted, individually or collectively, in interfering with the liberty of action of any of their number, is self-protection . . . [that is], to prevent harm to others."[3] Power may not be used for man's own good, either physical or moral. Mill objected to the despotism of both government and custom.

His position, of course, left open many questions on which his critics, such as James Fitzjames Stephens, were quick to pounce.[4] What is a harm to others? Does it include a moral outrage or a vulgar display? Mill grappled with this issue, making clear that he favored decriminalizing (as we would say) gambling, public drunkenness, the purchase of opium, or the practice of polygamy. But at the same time he accepted the punishment of public "offenses against decency," which, being a modest Victorian gentleman, he did not define. He did make it clear, however, that his enlarged view of liberty was reserved for civilized adults and should be denied to children and "barbarians."[5] Moreover, he, unlike some of his more rigorously libertarian followers, recognized that men are not isolated individuals. If a person degrades his faculties and habits, he brings evil onto those dependent on him and becomes a burden on "their affection or benevolence." How, then, can we draw the line between individual liberty and social obligation? Mill's solution was to propose that a man should only be constrained if he violates a "distinct and assignable obligation to any other person or persons."[6] But he did not clearly specify, and in fact no one can specify, the difference between a distinct and an implied obligation. I have a distinct obligation to support my wife and children and to refrain from abusing them, but I also have, I think, an obligation to live among them soberly, decently, and respectfully, and so drunkenness, drug abuse, and polygamy are wrongs that cannot be entirely decriminalized. Mill is silent on these complexities.

His silence did not induce a like silence in his more ardent followers. They took the principle of liberty to its ultimate conclusion: begging, pornography, and nude dancing are forms of protected speech; drug abuse is purely a private matter; the mentally disturbed have the same rights as the mentally competent; and a family is a contract that can have any terms its members choose. It is unlikely that Mill would have agreed; he surely would have said some of these things were offenses against decency and others a violation of a "distinct and assignable obligation," but the moral capital he had acquired and on which his libertarian and utilitarian views depended was assumed to exist without the necessity of any defense.

Equality

Originally philosophers meant only that human *nature* was everywhere essentially the same, such that differences in race or ethnicity were insufficient to deny to others the same essential rights as free Englishmen. Accordingly, slavery was everywhere and always wrong.

But in time, this view was extended to suggest that human *cultures* were everywhere equally worthy. Whatever the customs and mores of other cultures, they were the product of social learning. This view, when linked to moral positivism, implied that nothing in another culture could be criticized on the basis of any universal or objective standards. It was a view often advanced by people rightly worried about the rise of doctrines of racial supremacy and the spread of ethnic persecution,[7] but it was also endorsed by scholars whose chief interest was in science. Some of these were quite conservative politically, as witness the famous phrase of Yale sociologist William Graham Sumner: "the mores can make anything right."[8]

The adoption of cultural relativism obliterated the distinction Mill had made between civilized and barbarian people; indeed, it made the word "barbarian" not only pejorative but meaningless. And so it was not long after Sumner wrote that Ruth Benedict could discuss, dispassionately if not quite acceptingly, cannibalism and infanticide.[9] In its most extreme form, radical egalitarianism not only challenged xenophobia, it replaced it with xenophilia (i.e., a love of that which is foreign or exotic). We are all familiar with the remarkable tendency of highly educated people to declare that a custom they find loathsome in the United States is charming if found abroad.

Radical egalitarianism also contributed to the assault on patriotism. Since love of country may imply hatred of foreigners, no one

in one's own country should give way to such an emotion. Of
course, people in other cultures regularly and enthusiastically give
way to patriotic outbursts, but that is entirely proper since they are
the product of a culture we ought to understand whereas we are
the product of prejudices we ought to overcome.

Culture

Originally culture was understood to mean, in Matthew Arnold's
famous phrase, "the best that has been known and said"; it is "the
study of perfection, and perfection which consists of becoming
something rather than in having something, in an inward condition
of the mind and spirit."[10] In the 19th century, English life was
criticized for what Arnold and others saw as its tendency to weaken
high culture in the name of progress, but there was never any doubt
that the criticism was based on an understanding that a high culture of the spirit was possible and ennobling. So great a figure as
Goethe could say that "one ought, every day at least, to . . . read a
good poem, see a fine picture"[11] without anyone sniggering at the
sentiment or demanding to know what Goethe could possibly mean
by words such as "good" or "fine."

In the 20th century high culture became identified, in certain
quarters, with bourgeois philistinism. Now, the bourgeoisie has
been in trouble at least since Rousseau attacked it for being, in
Allan Bloom's phrase, "unpoetic, unerotic, unheroic."[12] To Rousseau, bourgeois man was a mercenary disguised as a moralist, neither a natural man nor a true citizen.

At first this view was merely an attack on the bourgeoisie for
lacking noble sentiments. But by the 20th century it had been
transformed into an attack on those sentiments themselves. The
radicalized view of culture broke with the idea that any culture was
high or, if high, good. The continued cultural aspirations of the
bourgeoisie were increasingly viewed as a love of *kitsch* masquer-
ading as an understanding of art or, even worse, as the mobilization
of culture as an instrument of class oppression.

George Grosz remarked that "the bourgeoisie . . . have armed
themselves against the rising proletariat with . . . 'culture' " and
Simone Weil made much the same point when she said that "cul-

ture is an instrument wielded by teachers to manufacture teachers." Movie critic Pauline Kael was only slightly more sympathetic when she remarked that "one of the surest signs of the philistine is his reverence for the superior tastes of those who put him down."[13]

Several alternatives to high culture were proposed. The earliest was romanticism, that is, a rebellion against classic forms and conventions and against rationalism, manifested in a heightened interest in nature, spontaneity, imagination, and self-expression. Another was decadence, defended by Oscar Wilde with this characteristically perverse yet elegant sentiment: "There are only two ways by which man can [attain civilization]: one is by being cultured, the other is by being corrupt."[14] A third was the idea of the avant-garde. Now, this phrase usually refers to whatever defies accepted conventions in the name of a superior vision; but since there is today no convention that has not long since been defied, it is not clear that an avant garde is any longer possible. When Marcel Duchamp displayed *Nude Descending a Staircase* at the 1913 Armory Show, people were still capable of being puzzled or shocked: they were told they were looking at a painting of a woman but they saw nothing of the kind. (Duchamp was later to explain that "my position is the absence of position." Oh.) We now look at the descendants of such paintings and murmur that they are "interesting."

For many, being avant-garde is simply to be against tradition, or more generally against any form or structure that might ever become a tradition. But for some, being avant-garde was a political act. Playwright Eugene Ionesco said that the avant-garde man is like an enemy inside a city he is bent on destroying because "an established form of expression is also a form of oppression."[15]

These many tendencies—extreme understandings of liberty and equality, relativistic views of human nature, diverse challenges to high culture—were, of course, quite different and often opposed. Some represented a challenge to the entire Enlightenment project. But they had in common a certain foundational logic that I describe as the radicalization of the central ideas of the Enlightenment. To the rationalists, reason is supreme, and so nothing can stand against it, including faith, imagination, and tradition. If rights are fundamental, then rights are trumps and nothing can overrule them, including duties and conventions. If men are equal in some respects, they have a claim to be equal in all respects. If one culture is good, all must be.

The defenders of reason limited its range to science and boasted of its accomplishments; the critics of reason agreed that its range was limited but argued that its products were threatening technologies, obscure philosophies, and a false sense of comprehension. At most, therefore, reason's realm should extend no further than science and technology; since reason is to be understood as having nothing to say about art or morality, then art and morality are both left to the realm of the imagination, and in that realm the decadent, the romantic, or the avant-garde have equal or superior claims to those of the aristocracy or the bourgeoisie.

This radicalization of the central doctrines of the Enlightenment, however inconsistent its results, produced tendencies that, taken together, can be called, with great over-simplification, modernism. But modernism consisted only of ideas consigned to books, discussed in salons, debated in universities, or hung in museums. However much they may have gained intellectual adherents, it is not obvious why they should have acquired so much influence beyond those small circles who read the books, belonged to the salons, taught at the universities, or visited the museums.

What is striking, however, is that modernism—that is, the radicalization of the Enlightenment—gave rise to an oppositional culture that has been far more pervasive than one would predict simply knowing of the ideas themselves. For centuries—perhaps for millennia—ordinary men and women have had a keen sense of the limits of reason, a firm attachment to the fundamental virtues of daily life, a desire for liberty tempered by moderation, a willingness to judge other people on the basis of standards they thought were universal, and an attraction to art and music conventionally understood.

History: Eventful Shifts in Moral Sentiments

That intellectuals should stand in opposition to their culture is hardly novel; Socrates was a critic of Athens, Machiavelli of Florence, and Rousseau of France. What is novel is when intellectual opposition gives rise to a more general adversary culture. For that to take place, reason alone is insufficient. Powerful events must occur. Virginia Woolff said that in December 1910 "human nature changed." As Gertrude Himmelfarb has explained, she was right about the change, but wrong about the date.[16] She should have put it sometime in the period 1914 to 1918. The normal opposition to popular culture of an aesthetic and philosophical elite became a massive and compelling indictment when that culture seemed to spawn the Armageddon of World War I. Men enthusiastically volunteered for service in the Great War; supposedly two-thirds of all Oxford undergraduates enlisted. The horrors of trench warfare, the blundering of incompetent generals, the inability of political leaders to explain the cause for which men were dying; these events, like none before them, discredited honor, duty, and country; reason and science; authority and bureaucracy. After World War I, Oxford undergraduates took an oath swearing never again to fight for king and country.

Modris Eckstein[17] has observed that the impulse toward liberation evident in arts, fashion, and mores in 1900 was greatly enlarged by the war and intellectual reaction to it: "Introspection, primitivism, abstraction, and myth making in the arts and introspection, primitivism, abstraction, and myth making in politics, may be related manifestations." This was especially the case in defeated Germany but to some extent in the West generally. The British tradition of duty and propriety persisted, perhaps because of the vast inertial forces behind it, and this made postwar London more sane than postwar Berlin. But the war cut away the confident foundations on which this tradition had long rested, thus leaving habits to sustain themselves without the aid of convictions. Stephen Spender described the result in a compelling metaphor: "The war had knocked the ball-room floor from under middle-class English life. People resembled dancers suspended in mid-air yet miraculously able to pretend they were still dancing."[18] Young people especially noticed that the floor was no longer there—nor, for that matter, the walls or the ceiling—and so began to express their cynicism about convention in all its forms.

The 1920s was the inevitable cultural aftermath of the Great

War. In that decade the habits of thought that most of us associate with the 1960s first acquired widespread acceptance and began to form a culture much broader (however thinner and less developed) than that of the expatriate intellectuals who had fostered it. How that culture might have evolved if left undisturbed we shall never know because the Great Depression and the Second World War intervened.

The cultural critique of bourgeois life and Victorian principles became to some a massive and persuasive indictment when the economic order collapsed. Unemployment, privation, ruination, all evident on any street corner and every farm, took away from the assumptions of the Enlightenment their last line of defense, namely, their claimed capacity to improve the material well-being of society. Not only was the West's moral capital exhausted, its economic capital had been spent, too. The Second World War briefly and compellingly restored a sense of purpose and, in time, material abundance, but the moral score was still to be settled. In the 1960s that settlement resumed in earnest.

When it resumed, it did so with access to an unprecedented number of potential recruits. With the return of prosperity and the aid of the GI Bill, enrollment in American colleges and universities quadrupled between 1955 and 1975, rising from 2.7 million to 11.2 million. The great majority of these students were affected only marginally, if at all, by the oppositional culture around them, but their numbers were so great that if only, say, 2 percent were strongly affected, the result would be the recruitment of a quarter of a million people every four years to an enterprise that once commanded the attention of a handful of people in literary salons and fringe political associations.

From Enlightenment to Postmodernism: The Radicalization of Individualism

Was this radicalization inevitable and, if inevitable, what was its effect on ordinary people? After all, Asia and the Middle East have embraced science, technology, and markets; these regions also have intellectuals and they often radicalize inherited doctrines. Yet they seem to lack the oppositional culture of the West. I think the radicalization that occurred in the West was distinctive and inevitable. It was distinctive in the premises with which it began, and these premises have long constituted not only the strength of the West but, indeed, its very meaning. Founded on the idea of emancipation and self-discovery; endowed with a rights-based legal code, a market economy, and an advanced scientific establishment; supplied with a vast pool of potential recruits, the Western form of radicalization was individualistic. Inevitably events occurred that would place popular culture under the guidance of elite culture. Had it not been the Great War and the Depression, it would have been something else.

It is not easy to reckon up the balance sheet of this sea change in the culture of liberalism. I began by recalling the familiar facts of crime, drug abuse, divorce, and illegitimacy, but it is time to recall as well what else has changed. Slavery has been abolished and segregation rolled back; mass higher education has produced a vastly more sophisticated and talented population; and women are less often the victims of a sexual double standard. Against those gains we must measure the increased tolerance of drug experimentation, the social marginalization of religious believers, the heightened skepticism about institutional authority, and a certain confusion over sexual roles.

Nor is it easy to judge the effects of this transformation. Though buffeted by culturally hostile forces and convinced that they are raising children and maintaining families with little cultural support, the average person is leading a life that is governed by far more powerful forces than intellectual fashion. Family, personality, neighborhood, and work are shaped by our natural and largely ineradicable desire for merited social approval, our deep attachment to those close to us, and the fundamental moral sentiments that incline us to sympathy, fairness, duty, and self-control.

But some people are inordinately vulnerable to modernism (or now, to post-modernism) because of their immaturity, their marginality, or their temperament. People who are young, who are impulsive and thrill-seeking, who are part of weak families and cultures, or who are aggrieved by their social subordination are attracted to, or lack sure defenses against, one or another version

of modernism—the anti-bourgeois, the romantically self-indulgent, the radically egalitarian, the hyper-rationalistic. Myron Magnet has argued that modernism changed the Haves as well as the
Have-Nots but changed the Have-Nots the most. When the Haves
fought for personal liberation, the Have-Nots wound up getting
social isolation.[19] The degree to which it occurred varied from case
to case, but let there be no doubt that it was explicitly urged. Norman Mailer's essay, "The White Negro," called on every man to
give up the "sophisticated inhibitions of civilization," divorce himself from society, and "follow the rebellious imperative of self."[20]
This message wasn't left hanging in generalities; Mailer, and others, soon got down to specifics. Almost every new drug—heroin,
cocaine, LSD, speed—was initially endorsed by elite users, only to
be abandoned by them just about the time they caught on with a
less privileged mass public. Theories that single-parent families are
desirable alternative lifestyles were not invented by single mothers
but by intellectuals who thought that they were removing a stigma
from an oppressed class.[21] (American intellectuals are sometimes
themselves the victims of this trickle-down culture: they embraced
existentialism and post-modernism just about the time when their
French creators had discarded them.)

I have elsewhere used the children's game of crack the whip as a
metaphor for this process of cultural transmission and amplifica-
tion.[22] A line of children hold hands; at the end of the line the first
child turns slowly, carefully; each succeeding child down the line
turns faster, less carefully; at the end of the line the last child races,
stumbles, and falls.

In our parochial lives we are only moderately touched by the
modernist waves; the degree of that change depends on our inner
bearings, our social resources, and unpredictable circumstance. We
all feel the tension between individual assertion and communal obligations. Individualizing and collectivizing forces tug at each of us.
What is growing up in a family but a continuous effort to balance
duty and loyalty with freedom and individuality?

Culture does not produce those claims, but it gives us a variety
of ways of balancing them. What our critics abroad in the worlds
of Islam and Confucianism remind us is that the West has irrevoca-
bly cast its lot with a culture that makes it easy, and seemingly

natural, for the individual to triumph over the group. Those critics are right, as is evident in the writings of almost any modern liberal thinker. The claims of family and community are often greeted suspiciously as sources of cultural reaction and political conservatism because they seem to imply traditional roles for women, neighborhood intolerance for diversity, and bourgeois hostility to free expression. Since there is some truth behind all of these suspicions, such complaints cannot be dismissed.

But those critics must also shoulder some burdens. They are defending a theory of rights and individualism that has converted some of our streets to a threatening gauntlet of aggressive panhandlers, adorned our buildings with unsettling graffiti, defended drug use as an entirely personal choice, stigmatized the two-parent family as archaic, and supplanted the belief in personal responsibility with the doctrine of social causation.

Abroad our critics watch and wait. The worlds of Islam and Confucianism scorn the choice we have made and wager that in time—a century or two—their way will be proved superior. Their claims cannot be ignored.

Islam and Confucianism are alike in elevating the collectivity over the individual. The distinctive feature of Islam is its denial of any possible distinction between religion and society, between church and state, and thus between religious law and secular law. Islamic law requires submission to God in the public as well as the private sphere. The consequence of this submission is to elevate duties over rights. Though Islam, Judaism, and Christianity have certain prophets in common, Christianity and Judaism were transformed by the Greco-Roman culture in which they were embedded into religions that acknowledged, albeit slowly and reluctantly, a separation between church and state and permitted the emergence of a political philosophy based on the maintenance of a separate sphere of individual rights. The post-Enlightenment Western intellectual could practice science, philosophy, or art divorced from religious authority, but the Muslim intellectual, at least in the fundamentalist view, cannot.

Confucianism is not a religion but a doctrine that tells the superior man how he ought to live. The goal is the achievement of harmony, not the assertion of individuality or the defense of rights.

In contemporary society the Confucian ethic implies a reliance on authority and tradition more than on rights and contracts, a desire for harmony more than conflict, a preference for group affiliation more than personal self-expression, and an instinct for nationalism over cosmopolitanism.

However different, Islam and Confucianism have in common an orientation—religious in one case, secular in the other—toward a larger collectivity. Their ideas, like those of the Enlightenment, can also be radicalized, but their radicalism leads not to the ills of modernism but to the ills of traditionalism.

Today many in the West, and especially in America, look longingly at Islam and Confucianism. We sometimes envy the extent to which those worlds appear to repress crime, eliminate drugs, revere families, and respect authority. Four strokes of the cane in Singapore were greeted with cheers in New York City and Los Angeles.

Some leaders in those cultures already believe that we have lost; not a few people in our culture may be inclined to agree. I think they are wrong. The skeptics here and the boasters abroad may vastly underestimate the capacity of a free society to sustain what is truly human and to correct its own errors and vastly overstate the capacity of a communal society to liberate the human spirit, establish political legitimacy, or sustain economic growth. Thirty years ago America was scorned as a nation that denied many of its own citizens full participation in its political life. We changed. Twenty years ago America was criticized for its inability to sustain a manufacturing economy; American automobile companies and their workers, it was said, could no longer compete. We changed. Ten years ago America was told that it had over-extended itself with military commitments that would bankrupt us. They didn't; we won the Cold War. Five years ago America was told that it had embraced an inefficient welfare state and a cumbersome legal system that would inevitably suffocate individual initiative. Then there was an election, and we began to change.

The present challenge is more profound, for it is cultural, not economic or political, and culture is difficult, if not impossible, to change according to plan. But the West has faced cultural challenges before. In the 1930s the leaders of Germany, Italy, and the Soviet Union dismissed the English and the Americans as timorous, effete people whose will to fight had been eroded by bourgeois democracy and self-indulgent habits. They were wrong; it was they who failed.

The decadent, individualistic, intemperate West is always being underestimated. I believe that, costly as its embrace may be, freedom is man's universal hope; its defense, his steady preoccupation. That hope will be easier to sustain and its defense more readily accomplished if all of us, but especially the intellectuals, recognize that the exercise of freedom presupposes the maintenance of a natural moral order that deserves respect and reaffirmation, an order that arises from the familial seedbeds of virtue.

Notes

1. Paine quoted in Gordon S. Wood, *The Radicalism of the American Revolution* (New York: Alfred Knopf, 1992), 217. See in general Wood's splendid analysis at pages 213–25.

2. David Hume, *A Treatise of Human Nature*, ed. L.A. Selby-Bigge and P.H. Nidditch (Oxford: Clarendon Press, 1978), 469.

3. John Stuart Mill, *On Liberty*, ed. David Spitz (New York: W.W. Norton, 1975), 10–11. First published in 1859.

4. James Fitzjames Stephens, *Liberty, Equality, Fraternity*, ed. Stuart D. Warner (Indianapolis, IN: Liberty Fund, 1993). First published in 1873.

5. Mill, *On Liberty*, 11.

6. Ibid., 75.

7. Cf. Carl N. Degler, *In Search of Human Nature* (New York: Oxford, 1991).

8. William Graham Sumner, *Folkways* (New York: Dover, 1959). First published in 1906.

9. Ruth Benedict, *Patterns of Culture* (Boston: Houghton Mifflin, 1934).

10. Matthew Arnold, *Literature and Dogma* (1873) and *Culture and Anarchy* (1869).

11. Goethe, *Wilhelm Meister's Apprenticeship*, trans. Thomas Carlyle (1795), bk. 5, ch. 1.

12. Allan Bloom, *Giants and Dwarfs* (New York: Simon & Schuster, 1990), 211.

13. George Grosz, "The Art Scab," in *Art is in Danger*, trans. Paul

Gorrell (1987); Simone Weil, *The Need for Roots* (1949); Pauline Kael, *I Lost It at the Movies* (1965).

14. Oscar Wilde, *The Picture of Dorian Gray* (1891), ch. 19.

15. Eugene Ionesco, "Talk About the Avant Garde," in *Notes and Counter Notes* (1962).

16. Gertrude Himmelfarb, *The Demoralization of Society* (New York: Knopf, 1995).

17. Modris Eckstein, *Rights of Spring* (Boston: Houghton Mifflin Co., 1989).

18. Quoted in ibid., 256.

19. Myron Magnet, *The Dream and the Nightmare* (New York: Morrow, 1993), 16.

20. Norman Mailer, "The White Negro," in *Advertisements for Myself* (New York: Putnam, 1959).

21. See, for example, Stephanie Coontz, *The Way We Never Were: American Families and the Nostalgia Trap* (New York: Basic Books, 1992), for a summary of the views of family life that became common in the 1960s and 1970s. At pages 241–43 she speaks approvingly of single-parent families as "alternative family forms" that are "flexible, effective ways of pooling resources and building community" that should not be condemned for "failing to conform to an idealize white model." Alvin Toffler, though of late much celebrated by conservative politicians such as Newt Gingrich, echoes the same themes: the nuclear family belongs to the "Second Wave"; modern, "Third Wave" families will include single-parent families, communal families, polygamous families, and aggregate families. Toffler, *The Third Wave* (New York: Bantam, 1980), ch. 17.

22. James Q. Wilson, "What To Do About Crime," *Commentary* (March 1994). Reprinted in James Q. Wilson and Joan Petersilia, eds. *Crime* (San Francisco: ICS Press, 1994).

CHAPTER 2

Liberal Virtues and the Formation of Civic Character

William A. Galston

Tensions within Liberalism

For two generations, scholarly inquiry has been dominated by the belief that the liberal polity does not require individual virtue. On the theoretical plane, liberalism has been understood by many as the articles of a peace treaty among individuals with diverse conceptions of the good but common interests in preservation and prosperity. On the level of basic institutions, the liberal constitution has been regarded as an artful contrivance of countervailing powers and counterbalancing passions. In the arena of liberal society, individual behavior has been analyzed through the prism, and public policy guided by the precepts, of neoclassical economics.

The conclusion that liberalism could be severed, in theory and in practice, from the concern for virtue was shared by scholars of widely divergent orientations. While Leo Strauss was on the whole sympathetic, and C. B. Macpherson hostile, to the liberal polity, they converged on an interpretation of Locke that stressed his effort to liberate individual acquisitiveness from traditional moral constraints.[1] Martin Diamond and Gordon Wood could agree on the essentials of the interest-based "new science of politics" that displaced civic republicanism and undergirded the Constitution.[2] The understanding of modern liberal society as an agglomeration of self-interested individuals and groups formed a common point

This essay is based upon, and extends, the analysis of liberal virtues in *Liberal Purposes*, Chapters 10 to 12.

of departure for defenders of pluralism (such as Robert Dahl in his 1950s incarnation) and critics, led by Theodore Lowi.[3]

Although the various analysts of liberalism were not in agreement on a specific conception of virtue, they were united in the belief that liberal theory and practice stood in tension with virtue however conceived. For Strauss and many of his followers, liberalism placed in jeopardy both the restraints on passion that should govern the daily life of the many and the striving for excellence that should guide the activities of the few. For J. G. A. Pocock and his allies, liberalism represented the evisceration of republican virtue, understood as the disposition to subordinate personal interests to the common good.[4] For Charles Taylor and his fellow communitarians, liberalism undercut the very possibility of community and thus the significance of the virtues, understood as the habits needed to sustain a common life.[5] To the extent that virtue could nonetheless be found in the actual practices of liberal society, it was to be understood, argued Irving Kristol and many others, as the residue of an older moral and religious tradition at odds with—and under relentless assault by—liberalism's most fundamental tendencies.[6]

The proposition that liberalism does not rest on virtue is not the arbitrary invention of contemporary scholarship. Albert Hirschman has traced the emergence in 17th- and 18th-century social thought of the thesis that republican government could best be secured, not through civic virtue, but rather through the liberation of the commercial-acquisitive "interests" of the middle class in opposition to the politically destructive "passions" of the aristocracy.[7] The most famous *Federalist* papers (nos. 10 and 51) contain memorable formulations of the need to counteract interest with interest and passion with passion. Immanuel Kant, who was at once the profoundest moral philosopher and the most devoted liberal theorist of his age, argued vigorously for the disjunction between individual virtue and republican government:

> The republican constitution is the only one entirely fitting to the rights of man. But it is the most difficult to establish and even harder to preserve, so that many say a republic would have to be a nation of angels, because men with their selfish inclinations are not capable of a constitution of such sublime form. But [this is an error: republi-

can government] is only a question of a good organization of the
state, whereby the powers of each selfish inclination are so arranged
in opposition that one moderates or destroys the ruinous effect of the
other. The consequence . . . is the same as if none of them existed,
and man is forced to be a good citizen even if not a morally good
person. The problem of organizing a state, however hard it may
seem, can be solved even for a race of devils, if only they are intelligent.[8]

In spite of the considerable evidence for the proposition that the
liberal-republican polity requires no more than the proper config-
uration of rational self-interest, this orthodoxy has in recent years
come under attack from scholars who argue that liberal theory,
institutions, and society embody—and depend upon—individual
virtue. Judith Shklar has traced the emergence of liberalism to a
revulsion against the cruelty of religious wars—that is, to a decision
to replace military and moral repression with a "self-restraining
tolerance" that is "morally more demanding than repression".[9]
Rogers Smith has found in Locke a core conception of "rational
liberty" on which a distinction between liberty and license and an
account of individual excellence are based.[10] Summarizing a pains-
taking reexamination of the neglected *Thoughts Concerning
Education*, Nathan Tarcov concludes: "Instead of a narrowly cal-
culating selfishness, Locke teaches a set of moral virtues that make
men able to respect themselves and be useful to one another both
in private and in public life."[11] Ronald Terchek extends this thesis
to Adam Smith and John Stuart Mill, whom he interprets as recom-
mending "the cultivation of those habits which turned us toward
the practice of virtue."[12] J. Budziszewski offers a general argument
for the proposition that liberalism and the cultivation of the virtues
can be logically compatible and even mutually supportive.[13] In
Harvey Mansfield Jr.'s striking rereading of the *Federalist*, the automatic or mechanical view of our constitutional arrangements is
replaced by a focus on well-ordered souls as the foundation of sus-
tainable republican government: "Not only are the people expected
to be virtuous but also those who run for office."[14] James Q. Wilson's survey of contemporary public policy dilemmas concludes
that economic diagnoses and prescriptions, which treat individual

dispositions as fixed and exogenously determined "tastes," are at best one-sided. The challenge of social policy is not just the manipulation of incentives but also the formation of character: "In almost every area of important public concern, we are seeking to induce persons to act virtuously. . . . In the long run, the public interest depends on private virtue."[15]

If this line of argument is correct, there is a tension at the heart of liberalism. The liberal state must by definition be broadly inclusive of diversity, yet it cannot be wholly indifferent to the character of its citizens. As Thomas Spragens has noted, "A citizenry without public spirit, without self-restraint, and without intelligence accords ill with the demands of effective self-governance."[16] To quote Judith Shklar once more, the alternative before us

> is not one between classical virtue and liberal self-indulgence. . . . Far from being an amoral free-for-all, liberalism is, in fact, extremely difficult and constraining, far too much so for those who cannot endure . . . the risks of freedom. The habits of freedom are developed, moreover, both in private and in public, and a liberal character can readily be imagined.[17]

The challenge, then, is to give an account of individual virtue that supports rather than undermines liberal institutions and the capacious tolerance that gives liberal society its special attraction.

The thesis that liberalism rests in some measure on virtue is not the palpable absurdity that the liberal polity requires an impeccably virtuous citizenry, a "nation of angels." Nor is it incompatible with the mechanical-institutional interpretation of liberalism, for clearly the artful arrangement of "auxiliary precautions" can go some distance toward compensating for the defect of better motives. Nor, finally, does this thesis maintain that the liberal polity should be understood as a tutelary community dedicated to the inculcation of individual virtue or excellence. The claim is more modest: that the operation of liberal institutions is affected in important ways by the character of citizens (and leaders), and that at some point, the attenuation of individual virtue will create pathologies with which liberal political contrivances, however technically perfect their design, simply cannot cope. To an extent difficult to measure but impossible to ignore, the viability of liberal society depends on its ability to engender a virtuous citizenry.

While this requirement is not unique to liberal societies, it poses special difficulties for them. The liberal way of life frees individuals from traditional restraints and allows them to pursue their own conceptions of happiness. To the extent that the liberal virtues are not simply consistent with individual self-interest, processes of forming and maintaining them will come into conflict with other powerful tendencies in liberal life. The liberal virtues are the traits of character liberalism needs, not necessarily the ones it has. Yet these virtues need not be imported from the outside, for they are immanent in liberal practice and theory. The tension between virtue and self-interest is a tension within liberalism, not between liberalism and other traditions.

The Classical Conception of Virtue

The classical conception of the relation between virtue and politics was spelled out by Aristotle. Individual virtue (or excellence— the Greek *arete* will bear both meanings) is knowable through everyday experience, definable through philosophic inquiry, and is always and everywhere the same. For Aristotle, the virtues are not just Greek, but rather human, virtues. Political life must be seen as in large measure a means to the attainment of virtue, understood as an end in itself. Once the threshold conditions of physical and material security are met, the political community should structure its institutions and policies to promote virtue in its citizens, and its worth as a community depends on the extent to which it achieves that goal.

Aristotle was under no illusion that the communities of his day were actually organized in pursuit of virtue. Some, like Sparta, were devoted to military victory; others, to commercial prosperity; most had no single discernible goal. Each nonetheless had a largely tacit, operative conception of the virtuous individual as the good citizen whose character and conduct were most conducive to the preservation of the community and of its way of life. In this understanding, the relation of politics and virtue are reversed: virtue becomes the means, and the political community provides the end.

This reversal gave rise to the question explored by Aristotle in Book III of the *Politics*: Are the virtues of the good human being and of the good citizen identical or different? It turns out that they are nearly always different, a conclusion that generates a double dilemma. If a community is notably imperfect, the citizen who shapes himself in its image and devotes himself to its service will undergo a kind of moral deformation. Conversely, the virtues of the good human being *simpliciter* may not only not promote, but may actually impede, the activities of the particular community in which he happens to find himself.

Liberal theorists were not unaware of this dilemma, and they responded to it in two very different ways. Some, such as John Stuart Mill, retained a place for the Aristotelian conception of virtue as an intrinsic good but argued that the practice of virtue, so understood, would also be supportive of the liberal polity. In a liberal order, the same virtues are both ends and means: the good human being and the good citizen are identical.

The other liberal strategy was to cut the knot by denying the very existence of intrinsic virtue, that is, by reinterpreting virtue as purely instrumental to the nonmoral goods that constitute the true ends of liberal politics. Thus Hobbes says:

> All men agree on this, that peace is good, and therefore also [that] the way, or means, of peace, which . . . are justice, gratitude, modesty, equity, mercy, and the rest of the laws of nature, are good. . . . But the writers of moral philosophy, though they acknowledge the same virtues and vices, [do not see] wherein consisted their goodness; nor that they come to be praised as the means of peaceable, sociable, and comfortable living.[18]

During the past two decades, John Rawls has moved between the Hobbesian and Millian strategies. For Rawls, the ultimate justification—and overriding objective—of the liberal polity is the attainment of justice, viewed not as an individual virtue but as a social state of affairs. Rawls rejects "perfectionism"—the thesis that society should be so arranged as to maximize the achievement of individual virtue or excellence. Yet justice as a virtue predicated of individuals does occupy a place within his overall theory. Individuals are presumed to have a capacity for a sense of justice—that is, the ability to accept and to act upon the agreed-on principles of social justice, which in turn supply the substantive content of individual justice. As this conception is developed in *A Theory of Justice*, the engendering of just individuals is not the goal of liberal society but rather the means to the preservation of that society. That is why each member of a well-ordered liberal society wants the others to have a developed sense of justice. And more broadly, Rawls declares in a Hobbesian spirit, "a good person has the features of moral character that it is rational [i.e., instrumentally rational] for members of a well-ordered society to want in their associates."[19] In his more recent work, however, he has placed increased emphasis on the development and exercise of "moral personality" as an intrinsic good or end in itself. The very practices that help sustain a just society also express our nature as free and equal rational beings who have realized their innate capacity for justice.[20]

In the liberal tradition, then, we find traces of both sides of the Aristotelian conception—virtue as end and as means. It would be surprising, however, if on closer inspection the liberal canon of the virtues turned out to mirror the classical enumeration. Indeed, I shall argue (*pace* Hobbes) that it does not. The liberal virtues are not simply the classical virtues justified on a different basis. They are in important respects different virtues.

Liberal Virtues as Means

I begin by examining the liberal virtues understood instrumentally, as means to the preservation of liberal societies and institutions. To fix terms, let me characterize the liberal polity as a community possessing to a high degree the following features: popular-constitutional government; a diverse society with a wide range of individual opportunities and choices; a predominantly market economy; and a substantial, strongly protected sphere of privacy and individual rights. And to avoid misunderstanding, let me briefly characterize the status of the propositions I am about to advance.

1. The discussion of the instrumental virtues in this section is a catalog, not of logical entailments within liberal theory, but rather of empirical hypotheses concerning the relationship between social institutions and individual character. I offer a most fragmentary evidence in support of these hypotheses, an adequate test of which would require a far more systematic historical and comparative inquiry.

2. When I speak of certain virtues as instrumental to the preservation of liberal communities, I do not mean that every citizen must possess these virtues, but rather that most citizens must. The broad hypothesis is that as the proportion of non-virtuous citizens increases significantly, the ability of liberal societies to function successfully will progressively diminish.

3. The fact (if it is a fact) that the instrumental virtues are socially functional does not mean that they are individually advantageous. To be sure, there is some overlap between these two objectives. The liberal virtues demand less self-discipline and sacrifice than do the virtues of classical antiquity, of civic republicanism, or of Christianity, and the practice of many of these social virtues will simultaneously make it easier for individuals to succeed within liberal communities. Still, these virtues are not reducible to self-interest, even self-interest "rightly understood." Thus, while the liberal virtues do not presuppose a specific moral psychology, they do at least imply the rejection of any comprehensive egoism.

General Virtues

Some of the virtues needed to sustain the liberal state are requisites of every political community. From time to time, each community must call upon its members to risk their lives in its defense. Courage—the willingness to fight and even die on behalf of one's country—is thus very widely honored, even though there may be occasions on which the refusal to fight is fully justified.

In addition, every community creates a complex structure of laws and regulations in the expectation that they will be accepted as legitimate, hence binding, without recourse to direct threats or sanctions. The net social value of a law is equal to the social benefits it engenders minus the social costs of enforcing it. As the individual propensity to obey the law diminishes, so does a society's ability to pursue collective goals through the law. Law-abidingness is therefore a core social virtue, in liberal communities and elsewhere. (This does not mean that disobedience is never justified, but only that a heavy burden of proof must be discharged by those who propose to violate the law.)

Finally, every society is constituted by certain core principles and sustained by its members' active belief in them. Conversely, every society is weakened by the diminution of its members' belief in its legitimacy. Loyalty—the developed capacity to understand, to accept, and to act on the core principles of one's society—is thus a fundamental virtue. And it is particularly important in liberal communities, which tend to be organized around abstract principles rather than shared ethnicity, nationality, or history.

Beyond the virtues needed to sustain all political communities are virtues specific to liberal communities—those required by the liberal spheres of society, economy, and polity.

Virtues of Liberal Society

A liberal society is characterized by two key features—individualism and diversity. To individualism corresponds the liberal virtue of independence—the disposition to care for and take responsibility for oneself, and to avoid becoming needlessly dependent on others. Human beings are not born independent, nor do they attain independence through biological maturation alone. A growing body of evidence suggests that in a liberal society the family is the critical arena in which independence and a host of other virtues must be engendered. The weakening of families is thus fraught with danger for liberal societies. In turn, strong families rest on specific virtues. Without fidelity, stable families cannot be maintained. Without a concern for children that extends well beyond the narrow boundaries of adult self-regard, parents will not effectively discharge their responsibility to help form secure, self-reliant young people. In short, the independence required for liberal social life rests on self-restraint and self-transcendence—the virtues of family solidarity.

Let us turn now from individualism to diversity, the second defining feature of liberal society. The maintenance of social diversity requires the virtue of tolerance. This virtue is widely thought to rest on the relativistic belief that every personal choice, every "life-plan," is equally good, hence beyond rational scrutiny and criticism. Nothing could be further from the truth. Tolerance is fully compatible with the proposition that some ways of life can be known to be superior to others. It rests, rather, on the conviction that the pursuit of the better course should be (and in many cases can only be) the consequence of education or persuasion rather than coercion. Indeed, tolerance may be defined as the ability to make this conviction effective as a maxim of personal conduct.

Virtues of the Liberal Economy

The liberal/market economy relies on two kinds of virtues—those required by different economic roles, and those required by liberal economic life taken as a whole. In a modern market economy, the basic roles are the entrepreneur and the organization-employee. The entrepreneurial virtues form a familiar litany—imagination, initiative, drive, determination. The organizational virtues are very different from (and in some respects the reverse of) the entrepreneurial. They include such traits as punctuality, reliability, civility toward coworkers, and a willingness to work within established frameworks and tasks. As economic units evolve, one of the great management challenges is to adjust the mix of entrepreneurial and organizational practices. Sometimes this takes the form of an organizational displacement (or routinization) of entrepreneurial charisma, as in the ouster of Steven Jobs as head of Apple Computer. Sometimes it requires just the opposite, as when a large, stodgy organization replaces a centralized structure with semiautonomous units and loosens individual task and role definitions in an effort to encourage more entrepreneurial practices on the part of its employees.

There are three generic (as distinct from role-specific) virtues required by modern market economies. The first is the work ethic, which combines the sense of obligation to support personal independence through gainful effort with the determination to do one's job thoroughly and well. The second is the achievement of a mean between ascetic self-denial and untrammeled self-indulgence—call it a capacity for moderate delay of gratification. For while market economies rely on the liberation and multiplication of consumer desires, they cannot prosper in the long run without a certain level of saving, which rests on the ability to subordinate immediate gratification to longer-run self-interest.

The third generic economic virtue is adaptability. Modern market economies are characterized by rapid, sweeping changes that reconfigure organizations and occupations. Patterns of lifelong employment within a single task or organization, common for much of this century, are being displaced. Most individuals will change jobs several times during their working lives, moving into new occupations, new organizations, and even new sectors of the economy. To be sure, collective political action can help regulate the pace of change, ameliorate its consequences, and share its costs. Still, domestic and international pressures combine to make the fact and basic direction of economic change irresistible. Thus, the disposition to accept new tasks as challenges rather than threats and the ability to avoid defining personal identity and worth in reference to specific, fixed occupations are essential attributes of individuals and economies able to cope successfully with the demands of change.[21]

Virtues of Liberal Politics

Let us examine, finally, the sphere of politics, which calls for virtues of both citizens and leaders.

Virtues of citizenship. Some generic citizen virtues have already been identified: courage, law-abidingness, loyalty. In addition to these are the citizen virtues specific to the liberal polity. Because a liberal order rests on individual rights, the liberal citizen must have the capacity to discern, and the restraint to respect, the rights of others. (Invasion of the rights of others is the form of *pleonexia* specific to liberal political life.) Because liberalism incorporates representative government, the liberal citizen must have the capacity to discern the talent and character of candidates vying for office, and to evaluate the performance of individuals who have attained office. Liberalism also envisions popular government, responsive to the demands of its citizens. The greatest vices of popular governments are the propensity to gratify short-term desires at the expense of long-term interests and the inability to act on unpleasant truths about what must be done. To check these vices, liberal citizens must be moderate in their demands and self-disciplined enough to accept painful measures when they are necessary. From this standpoint, the willingness of liberal citizens to demand no more public services than their country can afford and to pay for all the benefits they demand is not just a technical economic issue, but a moral issue as well. Consistently unbalanced budgets—the systematic displacement of social costs to future generations—are signs of a citizenry unwilling to moderate its desires or to discharge its duties.

The liberal citizen is not the same as the civic-republican citizen. In a liberal polity, there is no duty to participate actively in politics, no requirement to place the public above the private and to systematically subordinate personal interest to the common good, no commitment to accept collective determination of personal choices. But neither is liberal citizenship simply the pursuit of self-interest, individually or in factional collusion with others of like mind. Liberal citizenship has its own distinctive restraints—virtues that circumscribe and check, without wholly nullifying, the prompting of self-aggrandizement.

Virtues of leadership. The need for virtue and excellence in political leaders is perhaps more immediately evident than is the corresponding requirement in the case of citizens. The Founders saw popular elections as the vehicle for discerning and selecting good leaders. Thomas Jefferson spoke for them when he wrote to John Adams:

[T]here is a natural aristocracy among men. The grounds of this are virtue and talents. . . . The natural aristocracy I consider as the most precious gift of nature, for the instruction, trusts, and government of society. . . . May we not even say, that that form of government is the best, which provides the most effectively for a pure selection of these natural *aristoi* into the offices of government? . . . I think the best remedy is exactly that provided by all our constitutions, to leave to the citizens the free election and separation of the *aristoi* from the *pseudo-aristoi*.[22]

The leadership virtues specific to liberal polities include patience—the ability to accept, and work within, the constraints on action imposed by social diversity and constitutional institutions. Second, the liberal leader must have the capacity to forge a sense of common purpose against the centrifugal tendencies of an individualistic and fragmented society. Third, the liberal leader must be able to resist the temptation to earn popularity by pandering to immoderate public demands. Against desire the liberal leader must counterpose restraints; against the fantasy of the free lunch he must insist on the reality of the hard choice; against the lure of the immediate he must insist on the requirements of the long-term. Finally, while the liberal leader derives authority from popular consent, he cannot derive policy from public opinion. Rather, he must have the capacity to narrow—so far as public opinion permits—the gap between popular preference and wise action. The liberal leader who disregards public sentiment will quickly come to grief, but so will the leader who simply takes that sentiment as the pole-star of public policy. Through persuasion, the liberal leader tries to move the citizenry toward sound views. But the limits of persuasion must constitute the boundaries of public action, or else leadership becomes usurpation.

As the authors of the *Federalist* insisted, and as experience confirms, there are also specific virtues required for the successful conduct of the different offices in a liberal-constitutional order: optimism and energy in the executive, deliberative excellence and civility in the legislator, impartiality and interpretive skill in the judge.[23] And, as Jefferson suggested, the ultimate test of systems of election or appointment is their tendency to select officeholders with the appropriate virtues. For that reason, it is appropriate and necessary to inquire whether particular systems of selection (e.g., presidential nominating primaries) tend on balance to reward the kinds of personal traits that their corresponding offices require.

General political virtues. There are two other political virtues required of liberal citizens and leaders alike. While not all public policies need be made in the full light of day, liberal politics rests on a presumption of publicity—that is, on a commitment to resolve disputes through open discussion unless compelling reasons can be adduced for restricting or concealing the policy process. Thus, a general liberal political virtue is the disposition—and the developed capacity—to engage in public discourse. This includes the willingness to listen seriously to a range of views that, given the diversity of liberal societies, will include ideas the listener is bound to find strange and even obnoxious. The virtue of political discourse also includes the willingness to set forth one's own views intelligibly and candidly as the basis of a politics of persuasion rather than manipulation or coercion.

A second general political virtue is the disposition to narrow the gap (so far as is in one's power) between principles and practices in liberal society. For leaders, this means admitting and confronting social imperfections through a public appeal to collective convictions. For citizens it can mean either such a public appeal or quiet acts that reduce the reach of hypocrisy in one's immediate community. For both, it can lead to a tension between social transformation and law-abidingness, which can be resolved prudentially only with reference to the facts of specific cases. This is a tension rather than a contradiction between these two liberal virtues because the virtue of law-abidingness embodies, not the absolute priority of law, but rather a presumption in favor of the law that can be rebutted in a narrow range of instances.

Liberal Virtues as Ends

The thrust of the argument thus far has been to specify the virtues instrumental to the preservation and operation of the liberal polity. Let us turn now from pondering liberal virtues as means to examining them as ends. The question is whether there is a conception of the virtuous or excellent individual linked intrinsically to liberal theory and seen as valuable, not instrumentally, but for its own sake.

It might be thought that the answer must be negative. After all, it is characteristic of both liberal societies and liberal theories to be open to a wide variety of life plans and to their corresponding excellences. Yet the liberal tradition is by no means silent on this question. Indeed, it suggests three conceptions of intrinsic individual excellence, overlapping yet distinct.

The first is the Lockean conception of excellence as rational liberty or self-direction. As persuasively reconstructed by Rogers Smith, rational self-direction includes the capacity to form, pursue, and revise life plans in light of our personal commitments and circumstances. But it is a substantive, not merely instrumental standard:

> [I]f we value rational self-direction, we must always strive to maintain in ourselves, and to respect in others, these very capacities for deliberative self-guidance and self-control. Correspondingly, we must see the habitual exercise of these capacities as constituting morally worthy character and their enhancement as constituting morally praiseworthy action.[24]

The second non-instrumental liberal conception of individual excellence is the Kantian account of the capacity to act in accordance with the precepts of duty—that is, to make duty the effective principle of personal conduct and to resist the promptings of passion and interest insofar as they are incompatible with this principle. Judith Shklar has offered a fine sketch of Kant's morally excellent individual in action:

> At all times, he must respect humanity, the rational moral element in himself and in *all* other men. For his own sake, he must choose to avoid all self-destructive and gross behavior, and above all else, he must not lie. . . . To other men he owes no liberality or pity or *noblesse oblige* of any kind, because this might humiliate the recipients. What he does have to show them is a respect for their rights, decent manners, and an avoidance of calumny, pride, and malice . . . This is a thoroughly democratic liberal character, built to preserve his own self-respect and that of others, neither demanding nor enduring servility.[25]

The third liberal conception of individual excellence was adapted in different ways from romanticism by John Stuart Mill, Ralph Waldo Emerson, Henry David Thoreau, and Walt Whitman. It is the understanding of excellence as the full flowering of individuality. As Mill expounded this thesis, the excellence of individuality combines the Greek emphasis on the development, through activity, of human powers with the modern realization that the blend and balance of these powers will differ from individual to individual. Because liberal societies allow maximum scope for diversity, they are the most (though not perfectly) conducive to the development of individuality. And because liberal societies rest on individual freedom, they tend to foster the self-determination that is at the heart of true individuality. As Mill put it, "He who lets the world, or his own portion of it, choose his plan of life for him, has no need of any other faculty than the ape-like one of imitation. He who chooses his plan for himself, employs all his faculties."[26] Or, as George Kateb sums up the parallel argument within the Emersonian tradition,

> One must take responsibility for oneself—one's self must become a project, one must become the architect of one's soul. One's *dignity* resides in being, to some important degree, a person of one's own creating, making, choosing rather than in being merely a creature or a socially manufactured, conditioned, created thing.[27]

Can these three distinct, but recognizably liberal, conceptions of human excellence be made to cohere in a single unified view? Yes, to a point. They have a common core—a vision of individuals who in some manner take responsibility for their own lives. Each links excellence to a kind of activity. And all lead to a vindication of the dignity of every individual and to the practice of mutual respect. Beyond this common core, however, certain tensions become manifest. The exercise of Lockean rational liberty can lead to a wide range of deliberative outcomes, while Kantian duty usually prescribes a single course of conduct as generally binding. The pursuit of Emersonian individuality can tend toward a kind of poetic, even mystical self-transcendence at war with both the rationalism of Kantian morality and the prosaic, orderly self-discipline of Lockean liberty.[28]

It is possible, of course, to resolve these tensions by giving one conception pride of place and requiring the others to maintain consistency with the preferred standard. (This is the course that Rawls—like Kant—follows when he subordinates the rational pursuit of individual life-plans to the social requirements of moral right.) But it may be more advisable to accept a range of tension and indeterminacy—that is, to see the liberal polity at its best as a community that encourages all of these overlapping but distinct conceptions of individual excellence and provides an arena within which each may be realized, in part through struggle against the others.

Ways of Developing Liberal Virtues

The health of liberal polities is intertwined in complex ways with the practice of liberal virtues. Now assuming that these virtues are not innate, by what means are they to be engendered? And are they adequately developed in our own liberal community? A full examination of these issues lies well beyond the scope of the present discussion. But let me briefly discuss three alternative hypotheses.

The optimistic hypothesis claims that daily life in the liberal polity is a powerful if tacit force for habituation to at least the minimal requirements of liberal virtue. The sorts of things regularly expected of us at home, in school, and on the job shape us in the manner required for the operation of liberal institutions. And while hardly models of moral perfection, citizens of modern liberal communities are at least adequately virtuous—and not demonstrably less so than were citizens in times past.

The neutral hypothesis maintains that tacit socialization is not enough; that authoritative institutions such as families, schools, churches, the legal system, political leaders, and the media must deliberately and cooperatively foster liberal virtues; that these institutions are not now performing this task adequately; but that there is no reason in principle why they cannot do so once they come more fully to understand their responsibility.

Finally, the pessimistic hypothesis—associated with such thinkers as Daniel Bell—suggests that powerful strands of contemporary liberal culture tend to undermine liberal virtues, that in particular the various forms of liberal self-restraint have fallen victim to the imperatives of self-indulgence and self-expression.[29] From this perspective, the task of strengthening and renewing liberal virtues requires more than improving the formal institutions of moral and civic education. It requires as well a sustained effort to reverse corrosive tendencies fundamental to modern culture.

Evidence can be adduced for each of these hypotheses. Optimists can point to the demonstrable fact that our polity has generated—or at least has not thwarted the generation of—the minimal conditions for its survival over the past two centuries. Neutralists can argue that key social indicators—crime, drugs, family stability, and others—are headed in alarming directions and that the impact of major forces of socialization—in particular, television and popular culture—is on balance negative. And pessimists can observe that with the important exception of organized religion, most sources of social authority have a diminished confidence in their ability to establish, inculcate, and enforce social norms of conduct and character.

In a perspective study of contemporary city government, Stephen Elkin has argued that the operation of urban political institutions has a pervasive, and predominantly negative, effect on the character of the citizenry. In order for a commercial republic to move toward the "commercial public interest," it needs at the heart of the liberal democratic citizen "a disposition to think of political choice as involving the giving of reasons." Public choice is to involve "justification, not just the aggregation of wants and interest."[30] Unfortunately, modern city governments systematically fail to foster this disposition, for three reasons. These governments are executive-centered and are therefore not geared to eliciting reasoned argument from individual citizens, or to listening attentively if it happens to be forthcoming. They induce citizens to relate to one another as interest-bearers and as bargainers rather than as participants in a shared process of justification. And finally, many urban citizens relate to one another as "clients" whose interests are defined and mediated by bureaucratic experts.[31] These negative consequences of urban public life cannot be reversed without systematic reform in the characteristic institutions and procedures of city governments.[32]

Richard Dagger also looks to the city as the locus of citizenship, and he is equally discouraged by what he finds. In his view, three features of contemporary urban life are particularly destructive. The sheer size of most cities militates against individual interest in its affairs and against the development of mutual trust. The fragmentation of governmental responsibility breeds "confusion, disorientation, and a sense of impotence." Rapid mobility loosens the ties that bind individuals to the community and erodes the disposition to participate and cooperate. Like Elkin, Dagger argues that the negative consequences for citizenship of the modern city cannot be reduced without systematic reforms that ameliorate their causes.[33]

George Kateb takes a more optimistic view. He argues that representative democracy has a tendency to foster the kinds of character traits that liberal societies particularly need: independence of spirit, the democratization of social life, and a "general tolerance of, and even affection for, diversity."[34] Overall, liberal democratic society is taught, or teaches itself, a fundamental lesson about the nature of all authority:

> a pervasive skepticism . . . ; a reluctance to defer; a conviction that those who wield authority must themselves be skeptical toward their roles and themselves and that necessary authority must be wielded in a way that inflicts minimum damage on the moral authority of all people . . . [and] a tendency to try to do without authority wherever possible or to disperse or disguise it, and thus to soften it.[35]

While not insensitive to the very real difficulties inherent in such dispositions, Kateb is willing to defend them, not just as instrumentally necessary for liberal democracies, but also as intrinsically preferable to the sets of disposition associated with alternative forms of political organization—in particular, direct democracy.[36]

Robert Lane has undertaken what is probably the most thorough and systematic effort to assemble and assess the empirical evidence concerning the effects of liberal democratic life on character formation. He begins by defining, and defending, a model of "mature and developed personality" that has five components: cognitive capacity; autonomy; sociocentrism—the ability to understand and recognize the thoughts and claims of others as well as oneself; identity—some combination of self-knowledge, self-acceptance, and self-respect; and identification with normal values, as a necessary bulwark against sociopathic behavior.[37] Lane then examines in detail the effects of capitalist markets and democratic politics on the development of such a personality. His conclusion is a nuanced blend of hope and concern:

> The market has taught us much, including cognitive complexity, self-reliance, and a version of justice where work or contribution to the economy is rewarded. Through its emphasis on transactions it has eroded some of the sources of sociocentrism. By its destruction of sources of humane values, its instrumentalism, it has made identity hard to achieve and its amoralism has made difficult the identification with moral values. Democracy, too, has made people think; it has offered a promise of fate control which it only partially fulfills. While it embodies a form of sociocentrism, it does not model morality for the public, although its form of justice allows for beneficence, the justice of need. And its complex diversity makes identity hard to achieve, but once achieved, all the more valuable.[38]

In a parallel analysis focusing exclusively on the capitalist market, Lane examines—and largely rejects—recent pessimism about its effects. Consumerism has not perceptibly eroded the work ethic; modern industry requires as much cooperation as competition; individuals continue to have confidence in their efficacy—that is, in some nonrandom relation between the effort, contribution, and skill they display and the rewards they receive; the capacity to innovate, and to take the initiative, is higher among workers in market economies than in command economies; and the ability to question authority by adopting a skeptical stance toward authoritarian morality remains high.[39]

These findings help us focus the debate between optimists, pessimists, and neutralists. It is surely important, as the optimists insist, to take a long view—to recall that America has survived social conflict and dislocation as severe as any we are now experiencing, and to recognize that our current civic culture retains many healthy elements that help sustain personal liberty while warding off public oppression. But it is at least as important to give sustained attention to the phenomena on which neutralists dwell: rising rates of drug use, crime, and family breakdown; inadequate levels of public education, public provision, and public involvement; greed and short-sightedness in public and private affairs; and the growing barbarization and tribalization of American life. Nor can we afford to ignore the pessimists' thesis that these problems are structural rather than accidental—for example, that media-driven patterns of consumption and self-involvement are steadily breaking down the habits of restraint and responsibility on which the liberal polity (like any other) inescapably depends.

In *Federalist 55*, James Madison reminds us that,

> As there is a degree of depravity in mankind which requires a certain degree of circumspection and distrust, so there are other qualities in human nature which justify a certain portion of esteem and confidence. Republican government presupposes the existence of these qualities in a higher degree than any other form. Were the pictures which have been drawn by the political jealousy of some among us faithful likenesses of the human character, the inference would be that there is not sufficient virtue among us for self-government.

Madison speaks of "human nature." But he was under no illusion that the balance between depravity and estimable qualities that we actually observe in individuals is just given by nature. While we are endowed with certain capacities for virtue, we become virtuous only under certain circumstances—through appropriate upbringing, education, and experience. What is most striking about our constitution—a point Mary Ann Glendon has stressed—is its failure to provide for, or even to mention, these formative forces.[40] Our national political institutions presuppose the existence of certain kinds of individuals but do nothing to produce them.

There are, I think, three linked explanations for this odd hiatus. The first is that Madison and others saw American society—families, communities, and daily life—as fundamentally healthy, as productive of adequately virtuous citizens, and they assumed (or at least hoped) that these institutions would remain healthy of their own accord. Second, the federal, as opposed to purely national, design of our new political institutions was meant to leave nearly all social questions to states and local communities. Third, the rise of liberal democracy, in contradistinction to classical republican-ism, meant an emerging (though constantly contested) demarca-tion between the public and private realms. The formation of character, including public character, was left to institutions such as families and religious communities which were to be signifi-cantly free from public direction.

In essence, in the American liberal democratic order, as opposed to totalitarian or even classical republican regimes, semi-autono-mous families play a key role in the formation of citizens. It follows directly that if families become less capable of performing that role, the well-being of the entire community is jeopardized. There is evi-dence that the family breakdown of recent decades is yielding just that result.

Among these liberal virtues is what I have called "indepen-dence"—the disposition to care for, and take responsibility for, oneself and to avoid becoming needlessly dependent on others. A growing body of evidence suggests that in a liberal democracy, the family is the critical arena in which independence is fostered. For example, after correcting for other variables such as educational attainment, the children of long-term welfare-dependent single parents are far more likely to become similarly dependent them-selves.

Equally suggestive is the evidence concerning the difficulties that many young unwed mothers experience in raising their sons. The absence of fathers as models and co-disciplinarians contributes to the low self-esteem, anger, violence, and peer-bonding through gang lawlessness characteristic of many fatherless boys. The ero-sion of the two-parent family structure thus threatens to generate a growing subset of the population that cannot discharge the basic responsibilities of citizenship in a liberal democracy.

One key function of strong families in liberal democracies is the encouragement of civic character and competence in young people. A second, closely related, function is the linking of the young to the broader community. More than two centuries ago Edmund Burke suggested that the seeds of public concern are sown in the sense of connection we feel to our family and kin. A half century after the founding, Tocqueville's observations led him to conclude that America's families helped mute self-centered egoism and link individuals to their political institutions. Recent sociological studies confirm a strong correlation between family solidarity and the sense of obligation to a wider community and society.

In this connection, among others, the decline of stable marriages is a worrisome sign for our polity. Various studies suggest, for example, that children of divorced parents experience greater than average difficulty in making commitments and forging bonds of trust with others. Taken in conjunction with the Burke/Tocqueville thesis, these observations generate the prediction that in the aggregate, today's young people would feel a lower sense of connection to the political community than did those of previous generations. A recent *Times Mirror* study is consistent with this prediction. As Glendon summarizes its principal finding, the current group "knows less, cares less, [and] votes less" than young people at any time during the past half century.[41]

Pondering these developments, along with many others tending in the same direction, we have at least as much food for concern as for celebration. It is fashionable, and all too easy, to denigrate this stance by pointing out that cultural pessimism is a pervasive theme of human history in nearly every community and in nearly every generation. But the fact remains that political communities can move, and throughout history have moved, from health to disrepair for reasons linked to moral and cultural decay. In the face of this, contemporary American liberals cannot afford to be complacent. We cannot simply chant the mantra of diversity and hope that fate will smile upon us. We must try as best we can to repair our tattered social fabric by attending more carefully to the moral requirements of liberal public life and by doing what is possible and proper to reinforce them.

Notes

1. Leo Strauss, *Natural Right and History* (Chicago: University of Chicago Press, 1953); C. B. Macpherson, *The Political Theory of Possessive Individualism* (London: Oxford University Press, 1962).

2. Martin Diamond, "Democracy and *The Federalist*: A Reconsideration of the Framers' Intent," *American Political Science Review* 53:

52–68; Gordon Wood, *The Creation of the American Republic, 1776–1787* (New York: Norton, 1969).

3. Robert Dahl, *A Preface to Democratic Theory* (Chicago: University of Chicago Press, 1956); Theodore Lowi, *The End of Liberalism* (New York: Norton, 1969).

4. J. G. A. Pocock, *The Machiavellian Moment* (Princeton: Princeton University Press, 1975); Quentin Skinner, "The Idea of Negative Liberty," in *Philosophy in History*, ed. Richard Rorty, J. B. Schneewind, and Quentin Skinner (Cambridge: Cambridge University Press, 1984).

5. Charles Taylor, "Atomism," in *Powers, Possessions, and Freedoms: Essays in Honor of C. B. Macpherson*, ed. Alkis Kontos (Toronto: University of Toronto Press, 1979); Alasdair MacIntyre, *After Virtue* (Notre Dame: Notre Dame University Press, 1981) and "Is Patriotism a Virtue?", *The Lindley Lecture* (University of Kansas: Department of Philosophy, 1984); Michael Sandel, *Liberalism and the Limits of Justice* (New York: Cambridge University Press, 1982) and the "The Procedural Republic and the Unencumbered Self," *Political Theory* 12 (1984): 81–96.

6. Irving Kristol, "The Adversary Cultures of the Intellectuals," in *The Moral Basis of Democratic Capitalism*, ed. Michael Novak (Washington, DC: American Enterprise Institute, 1980).

7. Albert Hirschman, *The Passions and the Interests* (Princeton: Princeton University Press, 1977).

8. Immanuel Kant, "Perpetual Peace," in *Kant on History*, ed. Lewis White Beck (Indianapolis: Bobbs-Merrill, 1963), 111–12.

9. Judith Shklar, *Ordinary Vices* (Cambridge, MA: Harvard University Press, 1984), 5.

10. Rogers Smith, *Liberalism and American Constitutional Law* (Cambridge, MA: Harvard University Press, 1985).

11. Nathan Tarcov, *Locke's Education for Liberty* (Chicago: University of Chicago Press, 1984); see also his "A 'Non-Lockean' Locke and the Character of Liberalism," in *Liberalism Reconsidered*, ed. Douglas Maclean and Claudia Mills (Totowa, NJ: Rowman and Allanheld, 1983).

12. Ronald Terchek, "The Fruits of Success and the Crisis of Liberalism," in *Liberals on Liberalism*, ed. Alfonso Damico (Totowa, NJ: Rowman and Littlefield, 1986), 18.

13. J. Budziszewski, *The Resurrection of Nature: Political Theory and the Human Character* (Ithaca, NY: Cornell University Press, 1986).

14. Harvey Mansfield Jr., "Constitutional Government: the Soul of Modern Democracy," *The Public Interest* 86 (1987): 59.

15. James Q. Wilson, "The Rediscovery of Character: Private Virtue and Public Policy," *The Public Interest* 81 (1985): 15–16.

16. Thomas Spragens Jr. "Reconstructing Liberal Theory: Reason and Liberal Culture," in *Liberals on Liberalism*, ed. Damico, 43.

17. Shklar, *Ordinary Vices*, 5.

18. Thomas Hobbes, *Leviathan* (New York: Macmillan, 1962), 124.

19. John Rawls, *A Theory of Justice* (Cambridge, MA: Harvard University Press, 1971), 436–37.

20. See William A. Galston, *Liberal Purposes: Goods, Virtues, and Diversity in the Liberal State* (Cambridge: Cambridge University Press, 1991), ch. 6.

21. This virtue should be not confused with Robert Unger's much broader strictures against identifying personality with external structure. See *Liberal Purposes*, ch. 3.

22. Thomas Jefferson to John Adams, 28 October 1813, in *Free Government in the Making*, ed. Alpheus T. Mason (New York: Oxford University Press, 1965), 385.

23. For a parallel account, see Mansfield, "Constitutional Government," p. 60.

24. Smith, *Liberalism and American Constitutional Law*, 200.

25. Shklar, *Ordinary Vices*, 233.

26. John Stuart Mill, *On Liberty*, ed. David Spitz (New York: Norton, 1975), 56.

27. George Kateb, "Democratic Individuality and the Claims of Politics," *Political Theory* 12 (1984): 343.

28. See Nancy Rosenblum, *Another Liberalism: Romanticism and the Reconstruction of Liberal Thought* (Cambridge, MA: Harvard University Press, 1987), ch. 2.

29. Daniel Bell, *The Cultural Contradictions of Capitalism* (New York: Basic Books, 1976).

30. Stephen L. Elkin, *City and Regime in the American Republic* (Chicago: University of Chicago Press, 1987), 149.

31. Ibid., 159–64.

32. Ibid., ch. 9.

33. Richard Dagger, "Metropolis, Memory and Citizenship," *American Journal of Political Science* 25, 4 (November 1981): 715–37.

34. George Kateb, "The Moral Distinctiveness of Representative Democracy," *Ethics* 91, 3 (April 1981): 359–61.

35. Ibid., 358.

36. Ibid., 369–74.

37. Robert E. Lane, "Markets and Politics: The Human Project," *British Journal of Political Science* 11, 1 (January 1981): 3–6.

38. Ibid., 15.

39. Lane, "Capitalist Man, Socialist Man," *Philosophy, Politics and Society*, fifth series, ed. Peter Laslett and James Fishkin (New Haven: Yale University Press, 1979), 57–77.

40. Mary Ann Glendon, "Virtues, Families and Citizenship," in *The Meaning of the Family in a Free Society*, ed. W. Lawson Taitte (Dallas: The University of Texas at Dallas, 1991).

41. Ibid., 67.

CHAPTER 3

The Oldest Virtue

Judith Martin

Morals Versus Etiquette

Whenever there is a contest between etiquette and acknowledged virtues, etiquette loses. Hardly anyone would dispute the proposition that morals are more important than mere manners, and the assertion that etiquette can and should be jettisoned for a higher good is commonly made and accepted in everyday life.

"I'm concerned about people's health" is a typical explanation offered by someone who admonishes others, sometimes even strangers in restaurants, that what they're eating is bad for them. The moral virtue of devotion to the well-being of others supposedly obliterates the rule of etiquette against minding other people's business.

"You want me to be honest, don't you?" has come to be the standard response from anyone challenged for the practice of telling friends that they look terrible, exhibit bad taste, give boring parties or sing off-key. Although these statements are proscribed by etiquette, which classifies them as insults, they are allegedly permissible when reclassified as morally virtuous truth-telling.

"This is more important," an activist will declare when called upon to defend cursing passersby for wearing fur or leather coats, or scolding coffee-drinkers for using styrofoam cups. The moral worth of his cause on behalf of animals or the environment is seen as overriding the etiquette injunction against humiliating people.

Since expressing one's feelings came to be considered a virtue

(under such names as assertiveness or self-esteem, which are supposed to suggest a laudable strength of character), simply succumbing to a desire to say or do something may be cited as good
reason for canceling the claims of etiquette. A common justification
for ignoring the etiquette rule against nosiness is the simple admis-
sion of curiosity. In those rare instances, nowadays, when someone
who asks personal questions is taxed with invasion of privacy, the
offender points out he was "wondering" or "interested in" what
another paid for his house, why he uses a wheelchair, or whether
he is planning to get a divorce. The justification given for almost
any uncivilized behavior by children, including annoying other
people and damaging their property, is their manifestation not just
of self-expression but of the creative spirit.

Even the failure to do something may be given a moral dimension that excuses ignoring the requirements of etiquette. Such
omissions as not visiting the dying, not attending funerals, and not
sending thank you letters in return for hospitality, favors, or presents were once perceived as evidence of rudeness, presumably
prompted by selfishness or sloth. Now the explanations ("I want to
remember him as he was," "Funerals give me the creeps," "I hate
to write letters," "People should do things just because they want
to, not because they expect to be thanked") imply that there is
virtue in the act of refusing to let the expectations of etiquette prevail over personal disinclinations. Indeed, these explanations imply
that it is anyone who expects that distaste for the duties of etiquette
to be overcome who is exhibiting a lack of compassion and respect.

In a bizarre twist, enforcing polite behavior has come to be considered a virtue that relieves anyone who engages in it from also
having to be polite. A new set of etiquette vigilantes who spot such
etiquette violations as smoking in the presence of nonsmokers without their permission or refusing to extend road courtesies to other
drivers will proudly report having used obscenities and threats in
order to make the violators "mind their manners."

Even among those who profess to value good manners (which
usually turns out to mean that they dislike being treated rudely
without necessarily being willing to behave politely themselves), it
is widely held that the decline of etiquette is a problem to be dealt

with only after the panoply of more serious social problems has been solved.

But what if the decline of etiquette *is* one of the most serious social problems, from which other serious social problems devolve merely as epiphenomena?

Manners and Morals as Partners

Throughout most of recorded history, theologians and philosophers extolled propriety and correct social behavior as virtues akin to morality. It is chiefly in this century that they came to regard etiquette as a dispensable frill, at best; at worse, they denounced it as a sin. Hypocrisy is the damning label now attached to any polite inhibition that disguises a sincerely held opinion or restrains a righteous impulse for action.

Obeisance to etiquette, far from being a weak and optional virtue, much less a sin, is the oldest social virtue and an indispensable partner of morality. Rather than being the crowning touch of good behavior in the upper reaches of a stratified society, etiquette is civilization's first necessity.

Since time immemorial, etiquette has been used to establish the principles of social virtue as well as the rules, symbols, and rituals of civilized life. Historically, it preceded the invention of the law as a restraint of individual behavior for the common good, surely making etiquette the oldest deterrent to violence after fear of retaliation. Developmentally, it still precedes the teaching of moral concepts in the socialization of children.

Evidence of the prehistoric practice of etiquette—such as communal eating and ceremonial burying of the dead—has served to define civilization in its earliest manifestations. Yet there persists a widespread belief that etiquette arose from the desire of Victorian killjoys to ruin private pleasures, to quash the freedoms achieved during the Enlightenment, and to enhance the power of rich snobs over the proletariat.

This notion ignores overwhelming evidence that etiquette exists in primitive societies as much as—and often in more rigid forms than—in industrialized societies. Contemporary romantics are given to disdaining the etiquette tradition of their own modern culture while waxing sentimental over similar practices in what they regard as more authentic cultures. But in present American society, etiquette rites are much more elaborate among the young and the poor (for example, in the dress codes, precedence systems, gestures of greeting, and modes of address in urban street gangs) than among the rich who have increasingly abandoned the very aspects of etiquette that are of vital concern on the streets.

The Ensemble of Fundamental Beliefs

Morals and manners are not conflicting but complementary, and sometimes overlapping, parts of the ensemble of fundamental beliefs and needs that we hold simply because we are rational agents blessed with practical reason. Moral beliefs include such concepts as duty, obligation, responsibility, and sacredness of the person, while manners include such beliefs and needs as communal harmony, cultural coherence, and dignity of the person. Ethics and etiquette refer to sets of imperatives commanding social behavior that derive their authority as rational prescriptive systems from morals and manners, respectively.

Hence, committing murder, which violates the sacredness of the person, is immoral, while causing humiliation, which violates the dignity of the person, is unmannerly. But such beliefs as compassion, respect, and toleration are shared by morals and manners and hence form the basis of imperatives of ethics as well as of etiquette.

In many everyday situations where conflicts between ethics and etiquette arise, giving precedence to etiquette may be the more virtuous choice. The likelihood of bringing about a higher good (i.e., *eudaemonia*) by rudely expressing one's concern for others' health, voicing unflattering criticism, and forcing confrontational consideration of moral issues is small (and, in some cases, such as the friend who sings off-key, nil). However, it is nearly a certainty that these morally righteous etiquette transgressions will cause embarrassment and hurt feelings, evils that manners seek to forestall. Is hypocrisy such a heinous sin that avoiding any small amount of it is worth sacrificing the feelings of people who had mistakenly assumed that they were pleasing others?

Conflicts may arise not only between ethics and etiquette but also within etiquette itself when contradictory rules may apply to a given setting. The same action may appear either necessary or proscribed, depending on the relative consideration given by the agent to various aspects of the situation. Complex judgment—wisdom—is then required in order to decide on a course of action that best serves the ends of manners.

Should patients show respect for their doctor by addressing him or her by title and surname, if the doctor is calling them by their first names? Is the doctor doing this because he lacks respect for his patients or because he believes that the manners of personal friendship put patients more at ease? Suppose the patients are offended, rather than put at their ease, by this inequity. Should they ignore it to spare the doctor embarrassment or correct it on the grounds that they owe it either to their own dignity or to the doctor to let him know that he is producing an effect opposite from what he intended to achieve?

Has a boss who calls women employees "honey" given evidence of evil intent, in which case he should be properly chastised, or is he of goodwill but ignorant of social conventions? How long after customs have changed is such ignorance excusable?

The Functions of Etiquette

In spite of the thoughtfulness required in weighing and interpreting one's own and others' actions in the interests of politeness, rules of etiquette cannot always be deduced from first principles. Persons who believe that etiquette is just following common sense in applying the mannerly injunction to be considerate of others fail to recognize that etiquette serves not only a regulative function but also symbolic and ritual functions.

Regulative Etiquette

Regulative etiquette is the most easily understood of the three functions because it resembles the law. Both the law and etiquette provide rules for the promotion of communal harmony, according to the principles of morality and of manners, respectively. The law addresses the most serious conflicts, including those threatening life, limb, and property, and dispenses such fierce sanctions as fines, imprisonment, and loss of life for violations of its rules. With only the sanction of shame at its command, etiquette addresses conflicts for which voluntary compliance is generally attainable; it thus serves to avert antagonisms that might escalate into violations of law. In this respect, etiquette resembles international law, which seeks to avert war, but has only the sanction of shame with which to enforce its rules upon sovereign states.

Because both etiquette rules and laws are fashioned to pertain to a particular time and social setting, they are subject to development and change, albeit slowly because of their inertia due to tradition. The principles, however, from which manners and morals derive their authority remain constant and universal. Even directly contradictory rules of etiquette prevailing in different societies at the same time, or at different times in the same society, may derive their authority from the same principle of manners.

Failing to take off one's shoes when arriving at a dinner party in Japan would show a lack of respect for the hosts, while seating guests with their backs to the most decorative part of the room is understood to honor them by having these objects serve as their background. But taking off one's shoes upon arriving at an American dinner party would be a demonstration of disrespect, and an American host who asks guests to remove their shoes in order to preserve the cleanliness of the carpet is disrespectful to the guests by showing more honor to his possessions than to them.

Treating women courteously once required men to allow them precedence and offer them assistance, including symbolic assistance for tasks that even men knew women could perform unassisted. Courtesy now forbids men from offering women special precedence or assistance in the working world where calling attention to their gender, and suggesting that it requires protection, puts women at a professional disadvantage. In the private realm, the old-time, gender-related courtesies still prevail, although they are increasingly falling into disuse. It is likely that precedence and assistance will soon come to be based solely on age and need, a system which creates new hazards by requiring people to guess these attributes in others who may well take insult from being categorized, accurately or not, as being old or helpless.

Does this change in customs mean that etiquette authorizes a woman offered a seat by a man, or a frail-appearing man offered a seat by a robust youth, to snap out, "I can stand just as well as you can"? No, because the injunction against reproving the author of an obviously well-intentioned gesture is an unalterable principle of manners.

Because etiquette is both voluntary and flexible, it is able to prevent or settle a myriad of minor disputes that would otherwise have to be handled by the law, often after first erupting into violence. A complex society cannot operate properly without using both etiquette and, where voluntary compliance fails, law. This has been demonstrated in recent years, when a declining belief in etiquette as a legitimate force in regulating social conduct has prompted American society to try to get along without it.

Many Americans came to believe—and to put into practice—the idea that any behavior not prohibited by law ought to be tolerated. As a result, people who found rude but legally permitted behavior intolerable have attempted to expand the law to outlaw rudeness. For this purpose, they escalated the consequences of rudeness to bring it into categories that were already given serious attention by the law. Thus, any insult became slander or libel, meanness became mental cruelty, and annoyances from tobacco smoke or noise became health hazards.

This attempt to redefine manners violations as moral violations poses a threat to the freedoms guaranteed by the Constitution. Freedom of expression, as we understand it, is compromised when mere obnoxiousness is outlawed. And yet the very practices of a democratic state, including such governmental business as legislative sessions and judicial proceedings, cannot be carried out effectively if there are no restraints on the rights of people to disrupt them. That is why there is no unlimited free speech even in legislative sessions or courtroom trials where free speech itself is the subject under discussion. If everyone were allowed to talk at once or were such provocative tactics as obscenities, personal invective, and a show of disrespect for authority permitted, the very purpose of the debate would be frustrated.

Our educational institutions have had a difficult time with the free speech-etiquette paradox. This can only be resolved once it is recognized that an institution may insist upon adherence to etiquette in order to further its mission, without these restrictions on the freedom of expression at certain times and places necessarily constituting an abridgement of rights guaranteed by law. It can allow people to attack ideas without allowing them to attack one another and freely protect the discussion of offensive topics without permitting the use of offensive speech.

Symbolic Etiquette

In the less easily understood symbolic function of etiquette, its rules are rarely deducible from first principles. Untutored people who raise such questions as "Why should I wear a tie when it doesn't serve any purpose?" fail to understand the rich vocabulary of symbolism provided by etiquette, which enables people to recognize essential attributes or intentions of others, such as that a man wearing a tie is treating the occasion seriously. Because the relation between symbols and the things they stand for is arbitrary, symbolic etiquette is a powerful means of communication. Even those who demand their own sartorial freedom from symbolism would not hire a defense lawyer who wore pajamas—which would serve the practical function of covering the body just as well as a suit—to court, or submit to an operation by a brain surgeon who wore a Dracula sweatshirt in his consulting room.

Ritual Etiquette

In its ritual function, etiquette serves the sacred as a means of satisfying those spiritual needs of ours that make us distinctly human. It provides for the ceremonies and traditions that serve to bind a society and to make such chaotically emotional occasions as weddings and funerals solemn and orderly. The powerful hold that such rites have on people is evidenced by their continuance even when their sacred purpose is explicitly denied or subverted.

At contemporary funerals, some speaker usually announces, "We're not here to mourn [the deceased] but to celebrate his life." Yet the observance that follows is a variation of the traditional funeral, with the eulogies given by laymen—friends or relatives—rather than by members of the clergy for the good reason that these functionaries are no longer apt to be acquainted with the people whom they are called upon to bury.

Wedding rites originally intended for young women passing from their fathers' protection to their husbands' have remained surprisingly unchanged; even though the bride may be self-supporting, a substitute must be found for an absent father, and she may be surrounded by her children rather than her girlish friends. And yet the intent of the ceremony, in making the union of the couple part of a wider commitment involving family and the community, is often abandoned, as evidenced by the typical bridal couple's excuse for a lack of consideration for the wishes and comfort of relatives and other guests: "Well, it's our wedding, so we get to do whatever we want."

The attitude that the wishes of others do not matter is exactly what manners is intended to counter. And no one has yet come up with a satisfactory substitute for family etiquette training in the earliest years of life to foster the development of the child in such manners principles as consideration, cooperation, loyalty, and respect and to teach the child such etiquette techniques as settling disputes through face-saving compromise. Within the family, the manners that are needed—although not always in evidence—are those associated with responsibility and compassion rather than individuality and strict justice: care of the helpless, respect for elders and for authority, allotment of resources on the basis of need, empathy with the feelings of others, the accommodation of differences.

From the earliest weeks of life, when an infant is taught to control hunger in order to meet the sleeping needs of parents and to fit into a social pattern in which people do not eat during the night; through babyhood, where etiquette skills include learning conventional greetings such as morning kisses and waving bye-bye; to toddler training in such concepts as sharing toys with guests, refraining from hitting, and expressing gratitude for presents, manners are used to establish a basis for other virtues.

The schools are not able to teach these principles, however valiantly they may try, because a mannerly attitude and etiquette skills are prerequisites for learning anything at all in a school setting. As a result of the ever-wider abandonment of home etiquette training, schools have become increasingly stymied by problems they identify as lacks of discipline and of commitment to moral behavior but which usually result from the children's failure to recognize that communal goals may outweigh individual desires and their ignorance of what is and is not acceptable behavior in the classroom.

Clinical psychology and the law have tried to compensate for the decline of etiquette training of children in the home. But they face an almost hopeless task, in that the language of mental health and legal rights obscures the discourse by presuming a world in which people's behavior is guided only by the rules of law and medicine. A society can hope to function virtuously only when it also recognizes the legitimacy of manners.

CHAPTER 4

The Roots of Declining Social Virtue: Family, Community, and the Need for a "Natural Communities Policy"

David Popenoe

To succeed, every society must have a very large percentage of adults who act as good citizens and uphold high moral standards. Yet, with a declining sense of civic obligation and rising social disorder, America today appears in this respect to be in a social recession. Especially over the past 30 years, we have seen a substantial weakening of social virtue. Trust in social institutions and support for public endeavors has withered. More dramatically, we have seen remarkable increases in the most repellent forms of antisocial behavior, especially violent crime. The social environment that has emerged seems to be generating alarming rates of such personal pathologies as suicide, substance abuse, eating disorders, psychological stress, anxiety, and unipolar depression.

According to a universally held and, I believe, correct understanding of the situation, high moral standards and prosocial behavior are largely learned in childhood. To find out what has gone wrong in America, therefore, we must look to the situation of children and the changing conditions of childhood. Unfortunately, what we find is cause for much apprehension. Historians have noted that the socialization of children has undergone more radical changes since 1960 than at any time in the past 150 years.[1] The result? A number of observers and national commissions have said that America may have the first generation of children in its history who are worse off in important behavioral and psychological respects than their parents were at the same stage of life.[2]

How can this social deterioration have happened? After all, there are fewer children in each family today and therefore more adults theoretically available to care for them; fewer children are born to teenagers and fewer are unwanted; children in some respects are healthier, materially better off, and they spend more years in school. In addition, there is more national concern for children's rights, for child abuse, and for psychologically sound childrearing practices.

The broad answer to what has gone wrong is that children are creatures of their environment, and the environment for childrearing in America has taken a marked turn for the worse. Much of the attention has focused on the institution of the family, which certainly has declined in major respects.[3] The break-up rate of families has skyrocketed, for example, as has the rate of births to unwed mothers. Adults—especially men—are less connected to family life than ever before. Parents are spending less time with their children. Is it any wonder that a weakened family is less able to produce children who have the character traits on which social virtue is based, children who are kind and considerate, trusting and trustworthy, responsible and hard working, honest and cooperative, and respectful of rules and authority?

A family focus is undoubtedly correct, as far as it goes. If parents fail, society fails. The social science evidence concerning what parents must do to raise socially responsible children will be reviewed below. But parents cannot do the job all by themselves. Just as the child is dependent on the family, the family is dependent on the surrounding community. Childrearing is a highly demanding, anxiety-producing, and difficult endeavor, one that throughout world history has never been left solely to parents (let alone a single parent) to the degree that it is in our society today. Parents normally have functioned in highly supportive communities, where the entire community is geared to the task. In the words of a commonly heard proverb, "It takes a whole village to raise a child."[4]

Parents need three types of social support in childrearing: emotional support in the form of love and acceptance from other adults, instrumental support such as the provision of information and advice and help with routine tasks, and the reinforcement of social expectations about what is and is not appropriate behavior.[5] For the moral development of children, no aspect of community support is more important than the community's ability to reinforce the social expectations of parents; that is, to express a *consensus of shared values*. Young people need to hear a consistent message about what is right and wrong from all the important adults in their lives; they need not only a social community but a *moral* community. As psychologist William Damon has noted, "The acid test of whether there is a community at all is the extent to which moral guidance for the young is shared among all who come in contact with them."[6]

Therein lies a childrearing problem of enormous magnitude in America today. How many communities do we have left that provide a consensus of shared values and in which the moral guidance of the young is shared by all? Pitifully few. Indeed, it is hard to think of communities that are more poorly designed for children than those of the United States. How we deal with this problem in the future will largely determine our nation's ability to persevere as a society with a measure of civic virtue. It is time for a radical shift in how we think about our communities and how we build them.

Raising a Moral Child

Let us begin with a review of the conditions of successful childrearing, looking at parent-child interaction, family structure, and the characteristics of family-supportive communities. A great deal is now known about the childrearing conditions that give rise to socially responsible children and adults who have competence, character, and social virtue.[7] The irony is that the more we learn about the optimum conditions of childrearing, the more we see these conditions being eroded before our very eyes.

Overestimating the effects on adults of the social environment within which they grew up is easy. Children can be very adaptable, and some successful adults come from the worst of social situations. Also, genetic endowment no doubt plays a much larger role in human behavior than most social scientists are willing to admit. Recent studies of identical twins reared in very different social environments[8] and siblings reared in the same social environment[9] should give all social scientists pause for reflection. They report a strong hereditability of most psychological traits, ranging from 50 percent to 70 percent, and there is certainly enough evidence for "constitutional factors" to provide an out for parents whose children do not turn out well and to recommend humility for parents whose children do. (The old saying is that parents tend to be cultural determinists—until their second child is born.) A useful formulation of the nature-nurture combination is that individual development is the result of individual organismic factors acting in relation to aspects of the environment which can facilitate or impede that development.[10] In any event, there is no evidence to suggest that genetic or biological changes explain why the present generation of children is worse off than their parents were at the same age. What has changed is the social environment in which children are being raised.

Parent-Child Interaction

The social science research of recent decades has pointed up three key dimensions of the parental socialization process as having particular importance for the development of socially responsible children: emotional attachment, prosocial behavior, and conformity to rules with respect for authority. First, many studies have concluded that, beyond the basic needs for physical protection and nutrition, a critical need of children growing up is to have warm, intimate "attachment" relationships with their parent or parents. As social psychologist Willard W. Hartup has concluded, "A child's effectiveness in dealing with the social world emerges largely from experience in close relationships."[11] The overriding importance of close relationships in childhood is contained in a series of propositions presented to UNESCO by Urie Bronfenbrenner, summarizing what he refers to as "the main findings of the scientific revolution that has occurred in the study of human development":

    1. In order to develop—intellectually, emotionally, socially, and morally—a child requires participation in progressively more complex reciprocal activity, on a regular basis over an extended period in the child's life, with one or more persons with whom the child develops a strong, mutual, irrational, emotional attachment and who is committed to the child's well being and development, preferably for life.

    2. The establishment of patterns of progressive interpersonal interaction under conditions of strong mutual attachment enhances the young child's responsiveness to other features of the immediate physical, social, and—in due course—symbolic environment that invite exploration, manipulation, elaboration, and imagination. Such activities, in turn, also accelerate the child's psychological growth.[12]

These findings were anticipated, of course, by such classic figures as Sigmund Freud and Charles Cooley and are heavily influenced by the pioneering work of the late John Bowlby and his followers, who have conducted the empirical research on "attachment theory."[13]

    There is growing evidence that early attachment experiences shape not only child development but also attitudes and behavior throughout one's life. People growing up without satisfactory attachment experiences are at higher risk of becoming anxious, insecure, or avoidant in social relationships, both as children and later as adults.[14] For example, a recent longitudinal study that followed people over a 36-year period found that the dimension of childhood correlating most closely with being socially accomplished as an adult (i.e., "having a long, happy marriage, children, and relationships with close friends at midlife") was having had "a warm and affectionate father or mother."[15] This factor was far more important than having grown up in a family with "parental harmony" or with a childhood that was "not difficult." Early attachment experiences are also important for developing a trusting view of others. Through attachment experiences people learn to desire the approval of others and to have the belief that—given certain conditions—they can count on such approval. This is an important basis of social trust.

Humans almost certainly have a genetic predisposition to engage in close relationships, but it is a predisposition that can be facilitated or impeded by the environment. A childrearing environment that generates strong attachments no doubt can be created by the mother—or by some other adult caregiver—alone. "Survivors" or "resilient children," the children from deeply deprived socioeconomic backgrounds who are successful as adults, typically have the common denominator of at least one adult who was devoted to their welfare.[16] But it is much more likely that strong attachments can be created when more than one adult is involved, as noted by Bronfenbrenner's third proposition:

3. The establishment and maintenance of patterns of progressively more complex interaction and emotional attachment between caregiver and child depend in substantial degree on the availability and involvement of another adult, a *third party* who assists, encourages, spells off, gives status to, and expresses admiration and affection for the person caring for and engaging in joint activity with the child.[17]

Although this proposition is written with the nonspecific "third party," it provides the justification—if any were needed—for the traditional role of the father in assisting the mother, which virtually every society has institutionalized through marriage. The most successful embodiment of this proposition in modern societies is the two-biological parent family where the father takes a strong interest in his children's and their mother's welfare.

It is the lack of a "third party," presumably, that is a major reason why single-parent families are less successful in child outcomes than their two-parent counterparts. Much has been written in recent years about the advantages, or lack thereof, of two-parent families. A 1992 front-page article in the *Washington Post* referred to "a searching reevaluation by social scientists" concluding that "the conventional two-parent household may be far less critical to the healthy development of children than previously believed." Some social scientists refer to "the misguided belief that children will receive better parenting in intact families." My reading of the research is that the relative success of the two-parent family can be considered a confirmed empirical generalization, indeed, about as confirmed a generalization as one can draw from the social sciences.[18] A review of research on the relationship between family structure and school achievement, for example, concluded, "I believe the consistency of the finding that living in a two-parent household is a benefit to achievement is evident; while not all differences reach significance, virtually none are found in the opposite direction."[19] Another research review concluded "research on antisocial behavior consistently illustrates that adolescents in mother-only households . . . are more prone to commit delinquent acts."[20] A third states, "What is clear is that the multiple economic, social, and psychological life stresses of being a single or a visiting or a remarried parent . . . weaken the family in its child-rearing and child-protective functions."[21] Finally, a recent nationwide study of teenagers, based on the 1988 National Health Interview Survey of Child Health, concluded that "young people from single-parent or step families were two to three times more likely to have had emotional or behavioral problems than those who had both of their biological parents present in the home."[22]

Beyond attachment, and the emotional security and ability to maintain close relationships that it brings, lies the second of the key dimensions of the parental socialization process: the need for children to develop "prosocial" patterns of behavior, that is, voluntary, altruistic behavior intended to benefit others, such as helping, sharing, and comforting. It is this behavior upon which the success of any society depends. As with attachment, there is evidence to suggest that humans are genetically predisposed to engage in prosocial behavior and that the seeds of prosocial behavior are manifest very early in a child's life, contrary to the classic notion that young children are born purely self-interested and amoral.[23] But again, the social environment can either facilitate or impede this inborn impulse.

Warm, supportive parenting of the type involved in attachment experiences provides a foundation for the development of prosocial behavior. In the words of several prominent psychologists, "Individual failures in moral development . . . begin with poor attachment bonds between an infant and its caretakers."[24] But good attachment is not sufficient. Prosocial behavior and moral values must be purposefully taught and reinforced by caregivers. This is especially true in individualistic and competitive societies such as the United States, where, compared to traditional societies, everyday life is not so marked by cooperation and helping among kin and neighbors.[25]

Social science research on prosocial behavior is of fairly recent vintage, most earlier work having focused on negative behaviors such as aggression and violence. The main conclusions of this research, few of which are counterintuitive, are as follows:[26] Children often learn by imitation or modeling, and the more consistently caring and altruistic the parent is, the more the child will be. Prosocial behavior can also be taught verbally, and children continually should be receiving such instruction. But instruction works much better when word and deed are allied; the words of parents who preach altruism but do not practice it themselves may have little lasting effect. It is also important to encourage (but not force) prosocial behavior in various ways so that children have the chance actually to practice it, especially in relationships among siblings. Prosocial and moral issues are encountered daily by children through their relationships with others, and these relationships can provide valuable learning experiences when guided and reinforced by adults.[27]

A most significant research finding is that prosocial behavior is heavily dependent on developing strong feelings of sympathy and empathy in children, on teaching them to take the perspective of the other.[28] Sympathy and empathy can be promoted in many ways, but one of the most important is through positive forms of discipline. Certain disciplinary techniques are more effective than others. By far the most effective in promoting sympathy, empathy, and thereby prosocial behavior involves the use of reasoning or "inductions," specifically pointing out the consequences of the child's behavior for other people ("Look at the way you hurt her; now she feels bad."). Such an approach takes time but is far preferable to "power-assertive" forms of discipline that involve physical punishment or the deprivation of privileges. Indeed, such punitive discipline, especially if used to excess, is actually detrimental for a child's prosocial development. Rather than an outward-looking empathy, it generates an inward-looking concern for the self and self-preservation.

The third key dimension of parental socialization is instilling in children a respect for authority and a sense of obligation to comply with social rules. A healthy family has its own set of rules, such as prohibitions against dishonesty, theft, and violence, that parallel those of the healthy society. In this respect the family is a miniature social system, with parents as the chief promoters and enforcers of social order. Some believe that children who have strong allegiance to family rules and social order will have difficulty developing an allegiance to the rules of larger social systems, but this is not the case. It is through relations with parents (and later other adults) that children learn about social rules in general and thereby develop a respect for society and its legitimate authority. Using other terms, this can be expressed as the development of conscience—an internalized constraint against certain actions, the violation of which generates anxiety.

The parents' task is to communicate and demonstrate to their children the purpose of social rules and, when necessary, enforce the rules by applying various sanctions, both positive and negative. In families where children are firmly attached and prosocial behavior has been promoted, negative sanctions are minimal. The close relationship that parents have with their children is normally enough to insure cooperation.

The outcome of this socialization process within the family is critically important for the larger society, which in the final analysis is based on regulation and hierarchy and the shared willingness of citizens to conform to social norms. "The child's respect for parental authority," notes William Damon, "sets the direction for civilized participation in the social order when the child later begins assuming the rights and responsibilities of full citizenship." Indeed, in Damon's view, "the child's respect for this authority is the single most important moral legacy that comes out of the child's relationship with the parent."[29]

The Strong Family

What kinds of families are best able to generate in their children emotional attachment, prosocial behavior, and respect for rules and authority? Analogous to the fashion in psychological research that has emphasized antisocial over prosocial behavior, there has been a great deal of sociological research on dysfunctional families but surprisingly little on strong, successful families. Recently, however, a number of family researchers have identified the characteristics of such families to be: "Enduring, cohesive, affectionate, and mutually-appreciative, and in which family members communicate with one another frequently and fruitfully."[30] Strong families are seldom "trouble free." Many have experienced health, financial, and other problems, but they are adaptable and able to deal with crises in a constructive manner.

This set of characteristics holds few surprises; it is one that any grandmother would probably present. One of the qualities most frequently mentioned by researchers is effective communication. In strong families, communication is clear, open, and frequent. "Family members talk to each other often, and when they do, they are honest and open with each other."[31] Another very important, underlying characteristic is commitment. In strong families there is a commitment to the family as a unit and a sense of the family as constituting a team with special identity and meaning. Members are willing to take action and sacrifice, if necessary, to preserve family well-being.[32] This same quality is found in strong, enduring marriages. Not only does each spouse consider the other a best friend, but each is committed to staying with the other for life.

Strong families also tend to have an "authoritative" disciplinary style.[33] Scholars agree that a child's moral capacities are best developed under an approach "in which firm demands are made of the child while at the same time there is clear communication between adult and child about the nature and justification of these demands."[34] Disciplinary styles can be arrayed on a continuum ranging from restrictive to permissive. When combined with a continuum of parent-child relationships ranging from "warm" to "cold," the authoritative style is sometimes referred to as "warm-restrictive" or "loving discipline." This disciplinary style encourages children to value adult approval, readily internalize rules, and abide by those rules.

The other major disciplinary styles have different child outcomes. An oversimplified summary of each follows: Warm-permissive parents tend to generate children who will be self-confident and socially outgoing, but who will frequently ignore or bend the rules ("affable but spoiled"); cold-restrictive parents tend to generate children who are anxious and sullen, but compliant; cold-permissive parents (probably the worst combination) produce children who are hostile and rule defying, with a high probability for delinquency. There is reason to believe that both the warm-permissive and cold-permissive approaches are on the increase, especially with the rapid growth of single-parent families in which one person has the sole responsibility for childrearing.

Compared to the others, the preferred warm-restrictive disciplinary style takes by far the most time. Parents must be able to make time for their children and be with them to provide both love and discipline. Indeed, the ability and willingness to spend time together are powerful factors underlying almost all aspects of the strong family. It takes a great deal of time to have the kind of warm, repetitive interactions on which successful family life is based, interactions which include many routines and family traditions and lead to the development of a rich family subculture that has lasting meaning for its members. This is why the "time famine" that currently faces so many American families is a national calamity.

Supportive Communities

Probably everyone in America would agree that strong family ties raise the probability of producing virtuous offspring. The chances of becoming a successful and socially responsible adult are increased substantially if one is raised in a loving, structured, supportive family environment. Much less well understood, however, is the fact that to be strong, a family requires a supportive environment of its own.[35] Strong families tend to be well connected to the local community. They have external resources in the form of friends, family, and neighbors, and they participate actively in community organizations; they are not as socially isolated as less successful families. Strong families that are fortresses in an alien community obviously can be found but these are exceptions. One of the most important distinguishing characteristics of families that abuse their children, for example, is social isolation.[36] Indeed, the recent increase in child abuse could well stem in part from the growing social isolation of families.

What kind of communities promote strong families? The list of characteristics of strong families noted above can just as well be applied to communities: "enduring, cohesive, and mutually-appreciative, and in which community members communicate with one another frequently and fruitfully." In short, communities that are stable, have a strong consensus of values, and in which people frequently interact with respect to those values are supportive communities.[37]

Turning to childrearing, the importance of the local community is summarized by Bronfenbrenner's fourth proposition about human development:

> 4. The effective functioning of child-rearing processes in the family and other child settings requires establishing ongoing patterns of exchange of information, two-way communication, mutual accommodation, and mutual trust between the principal settings in which children and their parents live their lives. In contemporary societies, these settings are the home, child-care programs, the school, and the parents' place of work.[38]

The central significance of the community for moral development is this: moral development in children takes place in part through repetition and reinforcement, and through adapting fundamental moral values to a variety of social circumstances beyond the family. As the child moves into the outside world, the moral lessons taught by the parents must be sustained by others. In an intensive 10-year study of 10 communities across America, Francis Ianni found the existence of a local consensus of values to be the key predictor of adolescent adjustment, a far stronger predictor than such variables as affluence or ethnicity. In his words:

> Congeniality among their values and clarity and consistency in their guidance are essential to the adolescent, who is engaged in a *search for structure*, a set of believable and attainable expectations and standards from the community to guide the movement from child to adult status. If the values expressed by different community sectors

are at odds . . . the teenager cannot be expected to accept their good will or trust their judgment.[39]

Yet all across America, community value dissensus is in the ascendancy. Much attention has focused on public schools and their failure to provide value reinforcement. Another important area of value conflict is between families and the world of work, which typically operates as if workers had no families. One of the most significant examples of value conflict in America today, of course, is between the values families try to teach their children and those commonly expressed through the mass media.

American parents today believe that they are a beleaguered lot, living in an increasingly hostile community environment where value consensus is more and more problematic. Their neighborhoods have become anonymous, their neighbors are disinterested, and crime and personal security are constant problems. They feel isolated and unappreciated and view their task as a lonely and risky one. Popular culture has become an enemy, not a friend. To make matters worse, their own parents now live at a distance, and they have fewer and fewer relatives on whom to rely for personal support.

Human Evolution and the American Experience

For a fuller understanding of the importance of the community for family functioning, it is useful to provide a brief excursus into human evolution. Human beings are tribal animals; our attitudes, instincts, and behaviors have been shaped by tribal experiences.[40] For most of our existence on earth, human personalities have been locked into close-knit and orderly social groupings, whether nomadic bands, small villages, or extended families. With the family as their basic building block, these groupings were glued together socially by strong loyalties and commitments based on family relatedness, a shared geographic area, a common religion, and a single ethnic group—forms of social connectedness that today we call "traditional."[41] Survival apart from such groupings was rare and individualism was unknown; the personal and the social were one.

From an evolutionary perspective, it is reasonable to say that we are biologically adapted in large measure to living an intense social life among our own kind, and we suffer when we do not have these strong, primordial ties. Put another way, our natural inclination is to want to have close personal ties and to be included in strong groups that have clear values and a stable social structure, a social situation which can provide us with a sense of identity and belonging. When we do not have close ties and strong groups we feel alienated, lonely, depressed, spiritually empty, and often worse—wretched, useless, and self-destructive.[42] The strength of social ties—what anthropologist Raoul Naroll refers to as a moralnet—varies from culture to culture around the world. Studies of these cultures have shown that the stronger the social ties, the fewer the social and personal problems.[43]

In the last few centuries, first in the West and later in other parts of the world, the culture of modernity—noted for its extreme individualism—has been transplanted onto our tribal human nature and our tribal social groupings. Modernity has brought enormous rewards. The creative impulses of individualism generated the growth of science and technology, and human beings have materially prospered as never before. The new focus on the individual brought political democracy, with considerable increases in individual dignity, personal liberty, interpersonal equality, and human justice. And the weakening of group ties has probably been instrumental in reducing inter-tribal warfare. Such warfare was elevated on the world scale to become the scourge of the 20th century. Indeed, human advances under the culture of modernity have been so impressive that it is thought today that civilizational progress and individual differentiation from the group go hand in hand; that individualism is the natural and progressive successor to tribalism and cultural collectivism.[44] And certainly, very few people today wish to return to the past.

Because of the tremendous successes of modernity, it is tempting to think that further progress rests on removing whatever tribalism remains, on getting rid for all time of "localism" and "parochialism" and enabling us all to pledge allegiance to but a single, universal human tribe. We must be very cautious about this strategy, however. The need for close ties and strong groups is an indelible part of human nature; it cannot be stamped out. As Michael Walzer recently has said:

> Tribalism names the commitment of individuals and groups to their own history, culture, and identity, and this commitment . . . is a permanent feature of human social life. The parochialism that it breeds is similarly permanent. It can't be overcome; it has to be accommodated, and therefore the crucial universal principle is that it must always be accommodated: not only my parochialism but yours as well, and his and hers in their turn. . . . our common humanity will never make us members of a single universal tribe. The crucial commonality of the human race is particularism.[45]

This broad issue could be addressed from many perspectives. The most important one is that modernity not only has rewards, as noted above, but also social costs: personal pathology and community disorder. These have become as much the hallmarks of modernity as material and technological growth and democracy. The negative impact has been greatest on children, who are the most sensitive expression of social conditions. At the personal level, radical individualism has an uneasy fit with our biologically-evolved human nature, and it is not at all certain that a further loosening of social ties in favor of individual choice will generate more human happiness and well-being. Indeed, we may not be as happy today as in times past. The generation of new personal "psychological" pathologies can be seen all around us. At the social level, while we may be making progress toward an international social order, our internal "tribal social order" has fallen on hard times. The gradual weakening of family and community ties, in short, of the traditional forms of social connectedness, has generated an alarming increase in community disorder.

The social costs (and perhaps also the rewards) of modernity are greater in the United States than anywhere else. This may not be the view of immigrants to this country from the Third World, who have not yet shared many of modernity's benefits, but it is the growing opinion of close observers of American society who have done careful, comparative examinations of recent social trends. Especially since the 1960s, a time when American society underwent

a massive attempt to rid itself of "tribal mentalities" and traditional social relationships, the social costs have grown. (So, of
course, have some important rewards, such as greater equality for
women and minorities.)

The United States has become possibly the most multi-tribal society of all time. In the sense of trying fully to blend together multiple ethnic, racial, and religious groupings, our diversity and
cultural pluralism are legendary. This is both our strength and our
weakness.[46] It is a strength because diversity can be stimulating,
generating creativity and achievement. It is a weakness because
diversity can be psychologically and morally overwhelming, generating moral relativism, hyper-individualism, and, ultimately, community and social decline. As fellow sociologist Peter Berger
recently has commented, "Pluralism creates a condition of perma-
nent uncertainty as to what one should believe and how one should
live; but the human mind abhors uncertainty."[47]

Tolerance of the strange and the diverse in America today has
become a social essential.[48] Indeed, tolerance and "intergroup relations" have become consuming goals of our nation (some might say
all-consuming because—as necessary as they are—they increasingly distract us from other important concerns and issues). Often
implicit in these goals is the weakening of group identities and
group ties, the idea being that people with weaker ties will be more
tolerant. But the emergence of a society in which all semblance of
tribalism is gone poses a serious threat to social order and further
human development because it mismatches with human nature. In
the words of political philosopher Michael J. Sandel, "Intolerance
flourishes most where forms of life are dislocated, roots unsettled,
traditions undone."[49] Along similar lines, ethicist Andrew Oldenquist has written, "Our social problems are not due nearly as much
to the competition of loyalties as to their absence. . . . they are due
to alienation, loss of belonging, to not having affiliations about
which one deeply cares."[50]

A major task of our age, therefore, is this: While seeking to maximize individual development and respond to the exigencies of an
ever-diversifying social environment, we must at the same time
maintain some semblance of tribalism—which boils down to protecting and cultivating the primordial institutions of family and

community.[51] This may sound like a tall if not improbable order, but it is the only reasonable choice we have.

American Communities and Family Life

American communities are strikingly unfit for children. If the building of American communities had been left to the wise planner in the sky, and if the needs and interests of children had been the primary goal, our residential communities would be very different from what now exists. The major drawbacks for children, considering the optimum conditions of childrearing discussed earlier, are as follows:

First, children need and want social stability and a stable social structure. They want to feel psychologically and socially secure in a place where they can "belong" and feel at home and where common values are shared by those with whom they come into contact. Yet American communities are transient, anonymous, diverse, and increasingly unfriendly and even hostile to children.

Second, children need and want a community where they feel physically secure, a place where they can freely play in the neighborhood without fear of bodily harm. Yet American neighborhoods are the most crime ridden of any industrialized society.

Third, children need and want a community that is accessible to them. Yet most American metropolitan environments are built at a scale that depends on the use of the automobile, a mode of transportation that is available to children only through adults.

Fourth, children need and want a community where their parents and other adults will be with them a great deal of the time. Yet most American communities are arranged in such a way that parents have to commute long distances to work, further extending their already long work hours. The typical American neighborhood is now filled during the day with empty homes.

Fifth, children need and want a rich local community life, with many community activities and events that draw families together to share good times. Yet community events across America, such as parades and community fairs, are in decline. The typical "community event" for most children has become a trip to the mall or movie complex or a few friends getting together to rent a video.

Sixth, children need and want free time, with a certain sense of carefreeness in which they can follow the path of their own imaginations. Yet the community lives of many American children have become increasingly regimented and scheduled through day care, school sports and other organized recreation, part-time jobs for teenagers, and many other activities that typically take place far from home (and often involve elaborate car-pool efforts).

The list could go on. Some of these drawbacks apply especially to the inner-city ghetto. But many apply to the type of community in which the average American now lives, the low-density suburb of a medium-sized metropolitan area. If not for children, we might ask, then for what or whom were such suburbs built? They were built primarily for economic efficiency; most residents would gladly leave such areas if they could find employment and services in smaller, more friendly places. They were built for the adult who has maximum use of the automobile, disregarding the situation not only of children but also the elderly, the poor, and the infirm and disabled. They were built by and for men, who are generally more mobile and whose lives, more than women's, are enriched by places of work (which have become the principle community for many). Women as well as children do not thrive in such areas. And they were built with the goal of privatizing family life, the opposite of what children want. The building of most American low-density suburbs involved simply constructing spacious houses on whatever land was vacant, with little thought given to the very real social needs of the majority of residents.

What can be done? How can we foster communities that are more oriented to the needs of children, communities—if you will—that have more of the qualities of a tribal village? There are two broad approaches to fostering community life in America. One focuses on residential areas or locality groups, people who live together in a common neighborhood or local area. The other focuses on nonresidential "interest" communities, or groups of people who live apart from one another but who constitute a network of social interaction and who share common interests and values. This second approach is the one being gradually played out in America, partly by default.

Historically, most residential areas have also been "functional communities" where people have networks of social interaction and share common values and interests. But physical proximity of residence is no longer the principal basis for social relationships among most adults. Increasingly unfulfilled by the locality group, people's strong desire for community largely has taken on a non-geographic dimension, what sociologists refer to as "dispersal of social ties." This reliance on nonresidential communities is not a wholly satisfactory solution to the problem, however, and it in some ways exacerbates it.

Nonresidential Communities

As residential areas in America have become increasingly diverse and amorphous, the strategy of Americans has been to give up on these as social communities and create "communities without propinquity" or far-flung social networks—communities of interest made up of like minded people who live in many different residential areas. This has been the characteristic strategy of urban dwellers. As cities grow and become more diverse, neighborhoods weaken and urbanites develop citywide social networks. Many cities still have remnants of a prior urban form, the mostly working-class "urban villages," but these are rapidly disappearing.

The best example of nonresidential communities in America today are those formed through religious institutions. More Americans belong to religious groups than to any other type of voluntary association. One reason is that, of all the social institutions, religious institutions are the only ones that are involved with the entire family during each stage of its life cycle. Typically, a strong local church will draw its parishioners from a great distance, and much of the social life of the members takes place through the church. When schools are added to the mix, the religious community becomes even more insulated from the locality; neighborhood schools in the residential community are given up in favor of private, religiously-oriented schools, a phenomenon that has grown like wildfire in recent years. The strength of such religious communities in

America today, fewer and fewer of which are organized along parish lines, is something that sets us apart from almost all other advanced, industrial societies. Especially outside of cities, fundamentalist Christian groups have become one of our strongest and most rapidly growing community types. They have also been quite successful, not incidentally, in maintaining social order and high moral standards among their members.

The important role of nonresidential communities in contemporary American life has been raised forcefully by the work of James S. Coleman and Thomas Hoffer in their comparison of public and private high schools.[52] They make the point that the comparative success of Catholic schools is due in large part to the fact that these schools are connected to functional communities made up of parents who share similar values about education and who interact to promote their children's educational achievement. They note that such functional communities greatly augment the resources available to parents in their interactions with the school and in their supervision of their children's schoolwork and their children's associations with others. It is important to point out that to be a fully functioning community, both sharing values ("value communities") and social interaction are essential. Many private schools constitute value communities but the community effect is weakened because parents do not interact much with one another. Public schools, in contrast, are typically attached to neighborhoods which lack both the value consensus and social network components.[53]

To promote academic achievement and moral behavior in children, it is undoubtedly important for schools to share the same values as the families who send them students. This proposition has long provided the impetus for those favoring "neighborhood schools." And, as neighborhoods themselves weaken as functioning communities, it has provided the impetus behind today's concern for "school choice" through use of vouchers. As Nathan Glazer recently has suggested, school choice permits "those who can create stronger communities to choose the schools in which the norms they respect and want to see realized can be enforced and will be generally accepted."[54] A major issue with school choice, however, is the potential negative consequences for those pupils who are left behind in the old neighborhood schools.

Other nonresidential sources of community are less encompassing of the full range of life activities. Examples are voluntary associations, such as adult service organizations and organizations based on ethnic heritage, and especially places of work. Much has been written about how the workplace in America has become a community for many people, especially those without families. In Japan, the workplace is much more community-providing than in the United States, although there the family is also strong. Much more can and needs to be done in America to make the workplace family-friendly. But the problem with the workplace as a source of community is the inherent instability of employment. Once a person is laid off—an all too familiar event in America today—that is the end of the community relationship.

A case can be made for fostering each of these nonresidential community forms. Without them, with what are people left? The problem is, however, that as each becomes stronger, the residential area grows weaker as a functioning community—toward a state of obsolescence in which each family and even each individual family member has its own set of personalized and non-overlapping nonresidential communities. A clear example is the shift to private schools and its inevitable consequences for neighborhood schools.

Residential Areas as Communities

Is it really such a good idea to largely give up on the residential community and shift to a wide range of nonresidential interest communities? I think not. We, as a nation, should be doing everything possible to bring neighborhoods and towns back to their historical, natural form—as functioning communities.

First, let us review why residential areas have declined as functioning communities:

1. Most residents no longer work in them
2. The distance between home and work has increased
3. They have become culturally diverse
4. They have a high turnover of population

5. Mothers are no longer at home during the day
6. The automobile has reduced pedestrian interaction
7. Security problems have grown, leading to increased privatization
8. Households have shrunk; with fewer people at home, the household becomes less attached to the locality.

An additional problem for childrearing families is that these families have become a distinct minority in most American localities; they now make up less than a third of all households nationwide, compared to more than 75 percent of all households in the last century.

These trends manifestly constitute a major structural change in society. Many of them cannot be undone; others could be modified, but we may not want to do that for other reasons. Such structural change constitutes a major obstacle to attempts to restore residential areas as important functioning communities in the lives of families.

With the deck so stacked, why is it nevertheless important to give serious consideration to such a restoration? Consider the social costs of the shift from residential to nonresidential communities. First, it is fundamentally unfair to our less privileged citizens. The more privileged in life tend to have more voluntary social relationships and connections outside of local areas, whereas the poor, the infirm, the handicapped, the elderly, and especially children—with their limited means and accessibility—are left behind to fend for themselves locally. For these segments of the population, the local residential area is still their main community, and there is little they can do about that fact. While for a well-heeled (especially male) adult there might be only a minimal negative impact from a home environment marked by unfriendliness, anonymity, and worse, for children and childrearing families the impact can be great. This form of inequality lies behind the recent "civic liberalism" proposals of Mickey Kaus. Rather than being so concerned with income inequalities and income redistribution, he argues, liberals should concentrate their efforts on building a public sphere in which all Americans can share and be respected as equals.[55]

Second, the shift to nonresidential communities generates neighborhood disorder, delinquency, and crime through a breakdown of informal social control.[56] One of the community changes today's parents most often note from the time they were growing up is neighborhood insecurity. For security reasons, children and teenagers are not able to wander freely about the neighborhood as they once were. Parents have deep concerns for their safety, and their whereabouts must now be known at all times. Juvenile delinquency has increased, and many teenage peer groups have become virulent. The social control of teenagers clearly depends not only on what is happening within the household but also on what is happening within the community.[57]

The amount of disorder in residential areas is strongly related to neighborhood upkeep and to the informal social control activities of residents, such as neighborhood watch and bystander intervention (e.g., being on the lookout for unruly behavior in public places and taking responsibility for reporting it, when necessary, to the police). It is very important in this regard for neighborhoods to be stable and cohesive, with citizens groups, block associations, and other neighborhood organizations and activities. Yet the shift by local residents to nonresidential sources of community severely weakens their neighborhood attachment. Neighborhood disorder, in turn, helps to generate neighborhood decline and makes the neighborhood a more likely target for outside criminals.[58] In the face of growing neighborhood decline and crime, residents tend to withdraw still further from the local community into their own private communities and private lives, setting off a spiral of neighborhood decay that can be seen today all across America.

Third, going beyond the immediate needs of children and other local residents, the weakening of residential communities exacerbates in some ways the problems of diversity in American life. As neighborhoods decline, caused either by market or government forces, those who are financially and temperamentally able move away, often leaving the old neighborhoods and local areas to the needy, the weak, and the disturbed. Not just neighborhoods but entire towns and cities are affected. The widespread geographic separation of rich and poor occurs, quite apart from considerations of common moral values. And America becomes differentiated into massive, isolated, lifestyle enclaves based mainly on wealth and privilege. Natural villages and towns of the past, by comparison, contained a broad mix of income groups, not within each neighborhood but within the local area. For better or worse, the citizens of these areas had to struggle—face to face—to create a common life.

Developing a Natural Communities Policy

To improve the conditions for childrearing in America today, nothing may be more important than trying to protect and cultivate those natural, tribal- or village-like communities that still remain—communities which have families as their basic building blocks and in which a mix of people through free association and sets of relational networks maintain a common life. This could be called a "natural communities" policy. It is a policy that, at minimum, enjoins both the market and the state from doing further damage to civil society. The wishes and concerns of local cultural groupings should be deeply respected, and functioning local communities should in some cases be protected from the intrusion of outsiders. Natural communities, like natural environments, should never be taken for granted. Social environments should be thought of as every bit as fragile and as worth preserving as natural environments, with a similarly intricate and easily damaged ecological network. Just as we now require environmental and family impact statements for some pending national legislation, perhaps we should also be thinking in similar terms about the impact of public policies on functioning social communities.

Unmistakably, the development of a natural communities policy faces a legal and social minefield. Unfortunately, the issues can barely be introduced here. There are the obvious concerns about racial and ethnic discrimination and about constitutionally guaranteed human rights. Many existing communities in America are far from "natural," including those at the top that function more to preserve property values than to promote a common life and those at the bottom, the urban and rural ghettos of the poor. This raises the serious issue of which existing communities, in fact, should be protected under a natural communities policy. Moreover, we must be concerned about community-supporting impulses running

awry, as sometimes happened in the "community action" programs of the 1960s when a handful of self-selected community
leaders benefited far more than community residents.[59]

Most importantly, the stability of American society rests precari-
ously on a balance between local autonomy and national solidarity.
From one perspective, the rise of strong, new "tribal" groupings
along racial and ethnic lines seems already to be pulling America
apart at the seams. Utmost care is necessary, therefore, to avoid
the furtherance of a "moral exclusiveness" in local communities.
Especially as children grow older, for example, they must be taught
the necessity of nested and overlapping group loyalties that extend
well beyond their local groupings.[60]

Also, a natural communities policy would have to be counterbal-
anced by a national solidarity policy that fosters those common
values and traditions that have held the nation together. This
should involve national and local service—the bringing together
of people from different backgrounds and requiring them to work
together to help build the nation as well as foster mutual respect
and tolerance, a policy strongly promoted by the Communitarian
movement.[61] And it should involve a strong, uniform national cur-
riculum to be incorporated into our primary and secondary schools,
along the lines suggested by Chester Finn, which includes not only
fundamental subjects such as math, science, and writing but also
our national and Western history and traditions.[62] Similarly, institutions of higher education should do more to promote national
solidarity through stressing our common Western values.

A natural communities policy would foster a certain kind of
"multiculturalism" in American life. I am not referring here to the
multiculturalism sometimes espoused on the nation's college cam-
puses, which centers around an "ideology of oppression" and involves a mostly individualistic power struggle to overturn the
dominant society.[63] I am referring instead to the multiculturalism
espoused by respectable and respected community leaders, persons
whose goal in life is to raise their own families in a decent and
orderly society. These are people who are working hard to achieve
the American dream but who at the same time cherish their own
cultures and cultural identity.[64]

The following are some specific goals that a comprehensive natural communities policy might include:[65]

1. *Foster residential stability.* Many studies have shown that the length of time spent in a community is the best predictor of community attachments: the longer one lives in a community, the more publicly attached to it one becomes.[66] People usually move for two reasons: jobs and housing. Obviously, it is important for this reason to maintain high levels of employment. Less obviously, much needless mobility is created by large areas that are homogeneous in housing type. Simply to find more appropriate space—for example, when children are added to a family or when one retires—it is necessary to leave the community entirely. Every local area, therefore, should be encouraged to provide a broad mix of housing types.

2. *Enforce community moral standards.* As a nation, we have become utterly preoccupied with individual rights. To be strong, local residential communities must necessarily be moral communities, and the assumptions that all rights rest with the individual and that local government should be morally neutral are antithetical to the continued existence of such communities. We do not need a new agenda of group rights, but we do need, as legal scholar Mary Ann Glendon has pointed out, "a fuller concept of human personhood and a more ecological way of thinking about social policy."[67] Without violating the Bill of Rights, local communities should have more autonomy in establishing and enforcing their own values and moral standards.

3. *Provide more public facilities.* The best communities are those with a rich measure of facilities and services available to all. This includes schools, hospitals, libraries, parks and playgrounds, youth centers, museums, and public transportation. The community with few public facilities and services need not wonder for long why its citizens are living in a myriad of diverse outside worlds, why they have scant local interest, and why they are quietly moving away.

4. *Favor the development of smaller cities and towns.* Studies have found that "the larger the community a person lives in, the less likely he or she is to say that it is 'a good place to live' . . . and to be fully satisfied with their immediate neighborhood."[68] Most people say they would prefer to live in a place smaller than that in

which they currently live, provided they had reasonable access to jobs and public services; it is the search for community that drives their preference. Small cities and towns, because they are closer to the "human scale," have measurable community-giving advantages over large urban agglomerations.

5. *Support local political and social autonomy.* To the extent possible, political decision making should be decentralized so local communities have more autonomy. Political autonomy and social autonomy are linked; one enhances the other. The subsidiarity principle should be followed: No political function or social task should be assigned to a unit that is larger than necessary to do the job.

6. *Promote functional balance.* Metropolitan conditions have fostered a tremendous specialization of local areas, with people living one in place, working at another, shopping at a third, and recreating at a fourth. There are obvious social advantages to bringing these functions into closer proximity with one another.

7. *Protect homogeneous neighborhoods.* I am not thinking here necessarily of racial and ethnic enclaves but of family-focused enclaves of people who share similar values and have a similar lifestyle.[69] American liberals have long looked askance at homogeneous neighborhoods (with the exception of those in which they live) as undemocratic. But people strongly prefer to live next door to others with whom they feel comfortable and can form close friendships,[70] and there is no reason they should not be allowed to—especially families with children. Provided they are functioning communities, homogeneous neighborhoods, possibly up to the size necessary to support neighborhood schools, should be protected and encouraged.

What should not be protected or encouraged are artificially homogeneous towns and cities. Most towns of the past in this country were quite heterogeneous, at least in terms of social class. Their children grew up among their own kind in their own neighborhoods, under a network of local social control, but as they grew older and extended their activities beyond the neighborhood, they came into contact with unlike people. Thus, as children matured, increasing diversity was introduced to them, especially at the high school and college levels. Because these towns contained a range of income groups and sometimes ethnic groups as well, the conflicting political interests arising from this diversity were dealt with largely at the local level.

All things considered, the best possible American residential community would be a moderately sized, functionally balanced, public-facilities rich, and politically bounded town that represented a microcosm of our society with a mixture of income, ethnic, racial, and religious groups. Within the town, each group would tend to live in its own separate neighborhoods, but all the groups would intermix in the public and political spheres. Unfortunately, we are drifting ever further from this community ideal.

Conclusion

The seedbed of social virtue is childhood. Social virtue is in decline in the United States for two main reasons—a decline in family functioning and a decline in community functioning. The two are closely linked. To help them have the knowledge, ability, time, and will to raise socially responsible children, parents must be attached to strong moral communities. Yet such communities, under a withering assault from state, market, and cultural influences, have fallen on hard times. When moral communities fail, families fail.

There is no evidence that realistic social alternatives exist for the traditional "tribal" structures of family and community. Whatever their condition, these primordial social structures remain powerful determinants of people's lives. To help restore social virtue, we as a nation should seek to protect and cultivate natural communities, preferably along residential lines. As individuals, we should seek to stay married, stay accessible to our children, stay active in our local communities, and stay put.

Notes

1. Steven Mintz, "The Family as Educator: Historical Trends in Socialization and the Transmission of Content Within the Home," in *Educa-*

tion and the American Family: A Research Synthesis, ed. William J. Weston (New York: New York University Press, 1989), 110.

2. National Commission on Children, *Beyond Rhetoric: A New American Agenda for Children and Families* (Washington, DC: U.S. Government Printing Office, 1991); The National Commission on the Role of the School and Community in Improving Adolescent Health, *Code Blue: Uniting for Healthier Youth* (Alexandria, VA: National Association of State Boards of Education, 1990).

3. See David Popenoe, "American Family Decline, 1960–1990: A Review and Appraisal," *Journal of Marriage and the Family* 55, no. 3 (1993): 527–42.

4. Cited in *The Responsive Community* 2, no. 3 (1992): 93.

5. Jay Belsky, "The Determinants of Parenting: A Process Model," *Child Development* 55 (1984): 83–96.

6. William Damon, "Common Sense on Morality and Today's Youth," *The Responsive Community* 2, no. 4 (1992): 87.

7. James Q. Wilson, *The Moral Sense* (New York: Free Press, 1993).

8. Thomas J. Bouchard Jr. and Matthew McGue, "Genetic and Rearing Environmental Influences on Adult Personality: An Analysis of Adopted Twins Reared Apart," *Journal of Personality* 58, no. 1 (1990): 263–92; Thomas J. Bouchard Jr., David T. Lykken, Matthew McGue, Nancy L. Segal, and Auke Tellegen, "Sources of Human Psychological Differences: The Minnesota Study of Twins Reared Apart," *Science* 25 (Oct. 1990): 223–28.

9. Robert Plomin, "Environment and Genes: Determinants of Behavior," *American Psychologist* 44, no. 2 (1989): 105–11; Judy Dunn and Robert Plomin, *Separate Lives: Why Siblings Are So Different* (New York: Basic Books, 1990).

10. F. D. Horowitz, *Exploring Developmental Theories: Toward a Structural/Behavioral Model of Development* (Hillsdale, NJ: Erlbaum, 1987).

11. Willard W. Hartup, "Social Relationships and Their Developmental Significance," *American Psychologist* 44, no. 2 (1989): 120–26.

12. Urie Bronfenbrenner, "Discovering What Families Do," in *Rebuilding the Nest: A New Commitment to the American Family*, ed. David Blankenhorn, S. Bayme, and J. B. Elshtain (Milwaukee, WI: Family Service America, 1990), 29–32.

13. John Bowlby, *A Secure Base: Parent-Child Attachment and Healthy Human Development* (New York: Basic Books, 1988).

14. The need for close relationships continues in adulthood and may be the most important factor in adult health and well-being. See James S.

House, Karl R. Landis, and Debra Umberson, "Social Relationships and Health," *Science* 241 (1989): 540–45.

15. Carol E. Franz, David C. McClelland, and Joel Weinberger, "Childhood Antecedents of Conventional Social Accomplishment in Midlife Adults: A 36-Year Prospective Study," *Journal of Personality and Social Psychology* 60, no. 4 (1991): 586.

16. Emmy E. Werner and Ruth S. Smith, *Overcoming the Odds: High Risk Children from Birth to Adulthood* (Ithaca, NY: Cornell University Press, 1992).

17. Bronfenbrenner, "What Families Do," 33.

18. David Popenoe, "The Controversial Truth: Two-Parent Families are Better," *The New York Times*, 26 December 1992; David Popenoe, "Scholars Should Worry About the Disintegration of the American Family," *Chronicle of Higher Education*, 14 April 1993, A48. See also Barbara Dafoe Whitehead, "Dan Quayle Was Right," *The Atlantic Monthly* 271, no. 4 (April 1993): 47–84.

19. Ann M. Milne, "Family Structure and the Achievement of Children," in *Education and the American Family: A Research Synthesis*, ed. William J. Weston (New York: New York University Press, 1989), 57.

20. David H. Demo and Alan C. Acock, "The Impact of Divorce on Children," *Journal of Marriage and the Family* 50, no. 3 (1988): 639.

21. Judith S. Wallerstein, "The Long-Term Effects of Divorce on Children: A Review," *Journal of the American Academy of Child and Adolescent Psychiatry* 30, no. 3 (May 1991): 359.

22. Nicholas Zill and Charlotte A. Schoenborn, "Developmental, Learning, and Emotional Problems: Health of Our Nation's Children, United States, 1988," Advance Data: 120 (Washington, DC: National Center for Health Statistics, 1990). For another report on this survey, with similar findings, see Deborah A. Dawson, "Family Structure and Children's Health and Well-Being: Data from the 1988 National Health Interview Survey on Child Health," *Journal of Marriage and the Family* 53, no. 3 (1991): 573–84.

23. R. L. Trivers, *Social Evolution* (Menlo Park, CA: Benjamin/Cummings, 1985); Christopher Badcock, *Evolution and Individual Behavior* (Cambridge, MA: Basil Blackwell, 1991); Judith Dunn, *The Beginnings of Social Understanding* (Cambridge, MA: Harvard University Press, 1988); Robert A. Hinde, *Individuals, Relationships, and Culture* (New York: Cambridge University Press, 1987).

24. Robert Hogan, John A. Johnson, and Nicholas P. Emler, "A Socioanalytic Theory of Moral Development," in *Moral Development. New Directions for Child Development*, vol. 2, ed. William Damon (San Francisco: Jossey Bass, 1978), 15.

25. Beatrice B. Whiting and Carolyn P. Edwards, *Children of Different Worlds: The Formation of Social Behavior* (Cambridge, MA: Harvard University Press, 1988); J. W. M. Whiting and Beatrice B. Whiting, *Children of Six Cultures: A Psychocultural Analysis* (Cambridge, MA: Harvard University Press, 1975).

26. Nancy Eisenberg, *The Caring Child* (Cambridge, MA: Harvard University Press, 1992); Nancy Eisenberg and Paul H. Mussen, *The Roots of Prosocial Behavior in Children* (New York: Cambridge University Press, 1989).

27. William Damon, *The Moral Child: Nurturing Children's Natural Moral Growth* (New York: The Free Press, 1988).

28. The direct evidence linking criminality with lack of empathy for others is very strong. See James Q. Wilson and Richard J. Herrnstein, *Crime and Human Nature* (New York: Simon and Schuster, 1985), chapter 7.

29. Damon, *The Moral Child*, 52.

30. Maria Krysan, Kristin A. Moore, and Nicholas Zill, *Research on Successful Families* (Washington, DC: Child Trends, 1990), 2; see also Maria Krysan, Kristin A. Moore, and Nicholas Zill, *Identifying Successful Families: An Overview of Constructs and Selected Measures* (Washington, DC: Child Trends, 1990).

31. Krysan, Moore and Zill, *Research on Successful Families*, 4–5.

32. Nick Stinnett and John DeFrain, *Secrets of Strong Families* (Boston, MA: Little Brown, 1985).

33. On this style, see Diana Baumrind, "Rearing Competent Children," in *Child Development Today and Tomorrow*, ed. William Damon (San Francisco: Jossey-Bass, 1989).

34. Damon, *The Moral Child*, 117.

35. Urie Bronfenbrenner, Phyllis Moen, and James Garbarino, "Child, Family, and Community," in *Review of Child Development Research*, vol. 7, ed. Ross D. Parke (Chicago: University of Chicago Press, 1983).

36. Robert T. Ammerman, in *Children at Risk: An Evaluation of Factors Contributing to Child Abuse and Neglect*, ed. Robert T. Ammerman and Michel Hersen (New York: Plenum Press, 1990); Gay Young and Tamra Gately, "Neighborhood Impoverishment and Child Maltreatment," *Journal of Family Issues* 9, no. 2 (1988): 240–254; James Garbarino and Deborah Sherman, "High Risk Neighborhoods and High Risk Families: The Human Ecology of Child Maltreatment," *Child Development* 51 (1980): 188–98.

37. Several studies have found that community instability, as measured by the social mobility of residents, is the best predictor of high ag-

gregate divorce rates. See Lynn K. White, "Determinants of Divorce: A Review of Research in the Eighties," *Journal of Marriage and the Family* 52, no. 4 (1990): 904–12.

38. Bronfenbrenner, "What Families Do," 36.

39. Francis A. J. Ianni, *The Search For Structure: A Report on American Youth Today* (New York: Free Press, 1989), 262.

40. See, for example: David Maybury-Lewis, *Millenium: Tribal Wisdom and the Modern World* (New York: Penguin Books, 1992).

41. This is not to say that all preliterate societies are or were "harmonious, peaceful, benign and content." See Robert B. Edgerton, *Sick Societies: Challenging the Myth of Primitive Harmony* (New York: Free Press, 1992).

42. See Andrew Oldenquist, *The Non-Suicidal Society* (Bloomington, IN: University of Indiana Press, 1986).

43. Raoul Naroll, *The Moral Order: An Introduction to the Human Situation* (Beverly Hills, CA: Sage, 1983).

44. Christopher Lasch, *The True and Only Heaven: Progress and Its Critics* (New York: W. W. Norton, 1991).

45. Michael Walzer, "The New Tribalism," *Dissent* (Spring 1992): 171.

46. See, for example, the collection of articles entitled "On the Importance of Being Tribal and the Prospects for Creating Multicultural Community," *Utne Reader* (July/August, 1992): 67–95.

47. Peter Berger, *A Far Glory: The Quest for Faith in An Age of Credulity* (New York: Free Press, 1992), 45.

48. For a recent statement of this issue, see "American Values: Life, liberty and try pursuing a bit of tolerance too," *The Economist*, 5 September 1992.

49. Michael J. Sandel, "Morality and the Liberal Ideal," *New Republic* 190 (7 May 1984), 17.

50. Oldenquist, *The Non-Suicidal Society*, 127.

51. This is closely related to the ideas of protecting "social capital" advanced by James Coleman; protecting "mediating institutions" advanced by Peter Berger and Richard Neuhaus; and protecting "civil society" advanced by Alan Wolfe. See James S. Coleman, *Foundations of Social Theory* (Cambridge, MA: Belknap Press, Harvard, 1990); Peter L. Berger and Richard John Neuhaus, *To Empower People: The Role of Mediating Structures in Public Policy* (Washington, DC: American Enterprise Institute, 1977); Alan Wolfe, *Whose Keeper: Social Science and Moral Obligation* (Berkeley, CA: University of California, 1989).

52. James A. Coleman and Thomas Hoffer, *Public and Private High Schools: The Impact of Communities* (New York: Basic Books, 1987).

53. Laurence Steinberg, "Communities of Families and Education," in *Education and the American Family: A Research Synthesis*, ed. William J. Weston (New York: New York University Press, 1989).

54. Nathan Glazer, "The Real World of Urban Education," *The Public Interest* 106 (1992): 75.

55. Mickey Kaus, *The End of Equality* (New York: Basic Books, 1992).

56. See Allan V. Horwitz, *The Logic of Social Control* (NY: Plenum Press, 1990).

57. One major empirical study concluded: "Communities characterized by sparse friendship networks, unsupervised teenage peer groups, and low organizational participation had disproportionately high rates of crime and delinquency." Robert J. Sampson and W. Byron Groves, "Community Structure and Crime: Testing Social Disorganization Theory," *American Journal of Sociology* 94, no. 4 (1989): 799.

58. Wesley J. Skogan, *Disorder and Decline: Crime and the Spiral of Decay in American Neighborhoods* (New York: Free Press, 1990).

59. Nathan Glazer, *The Limits of Social Policy* (Cambridge, MA: Harvard University Press, 1988).

60. See Oldenquist, *The Non-Suicidal Society*, ch. 10.

61. See "The Responsive Communitarian Platform: Rights and Responsibilities," 1991/92. *The Responsive Community* 2, no. 1 (1991/92): 4–20; and Amitai Etzioni, *The Spirit of Community: Rights, Responsibilities, and the Communitarian Agenda* (New York: Crown Publishers, 1993).

62. Chester Finn, *We Must Take Charge: Our Schools and Our Future* (New York: Free Press, 1991).

63. See Arthur M. Schlesinger Jr., *The Disuniting of America: Reflections on a Multicultural Society* (New York: W. W. Norton, 1992).

64. This is similar to the important distinction between "pluralistic" and "particularistic" multiculturalism made by Diane Ravitch in "Multiculturalism: E Pluribus Plures," *The American Scholar* (Summer 1990).

65. Several of these are further developed in David Popenoe, *Private Pleasure, Public Plight: American Metropolitan Development in Comparative Perspective* (New Brunswick, NJ: Transaction, 1989), ch. 10.

66. John Kasarda and M. Janowitz, "Community Attachment in Mass Society," *American Sociological Review* 39 (1974): 328–39; Robert J. Sampson, "Local Friendship Ties and Community Attachment in Mass Society: A Multilevel Systemic Model," *American Sociological Review* 53, no. 5 (1988): 766–79.

67. Mary Ann Glendon, *Rights Talk: The Impoverishment of Political Discourse* (New York: Free Press, 1991), 137.

68. Angus Campbell, *The Sense of Well-Being in America* (New York: McGraw Hill, 1981), 150.

69. See Oscar Newman, *Community of Interest* (Garden City, N.Y.: Anchor Press/Doubleday, 1980).

70. William A. V. Clark, "Residential Preferences and Residential Choices in a Multiethnic Context," *Demography* 29, no. 3 (1992): 451–66.

CHAPTER 5

Altruism, Civic Virtue, and Religion

Don S. Browning

The point of departure for this essay is the argument set forth in Alan Wolfe's important *Whose Keeper? Social Science and Moral Obligation.*[1] In this book, Wolfe puts forward a variety of arguments designed both to document the decline of civic virtue and to outline a remedy. He builds on the thought of Jürgen Habermas to show how the two great manifestations of the systems world, the state and the market, are impinging upon everyday life. The diverse logics of these systems, according to Wolfe, undercut our sense of obligation in both intimate family relations and distant relations in the world of public citizenship. His cure for these trends is to reinvigorate what he calls "civil society." Civil society, when it is strong, limits the spread of both state and market and functions as a support to the family—the real crucible of civic virtue. The discipline of sociology, he believes, has special insight into how moral virtue develops in modern societies and will have a major role to play in the revitalization of both civil society and civic virtue.

The general contours of Wolfe's position seem quite valid. Although I will offer an appreciative reading of Wolfe, I also will present four criticisms which, if taken to heart, would make his contribution even stronger. My concerns are systematic. I am not so much interested in focusing on Wolfe as I am in using his engaging perspective to advance a more systematic position. My criticisms have to do with (1) his thin view of culture, (2) his disconnection of the family from its biological basis, (3) his too complete rejection of the kind of deontological liberalism associated with the social philosophy of John Rawls, and (4) his belief that religion, and indeed tradition, can no longer play a significant role in the renewal of civil society. These four points are interconnected, do not necessarily undercut the essence of his argument, and constitute a point of departure for elaborating a constructive position relevant to the rejuvenation of civic virtue.

As a theologian with practical interests, I am concerned to show why Western religious traditions, specifically Christian theology, have something to contribute to this discussion. But practical theology strengthens its case if it can both incorporate and show the limitations of powerful social science perspectives such as Wolfe's.

Civic Virtue and the Systems World

Although the phrase "civic virtue" does not appear in Wolfe's book, he is clearly interested in what this concept represents. He is concerned with the deterioration of a strong sense of obligation and care for what he calls "distant relations."[2] By this he means individuals for whom we have some responsibility because they are members of the same nation or state but who are beyond the pale of our intimate relations in families, friendship circles, churches, and other voluntary organizations. Wolfe's explanation for the decline of civic virtue in this sense is complex. It entails a theory of how basic human altruism arises in families and becomes analogically extended to distant or nonfamilial relations. It is a theory that he shares with Aristotle, who developed it in his *Nicomachean Ethics* in reaction to Plato's theory of citizenship in *The Republic*. There are three parts to Wolfe's argument.

First, Wolfe's core explanation for the decline of civic virtue is the social trend which he calls "colonization." Colonization is a metaphor for the extension of the logics of the systems world into the intimate relations of civil society—family, friendships, neighborhoods, and voluntary organizations. The concept of colonization comes from the writings of Frankfurt *Schule* critical-theorist

Jürgen Habermas, especially his two-volume *Theory of Communicative Action*.[3] Colonization theory assumes that prior to the rise of modernity, the interactions of these spheres were face-to-face relations, where mutual recognition and free moral reconstruction were dominant over either market utility or state coercion. The formal theory of civil society was developed by Enlightenment thinkers such as Adam Smith, David Hume, and Adam Ferguson.[4] They saw this social sphere as a major source of protection against remnants of the monarchical or feudal state and a presupposition of the necessary constraints of an acquisitive market economy.

Habermas's theory of colonization says that with the rise of modernization, these spheres of face-to-face interaction have become corrupted by the spreading influence of both the cost-benefit efficiencies of markets in capitalist systems and the responsibility-suppressing, externally imposed rules and regulations of state bureaucracies. These two systems are especially disruptive to families, the birthplace of elemental altruism. State bureaucracies are more powerful in socialist countries such as Sweden; market systems are more powerful in capitalist countries such as the United States. In both places, it is a matter of these systems spilling over their native boundaries and, as Michael Walzer has described, shaping the logics of areas of life, such as the intimate sphere of families, which formerly had been protected from their influence.[5]

Wolfe gives detailed explanation and documentation of how state bureaucracies undermine what he calls the "public family" in countries such as Sweden and how market economies have much the same effect, but for very different reasons, on what he calls the "private family" in the United States.[6] Wolfe tries to document trends in both societies toward weakened charity, declining interest in having children signaled by lower birth rates, lessening involvement in the care of children and aging parents, dwindling concern for strangers and the homeless, and more concern with the demands of present generations at the expense of generations of the future. All of these humane qualities decline in the public family when these customary family functions are more and more given to the state to perform. On the other hand, they decline just as dramatically in the private family when it increasingly uses market-inspired cost-benefit calculations to measure the value of intimate relations.

The Chicago school of economics, specifically some of my academic neighbors such as Gary Becker and Judge Richard Posner, are directly indicted by Wolfe for systematically extending the rational-choice thinking of neoclassical economics to social arenas traditionally handled in noneconomic ways. This serves to give theoretical legitimation in countries with market economies for what is in fact happening anyway, that is, the increased use of the moral logic of self-interested rational calculation in "such areas as family size, arrangements for child care, patterns of marriage and divorce, and relations among grandparents, children, and grandchildren . . ."[7]

Wolfe's second main point is this: when a sense of care and obligation declines between family members, these qualities necessarily deteriorate in more distant relations as well. This is a point recently put forth as well by Mary Ann Glendon and Alice and Peter Rossi.[8] Traditionally, morality has been thought to move analogically from the affectional commitments of family members to the larger society. Wolfe believes that this must continue to be true in modern societies even though accomplishing this is an uphill battle.

> Being modern will always require some way of linking both intimate and distant obligations. Although in theory that balance could just as easily be found by engendering outward obligations inward, the proper balance will more realistically be found by extending inward obligations outward. . . . We need civil society—families, communities, friendship networks, solidaristic workplace ties, voluntarism, spontaneous groups and movements—not to reject, but to complete the project of modernity.[9]

Wolfe is clearly Aristotelian in seeing civic virtue as a matter of generalizing family and neighborhood affections to the wider community. Plato, in *The Republic*, argued that if the ruling class were to have sympathy for the entire community and not just its own families and children, couples should mate but have their children raised by the state. Since children and parents would not know each other, Plato imagined that this would lead his philosopher-kings to extend their altruistic sentiments to include all children and thus the entire state—not just their own offspring and relatives.[10]

Aristotle in his *Politics* did not respond kindly to Plato's thought experiment. Aristotle, as does Wolfe, believed that human sympathy spreads outward from special and embodied family relations. Aristotle believed "that which is common to the greatest number has the least care bestowed upon it."[11] If family and related intimate relations are weak, wider civic virtue will suffer as well. This preference for the Aristotelian in contrast to the Platonic view of the origins of civic virtue was fundamental to most of Christian history, especially after Aquinas's synthesis of Aristotelian philosophy with Christian theology. But the story is complicated, as we will soon see.

Wolfe's third point has to do with his proposed solution—the urgent need to revive civil society as a protection against the eroding effects of the state and market. Wolfe has a social interactional and social constructivist understanding of how civil society develops its culture and morality. Individuals in societies, in their interaction with one another and with groups on the margins, create their own rules. Learning and growth is important in this view of morality. In one place he writes, in italics, that this view sees *"moral obligation as a socially constructed practice negotiated between learning agents capable of growth on the one hand and a culture capable of change on the other."*[12] In deriving his theory of society, Wolfe champions interactionalists such as George Herbert Mead, Erving Goffman, and Alfred Schutz more than he does sociological structuralists such as Durkheim or Kantian structuralists such as Rawls and Kohlberg. His rejection of the latter is a matter to which I will soon return.

Some Foundations of Civic Virtue

Wolfe has a positive view of culture as a factor shaping human affairs. This is an attractive feature to a practically minded theologian, for where the concept of culture is developed, one generally finds tradition and religion trailing not far behind. But this is not so with Wolfe. This introduces my first criticism of Wolfe. His constructivist view of culture places heavy emphasis on how people create culture, but it places little emphasis on the role of historical inheritance in the creation of culture. He gives some attention to how cultures are united by stories, but these stories to Wolfe seem more created by societies in the present than inherited from the past.[13] If he had paid more attention to how the past—what Hans Georg Gadamer calls "effective history"—shapes the present, Wolfe would have called his view a *reconstructive* rather than a *constructive* theory of culture.[14] His view would have been closer to a hermeneutic theory which sees culture as reconstructing itself through a process of dialogue between the situation of the present and the classic religious and cultural sources of the past that have shaped that culture's history. In the additional criticisms that follow, we will see how classic expressions of our Western religious heritage have carried within them other crucial elements that Wolfe's important position neglects.

My second criticism has to do with Wolfe's failure to fully account for why families are the most basic seedbed of civic virtue. Specifically, it has to do with his neglect of the biological grounds of altruism. Wolfe sees no need to give a biological grounding to the social self or to his constructivist view of civil society.

> The long debate in Western philosophy about the nature of human nature is, from the standpoint of the social construction position on morality, misplaced. It is not how we are in nature that matters. . . . It is rather what we do with society that counts.[15]

But without saying more about the "nature of human nature," Wolfe cannot give an account of two of his most cherished assertions, that is, that families based on mother-father partnerships raise children on the whole better than nonfamilial settings and that generalized family affections make up the moral core of civic virtue. To show this, let us turn to a philosophically fine-tuned appropriation of insights from sociobiology. This will also, however, illustrate, how biological insights have been used in that theological tradition that has had most to do with shaping family theory in the Christian tradition—the thought of Thomas Aquinas.

The theory of inclusive fitness associated with the name of W. D. Hamilton and popularized by E. O. Wilson, Michael Ruse, and Peter Singer is the biology that suits this purpose.[16] It has recently been integrated into economic theory by Judge Richard Posner[17] and into law by Richard Epstein, Posner, and others.[18] This perspective has argued, with the use of elaborate mathematical models, that the core of altruism is grounded in the unconscious tendency among all species to sacrifice for others in direct proportion to the number of genes shared between the altruist and the recipient of his beneficial acts. All animals, including humans, are more likely to sacrifice for their children, brothers, and sisters— because they share 50 percent of their genes with them—than they are for uncles, aunts, and cousins with whom they share only a fourth or eighth respectively. But they are also more inclined to sacrifice for any close kin sharing a reasonably high percentage of genes than they are for unrelated persons or strangers. This view of the fundamental ground of altruism is called "kin altruism." Altruistic behavior, in this theory, is portrayed as a form of egoism. It is a complicated way of preserving oneself or, more accurately, one's genes.

Although biologists distinguish between reciprocal, group, and kin altruism, it is kin altruism which is said to account for parental investments in their children. Not only is kin altruism being used to explain rudimentary parental investment, it is also being employed to account for the relative absence of violence between parents and their children in comparison to nonblood-related acquaintances and strangers. Martin Daly and Margo Wilson in their *Homicide* employ a sophisticated form of inclusive fitness and kin selection theory to explain ground squirrels' capacity to differentiate between full and half sisters and show less hostility to full sisters.[20] They also apply it to explain why out of the 512 homicides in Detroit in 1977 only 32, or 6.25 percent, were between consanguineous relatives. The theory throws light on why cohabitants who were not blood relatives were eleven times more likely to be murdered than cohabitants who are kin.[21] They believe it explains why in a study in Canada they found a 40 percent higher abuse rate for children raised by one natural parent and one stepparent than children raised by both natural parents. It explains, they argue, why when homicide alone is considered children under two years of age were seventy times more likely to be killed when living with one stepparent than when living with both blood parents.[22] What explains these strange facts according to Daly and Wilson? The theory of kin selection and what it predicts about the altruism of natural parents for offspring who share their genes!

Of course, it should go without being said that under a variety of circumstances, natural parents do kill and abuse their children as children do kill and abuse their parents. But they do it much less than in nonconsanguineous relationships. When Wolfe rejects the role of nature in human nature, he is depriving himself of this support for his case about the importance of families in creating a basic altruism that, when generalized, is the core of civic virtue.

In addition, he need not be afraid that by including a biological dimension he is lapsing into determinism and undermining his constructivist view of society. Mary Midgley's philosophical reconstruction of sociobiological arguments in her *Beast and Man* has shown us the way out of this dead end. She contends that while humans have strong unconscious altruistic tendencies toward genetically related humans, they have other deep tendencies as well, such as a drive toward autonomy, pleasure, rest, and defense. It is precisely because humans have conflicting tendencies that rationality and culture play such an important role in mediating between the different directions of our human nature.[23] This was an argument that William James made many years before.[24] With this model of soft determinism at hand, Wolfe's constructivist view of culture can be retained but revised. Social interaction does not create culture and civil society *ex nihilo*. Instead, social interaction creates culture and civil society to accommodate, balance, and find various ways to organize certain central tendencies in humans, one of which is to act altruistically toward genetically related persons.

Moral philosophy and moral theology often have made use of similar biological insights in both the philosophy of Aristotle and its influence on the thought of Thomas Aquinas. It is commonly known that Aristotelian biology was crude by today's standards and very bad in its misogynistic depiction of women as intellectually inferior, material, passive, and unspirited.[25] But, as recent studies have observed, when Aristotle's family theory is taken as a whole, both his biology and his regard for women look much better, especially in comparison to Plato.[26] Aristotle taught, as does sociobiology, that by nature humans want to leave behind images of themselves.[27] He objected to Plato's removal of children from parents because it would make love "watery"; the qualities that inspire regard and affection are that "a thing is your own and that it is your only one. . . ."[28]

Aquinas incorporated these insights into his explicitly Christian moral theology. Families, for him, were natural phenomena created to accommodate the unusually long period of infant dependency. This required that each child should have "certain and definite parents," specifically "a tie between the man and a definite woman."[29] Furthermore, in his reflections in the *Summa Theologica* on "The Order of Charity," Aquinas explicitly follows the Aristotelian line that we have both a natural inclination and a moral obligation to love our children first and give them special privilege among life's various loves. Aquinas could do this by distinguishing between different kinds of love. For instance, a man should *honor* his father as his "creative principle" or source and as being, for this reason, nearer to God. But Thomas held that we should love our children more than our fathers in the sense of *caring* for them. He echoed Aristotle and anticipated modern biology when he wrote, "a man loves more that which is more closely connected with him, in which way a man's children are more lovable to him than his father, as the Philosopher states."[30]

Neither Aristotle nor Aquinas derived their ethics from their biology. But they both allowed biology to inform their ethics by attempting to stay within, as Midgley has said, our "central human needs and tendencies."[31] And even though they both saw the family as a seedbed of virtue, they both taught the necessity to transcend the family. Aristotle saw political discourse and action in the democratic polis as a greater good, and Aquinas saw life in the Kingdom of God as a greater good. Aquinas in particular saw family life as a good but not the final end of life. The enjoyment of the beatific vision of God was for him the final end, and the love between family members was both grounded in and pointed toward this greater love.[32] Aquinas was aware that the author of the gospel of Matthew had depicted Jesus as saying, "For I have come to set a man against his father, and a daughter against her mother. . . . He who loves father or mother more than me is not worthy of me; and he who loves son or daughter more than me is not worthy of me" (Matt. 10:35–37). But Aquinas, as have most Christian writers, did not believe that such words represented any fundamental contradiction between families and Christianity. He wrote that Jesus "commanded us to hate, in our kindred, not their kinship, but only the fact of their being an obstacle between us and God."[33]

Wolfe's reluctance to incorporate a biological dimension weakens his case for the contribution of strong families to altruism. It also leads him to overlook ways that Western religious traditions used their primitive biological insights to good effect. My point is not so much to champion the specifics of the biology of Aristotle and Aquinas as to suggest that in their thought we may have a model of how psychobiological theories can inform moral thinking in ways profitable for contemporary issues.

Social Construction and the Ethics of Principle

Wolfe believes that the free interaction of civil society can generate a morality that will provide both an alternative to as well as protection against the ethics of state coercion and market rational choice. I fully support him in attributing this potential to civil society. But I have reservations about his view of ethics and his rejection *in toto* of liberal ethics of the kind associated with Kant and Rawls. To suggest, as Wolfe's constructivist position does, that individuals in civil society "create their own moral rules through the social interactions they experience with others" does not leave us with criteria for judging when these rules are genuinely moral and when they are not.[34] Wolfe describes the process, but he does not give us criteria. Therefore, his theory of civil society and what it implies for civic virtue leaves us without moral substance.

Wolfe rejects the liberalism of Rawls without attempting to reconstruct it for his purposes. He criticizes Rawls and his moral-psychological counterpart, Lawrence Kohlberg, for overemphasizing abstract models of justice and rights. Their kind of liberalism assumes the moral and affectional glue of civil society but does not have the concepts to account for it.[35] He echoes the criticism of Carol Gilligan that Rawls and Kohlberg are "formal and abstract" and not sufficiently "contextual and narrative."[36] He seconds the criticism of Rawls's deontological liberalism voiced in Michael Sandel's *Liberalism and the Limits of Justice*; deontological liberalism sees moral judgments as ends in themselves totally independent of affects, desires, history, tradition, and the enhancement of particular nonmoral goods.[37] Against such a view, Wolfe writes, "In a world where people raise children, live in communities, and value friendships, a moral theory that demands rational cognition to the degree that Rawls's does is little help and may well be a burden."[38]

Wolfe does not realize that in rejecting Rawls and his understanding of justice as fairness, he has nothing to put in its place. His sociological description of how bonded members of a society create their own rules does not tell us how to distinguish moral from immoral rules; it overlooks the fact that members of a society sometimes happily make and accept, because of various manipulations, unjust rules. It also overlooks the truth that neo-Kantian concepts of justice, generalizability, and reversibility can be squared with positions that take genuine human affects, needs, and historical contingency into account. In these formulations—found in thinkers such as Frankena, Ricoeur, Etzioni, and the Catholic moral theologian Louis Janssens—justice is not defined as totally independent of a concern to actualize the good. In these formulations, all attempts to satisfy desire, meet needs, or pursue finite goods have to be done in ways consistent with, and under the direction of, the dominant deontological principle of justice.[39] It is true that such an act of justice does entail some transcendence over appetite, need, and particular social locations, but it does not necessitate their suppression. On the contrary, it requires only that they be guided to conform to the specifications of justice as fairness.

It is true that we often fail to attain this kind of justice, but it is precisely approximations of it that tell us that communities are on track. Nor do obligations to kin necessarily conflict with the obligation to nonkin. But it does require enlargement of the idea of justice. It simply entails a sense of justice between kin groups rather than only between individuals. It means that I must both allow and actively support the right of other families to discharge their duties to their children just as I claim the inclination and moral obligation to help my family.

It is also true that justice in this sense can be seen as quite interactional and social rather than just a thought experiment of an isolated individual. Habermas in *Communication and the Evolution of Society* develops a communicative or dialogical model of justice in contrast to what he calls a "monological" model. Justice is not simply what can be generalizable from the perspective of the individual thinker; it is what all who are part of the conversation freely agree can be justly generalized.[40] Habermas's theory of communicative justice and Wolfe's picture of civil society both have strong interactive features. But Habermas forcefully reworks Rawls's theory of justice into a communicative and interactive concept. I would add the need to see this communicative justice as guiding and measuring our affective quest for the good—including the central good of parental altruism toward children as the bedrock of later developmental and more public forms of altruism. Individuals who have the communicative capacity to participate in this kind of dialogical justice possess one of the central civic virtues. Possibly it is the most central civic virtue.

The neo-Kantian concept of generalizability and the sociobiological concept of kin altruism are not incompatible. The core of ethics may be the human capacity to generalize family affection and respect (the arena of our natural inclinations) to those outside the family. Stephen Pope in his important work on the relation of sociobiology to ethics has written that there are good biological and philosophical grounds for "affirming that relatively stable and secure bonds of love within the family create the emotional basis for a later *extension* of love to persons outside the family and that the utility of these early bonds continue powerfully to inform subsequent adult affectional bonds." (emphasis added)[41] It would be entirely justifiable to substitute the more neo-Kantian word "generalize" for Pope's word "extension." One also can substitute the word generalize for the word extension in the following words written by Mary Midgley:

> [T]he development of sociability proceeds in any case largely by this *extension* to other adults of behavior first developed between parents

and young. . . . wider sociality in its original essence simply is the power of adults to treat one another, mutually, as honorary parents and children. (emphasis added)[42]

Peter Singer in his book *The Expanding Circle: Ethics and Sociobiology* makes the same point. Universal ethical systems are not based on suppressing family commitments; they evolve from the use of disinterested reason in expanding these particular affections outward. Singer argues:

[E]thics evolved out of our social instincts and our capacity to reason . . . let us cling to the principle of equal consideration of interests. . . . which relies on the fact . . . that we are rational enough to take a broader point of view from which our own interests are no more important than the interest of others. . . ."[43]

Although this line of thinking gives more ethical content to Wolfe's radically constructivist view of both civil society and civic virtue, this synthesis of sociobiology and neo-Kantianism needs the support of additional beliefs. For us to generalize family affections outward to others, we must have certain beliefs that make us take nonkin as seriously as our blood kin. Although we seldom do this in the full affective sense that we apply to our children or parents, when instinct and reason are supplemented by certain beliefs, we do sometimes, quite profoundly, treat nonkin with the same equal regard that we are more likely to apply to our brothers and sisters, mothers and fathers, sons and daughters. What are these additional beliefs that are needed to support reason and our affections?

Civic Virtue and Religion

Wolfe acknowledges that civil society must have its beliefs about the meaning of life. He believes these generally take the form of unifying stories that "define identity" and "emphasize the need for some kind of restraint on individual desires. . . ."[44] But Wolfe believes that there is little role left in modern societies for religious stories. "Religion," he writes, "is no longer the source of moral authority it once was."[45] In fact, it is not just religion. He expands this point by writing, "In looking to religion, philosophy, literature, or politics to find the rule of moral obligation, we look in the wrong place."[46] The right place, he believes, is the free interaction of civil society as uncovered by sociology and conceived along Wolfe's constructivist lines.

Religion is, for Wolfe, all but dead. But civil society, he holds, must have at least its secular stories. They must unify distant or nonconsanguineous people by emphasizing the need for mutual dependence and self-sacrifice. But there is another moral function of stories that Wolfe does not mention—the need to provide beliefs about the moral status of individuals. Beliefs about the moral importance of other people, especially persons beyond our kin relations, are crucial, as I suggested above, to guide reason's extension of kin altruism to others.

The Kantian tradition proposes beliefs that tell us that all persons are rational beings with the capacity for freedom and deserving of universal respect. Such beings should be treated as ends and never as means only.[47] It can be argued that neo-Kantianism is a secular form of the Judeo-Christian narrative. This narrative grounds respect for the other on the belief that God made humans in the image of God. Christians claim that the religious status of personhood is the ground of the moral worth of humans. The sacred status of human personhood grounds morality, for Christians, even more profoundly than does human rationality.

Basil Mitchell has pointed out in his *Morality: Religious or Secular* that Judeo-Christian and Kantian ethics both base their ethics of justice on the status of persons as ends. The difference between them is that the Judeo-Christian tradition bases this on the *imago dei* in humans rather than on the thinner Kantian view of humans as rational beings.[48] Mitchell contends that the religious view adds moral weight and inclines those who base their moral action on this belief to take the other with even more seriousness.

My point is this: instinct and reason need the extension and reinforcement of unifying stories and their embedded beliefs. These stories, among other functions, must define the moral value of individuals. Beliefs about this, when deeply held, help reason generalize family affections and respect to distant relations. This is why civic virtue depends, in part, on narratives. Wolfe is perceptive in seeing the importance of stories for civil society and its civic virtue. But he is too optimistic in imagining that we can self-consciously invent new secular stories to take the place of the great religious stories that have shaped our culture.

Wolfe imagines society as creating itself something like Jean Paul Sartre envisioned the solitary individual defining herself. I recommend, instead, a hermeneutic model of historical reconstruction. Such a model sees societies standing in the present but, as Gadamer and Bellah have claimed, in a perpetual dialogue with the classics that have formed them out of the past.[49] Wolfe almost catches the spirit of the hermeneutical turn at the end of his book when he contends that modern persons will take social responsibilities seriously only when "society is understood as a gift."[50] One might think that Wolfe is speaking almost religiously about civil society or at least giving a strong pitch for the importance of inherited traditions. But what he gives, he also takes away. He soon adds a stunning qualifier: "Moreover, it is a gift that we give to ourselves, since no one put it in place for us."[51]

But is that true? Is it true that no one put our society in place for us? Isn't it rather that all societies are built on layer after layer of contributions that still shape our lives as living histories? Isn't it more likely that any powerful attempt to reconstruct (not just construct) civil society will be done out of a vital interpretive conversation with the religio-ethical narratives that have unified civil society in the past?

Civil Society, Civic Virtue, and a Black Pentecostal Church

It may be true that no one religious tradition will dominate our public stories as they have in the past. Yet I am constantly amazed by those polls which say that between 80 and 90 percent of Americans are vaguely evangelical Christian in their beliefs and believe both in a personal God that listens to prayers and in the divinity of Jesus Christ.[52] But my claim is modest. I do not say that Christian stories can be the unifying center for the whole of civil society. I do want to illustrate, however, how one religious community appropriates its Christian story in ways that empower its members' par-

ticipation in civil society. My motives are not apologetic in any
narrow sense; I am not arguing for the truth or superiority of Christianity as such. Rather, as a long-time religious liberal, I am saying
we can learn a great deal from this conservative church about how
local religious expressions, feeding on commanding religious traditions, can support the revitalization of civil society.

For ten months during 1988 and 1989, I studied a black Pentecostal Church called the Apostolic Church of God. It was located
eight blocks south on the very street I live on in Chicago's liberal
Hyde Park. It is only two blocks beyond the southern edge of the
University of Chicago where I teach. I give you the real name of the
church as I do the real name of the pastor, the Reverend Arthur
Brazier. I do this first of all because I have permission. I do it also
because both the church and the pastor are famous due to their role
in a widely studied community organization called The Woodlawn
Organization (TWO). I do it, finally, because part of the meaning-
fulness of the story is the way the spheres of our lives, both theirs
and mine, do and do not overlap even though we live in the same
neighborhood.

This church's story illustrates elements that go into the creation
of civil society and civic virtue, as I outlined these earlier. This
church has been a key mover in attempting to protect the Woodlawn neighborhood from the moral logics of both the market and
the state. Its theory and program illustrate the three elements of
civic virtue that I discussed previously—generalized family affections and obligations, justice, and a unifying narrative. Specifically, restoring the black family is central to the mission of
Apostolic Church. Furthermore, its official theology, devoid of the
jargon of deontological liberalism, still promotes a version of justice
that is analogous to it. Finally, its theological story helps its members handle the tensions between initiative and solidarity with distant others—a tension that besets the lives of its membership as
they seek to participate in the contradictions of a competitive democratic society with a liberal economic philosophy.

Apostolic Church of God is now approaching a membership of
8000.[53] In 1978 it had only 500 members. Arthur Brazier has been
its pastor for over 30 years. In the beginning, the church had less
than 100 members. During this period of fantastic growth, Brazier

was, in addition to his ministry, the head of TWO—the Saul-Alinsky–style community organization that fought to keep Woodlawn, one of Chicago's worst urban slums and ghettos, from collapsing. He and his church were in the forefront of promoting the control of teenage gangs, improving public education, enticing government loans for housing developments, and encouraging businesses to return to the neighborhood. He was also in the forefront of a major battle with the University of Chicago in its efforts to develop North Woodlawn for its use, thereby displacing its poor residents. This activity brought fame and scholarly attention to Brazier and TWO.[54] Brazier was a Pentecostal minister with a political concern; this was unusual and attracted interest. But few of his scholarly admirers paid attention to where Brazier's heart really rested. It was not primarily in his political activity; rather, it was in his church and his message to those who attended Sunday and Wednesday services.

Brazier's ministry can be usefully interpreted in light of Wolfe's theory of the pressures on civil society from both the state and the market. As Woodlawn's population became almost totally black by the early 1950s, both government and the market had its undermining effects. Markets, because of their cost-effectiveness mentality, began to withdraw. Pursuing business and industry in Woodlawn was not profitable, as William Julius Wilson has argued.[55] With jobs on the decline, men had less work and less to contribute to their families. Furthermore, the state-supported welfare systems had requirements that worked against male residency in families, in effect encouraging men to abandon their wives and children.

Apostolic Church is fully aware of the crisis of families in the black community. Its members are aware of teenage pregnancy, the fact that approximately 68 percent of all black children are born out-of-wedlock, and the growing feminization of poverty. The reconstruction of the black family is at the heart of its mission. Apostolic Church is a holiness church. Its official mission is to convert people, give them the gift of the Holy Spirit, turn them into sanctified saints, and help them live a life of moral purity. But a close second is its mission to reconstruct the black family and, within this, to reconstitute the role of black men in families.

In contrast to some political rhetoric of the 1992 presidential election, Apostolic Church spends little time speaking against single parents. Yet, it is clearly interested in reversing the trends toward single parenthood in the black community. Its strategy, however, is to concentrate on building up the self-image and responsibility of black men and enhancing their role in the black family. Its message seems successful; nearly 40 percent of the members of Apostolic Church are men, almost all of whom are under age 50. The women of the church are extremely supportive of the church's message to men and to families.

How are the three aspects of civic virtue discussed above stimulated at Apostolic Church?

First, Apostolic Church's family theology and ministry seem on the surface to be patriarchal. But to be fair, I must confess that, if really there, this patriarchy is subtle; the evidence for its presence is ambiguous and should remind us of the importance of context for the proper understanding of symbolic communication. Brazier's sermons and my various interviews with church members confirmed that men are depicted in this church as the moral and spiritual heads of their family. But, as it was in the classic verses of Ephesians 5, this headship is really one of servanthood, a concept quite different from standard patriarchal models in the Greco-Roman world that surrounded early Christianity.

Greek and Roman models of maleness emphasized the dominance and superiority of free men over women, slaves, and children. The message of Ephesians was different. It juxtaposed the message to spouses to "Be subject to one another out of reverence for Christ" (Eph. 5:21) with words such as "Husbands, love your wives, as Christ loved the church and gave himself up for her . . ." (Eph. 5:25). The members of Apostolic Church interpreted the idea of mutual submission to mean that wives and husbands are "to be in tune with one another." For the husband to be the spiritual and moral head meant that he was to take special leadership and responsibility for serving the family, parenting his children, and treating his wife and children with justice and respect.

In the end, the message was not so much one of male authority and power as it was one of male responsibility. An almost Rawlsian model of justice is supposed to reign, at this church, between husband and wife. Husband-wife relations, the official word says, are not a matter of 50–50, they "are a matter of 100–100."

Brazier is fully aware of the social systemic deficiencies and patterns of discrimination that both state and market have inflicted on black males. He leads the church in trying to change these systems—both state and market. He is for new jobs, humane welfare, better housing, job training, better transportation to take both men and women to where the jobs are—all the things that social-system reformers such as William Julius Wilson believe are important to cure the black ghetto of its ills.[56]

He also preaches a new family ethic, specifically aimed at men, and builds a community of support designed to implement it. In this way, his church contributes to civil society and civic virtue. It is a religio-cultural contribution. It seems to work. In addition to attracting large numbers of young men, Apostolic Church performs countless weddings each year, witnesses very few divorces among its congregation, sees few out-of-wedlock births among its teenagers, and supports large numbers of its children through high school and into higher education.

Apostolic Church is tolerant of alternatives to the blood-related mother-father partnership, but this family form is clearly the center of its emphasis. It does not, as some liberal feminists such as Judith Stacey do, champion so-called black matriarchy as a harbinger of the female-centered families of the future.[57] Nor does its rhetoric of male moral leadership in the family translate into a justification for the traditional (or more properly modern) breadwinning father and domestic and childrearing mother. The black wives in this church are nearly all employed outside the home and have been for decades. Parenting is something men are expected to be involved in, and it is not just left to women. In spite of the church's lapse into patriarchal-sounding language, its families, I grew to believe, were on the whole egalitarian, equal-regard families, but with a very strong emphasis on male responsibility.

Second, Apostolic Church has a theory of justice that has formal similarities to the deontological liberalism found in Rawls. I refer specifically to the reversible and generalizing characteristics of neighbor love, "you shall love your neighbor as yourself" (Matt. 19:19). This ethic is applied both to the area of intimate relations and public affairs. We saw this in the formula, quoted earlier, that husband and wife relations are not 50–50 (simple reciprocity) but 100–100 (full reversibility and equal regard). One sees this concern with justice in public affairs in the church's energetic support of liberal civil-rights organizations such as Operation Push.

In contrast to strict deontological liberal positions, in the theology of Apostolic Church the generalizability of neighbor love constitutes what I elsewhere have called the "inner core" of an ethic that is surrounded by a rich narrative "outer envelope."[58] The reversibility and generalizability of neighbor love guide affect and impulse. But this liberal-sounding ethic of neighbor love does not take over the church's entire ethical field. It is the highest and most abstract level of ethics for this church, but it is supported by many far more concrete ethical rules. Apostolic Church is a holiness church and its members are "saints" who have been grasped by the Holy Spirit. Saints are people "who have been set aside." They are forbidden to drink, smoke, lie, cheat, have premarital sex, or commit adultery. Women, however, are now permitted to wear jewelry and cosmetics, and everyone, no matter what their income, tends to dress well. The members of Apostolic Church are, for the most part, political liberals in that they support most liberal political causes—equal rights, fair housing, welfare, affirmative action, freedom of speech, etc. But they are cultural liberals in only certain limited ways. They preach an ethic of personal responsibility that leads them to temper their demands for government programs and guard against the temptations of a market-oriented popular culture. This is true even though, at the same time, the church works hard to prepare its members to work in business and industry—but to do so without conforming "to the ways of this world."

Third, the narrative outer envelope of Apostolic Church's religious ethic is complex and rich. It is the presence of this narrative that distinguishes this church's emphasis on justice from secular deontological liberalism in the strict sense. The theology of Apostolic Church is a synthesis of Calvinist themes of God's providence and the Wesleyan emphasis on sanctification. There is also a strong emphasis on both the goodness of creation and the doctrine of the atonement. The inner-core ethic of neighbor love (with all its analogies to deontological liberalism's emphasis on justice) is grounded, not on the rationality of humans, but in the faith that humans are created in the image of God and have added worth because Christ died for their sins. Furthermore, Brazier teaches that Christians are saved by the grace of God and not by their own actions. Nonetheless, moral behavior beneficial to others is a "sign" of salvation and a "mark" of the new freedom that Christians have in Christ.

Narrative and the Tensions of Modernity

I believe that the narrative outer envelope of Apostolic Church's ethic helps its people handle the tensions of life in a competitive democratic society. The members of Apostolic Church hear a message that empowers them to compete without turning either "winning" or "losing" in this society into an idolatry—a measure of their ultimate worth. Brazier's most paradigmatic sermon was preached on 2 Corinthians 8:9, "For you know the generous act of our Lord Jesus Christ, that though he was rich, yet for your sakes he became poor, so that by his poverty you might become rich." In interpreting this scripture, Brazier began with an emphasis on the richness of God—the richness of Being, if you will. When God became human and poor, humans who accept him became rich. Brazier was not speaking of richness in terms of money, clothes, houses, or high-salaried jobs. He was speaking about a "richness at the core of your selfhood." This is the meaning of receiving the Holy Spirit; it is a kind of enrichment, empowerment, and liberation of the self. It is somewhat analogous to the kind of empowerment of the self that comes from a parent's love or a therapist's unconditional acceptance. As one convert said about his conversion, "My mind cleared, I felt at ease, I had new energy, I felt refreshed and clean, I had a new sense of power."

This religious vision seemed to help the members of Apostolic Church handle both their jobs and their human relations. For instance, Brazier said in this sermon that it was permissible for a Christian to pursue wealth. In fact, those with the gift of the Holy Spirit will have a richer and more powerful self to do that very thing. The Christian with the Spirit will have the strength to pursue a good job, education, and a decent salary. The "Christian can do this *freely* precisely because salvation does not depend on material riches," just as it does not depend on worldly success. Hence, one is free to pursue a comfortable life because, in the end, it is not all that important. Furthermore, all saints must tithe, which in itself is a check on measuring oneself by material success.

This same way of thinking was applied by Brazier to personal relationships. A person with a rich self will have better love relations. Indeed, one can pursue these relationships precisely because one's salvation does not depend on them. In fact, if love relations are threatened, "you will have the power to try again, either with the person you have loved or someone new." This is because one's ultimate justification does not depend on one's love relationships. The theology of empowerment that Brazier preached worked to encourage energetic agency among his people in pursuit of both vocational and family goals. People are empowered to pursue these goods—yes, even to compete for them. But their competition is bounded by strong appeals to justice, a rich tradition of concrete moral rules, and a theology of grace that frees them from measuring themselves in any final way by their temporal successes or failures. I came to the conclusion that Apostolic Church was generally consistent with the great themes of the Christian tradition, but had reconstructed aspects of it to meet the unique needs of its situation. Its members were *reconstructing* both their religion and their civil society; they were not *constructing* it. This church had a rich sense of tradition—indeed, a "gift" from the past.

Apostolic Church was creating good citizens as well as sanctified "saints." Apostolic Church even today is Woodlawn's most powerful force for social reconstruction and is indirectly a political force throughout the entire community of Chicago. This is true even though Brazier never issues a political endorsement.

In presenting this case study, I have illustrated ways in which religion contributes to the revitalization of both civil society and civic virtue in a nation increasingly beleaguered by the overreaching systems of the state and market.

Notes

1. Alan Wolfe, *Whose Keeper? Social Science and Moral Obligation* (Berkeley: University of California Press, 1989).

2. Ibid., 19–23.

3. Jürgen Habermas, *Theory of Communicative Action*, Vols. 1–2 (Boston: Beacon Press, 1984, 1987).

4. Wolfe, *Whose Keeper?*, 13–19.

5. Michael Walzer, *Spheres of Justice* (New York: Basic Books, 1983), 12–13, 227–42.

6. Wolfe, *Whose Keeper?*, 52–60, 133–41.

7. Ibid., 54.

8. Glendon refers to the Rossis' research on this issue in her "Virtues, Families, and Citizenship," in *The Meaning of the Family in a Free Society*, ed. W. Lawson Taitte (Austin, TX: The University of Texas Press, 1991).

9. Wolfe, *Whose Keeper?*, 20.

10. Plato, *The Republic*, ed. Alan Bloom (New York: Basic Books, 1968), bk. 5, 461–65.

11. Aristotle, *Politics*, in *The Basic Works of Aristotle*, ed. Richard McKeon (New York: Random House, 1941), bk. 2, 1262a.

12. Wolfe, *Whose Keeper?*, 220.

13. Ibid., 94.

14. Hans-Georg Gadamer, *Truth and Method* (New York: Crossroad, 1982), 273.

15. Wolfe, *Whose Keeper?*, 215.

16. W. D. Hamilton, "The Genetic Evolution of Social Behavior," *Journal of Theoretical Biology* 7 (1964): 1–52; E. O. Wilson, *On Human Nature* (Cambridge: Harvard University Press, 1978); Michael Ruse, *The Philosophy of Biology* (London: Hutchinson, 1973); Peter Singer, *The Expanding Circle: Ethics and Sociobiology* (New York: Farrar, Straus & Giroux, 1982).

17. Richard Posner, *Sex and Reason* (Cambridge, MA: Harvard University Press, 1992).

18. Richard Epstein, "The Utilitarian Foundations of Natural Law," *Harvard Journal of Law and Public Policy* 12, no. 3 (1989): 713–51; Richard Posner, *Economic Analysis of Law* (Boston: Little, Brown, 1986).

19. Wilson, *On Human Nature*, 53–56; Carl Degler, *In Search of Human Nature* (New York: Oxford University Press, 1991).

20. Martin Daly and Margo Wilson, *Homicide* (New York: Aldine De Gruyter, 1988), 11.

21. Ibid., 20–23.

22. Ibid., 87–89.

23. Mary Midgley, *Beast and Man* (Ithaca, NY: Cornell University Press, 1978), 51–82.

24. For an interpretation of William James's view of humans as simultaneously the most instinctual and most rational of creatures, see Don Browning, *Pluralism and Personality* (Lewisburg, PA: Bucknell University Press, 1980), 164.

25. Maryanne Cline Horowitz, "Aristotle on Women," *Journal of the History of Biology* 9, no. 2 (1976): 183–213.

26. Arlene Saxonhouse, "Aristotle: Defective Males, Hierarchy and the Limits of Politics," in *Feminist Interpretation and Political Theory*, ed. Mary Shanley and Carole Pateman (University Park, PA: The Pennsylvania State University Press, 1991), 45–50.

27. Aristotle, *Politics*, bk. 1, 1128.

28. Ibid., bk. 2, 1126b.

29. Thomas Aquinas, *Summa Theologica* (New York: Benziger Brothers, Inc., 1948), III, "Supplement", q. 41, a. 1.

30. Aquinas, *Summa*, II, ii, q. 26, a. 1; Stephen Pope, "The Order of Love and Recent Catholic Ethics: A Constructive Proposal," *Theological Studies* 52 (1991): 257–62.

31. Midgley, *Beast and Man*, 193.

32. Aquinas, *Summa*, II, ii, q. 26, a. 9.

33. Ibid., q. 26, a. 7.

34. Wolfe, *Whose Keeper?*, 262.

35. Ibid., 103, 123.

36. Ibid., 124; Carol Gilligan, *In a Different Voice* (Cambridge, MA: Harvard University Press, 1982).

37. Michael Sandel, *Liberalism and the Limits of Justice* (Cambridge, MA: Harvard University Press, 1982), 15–65.

38. Wolfe, *Whose Keeper?*, 125.

39. William Frankena, *Ethics* (Englewood Cliffs, NJ: Prentice Hall, 1973); Paul Ricoeur, "Entre philosophie et théologie: La règle d'or en question," *Revue d'histoire et de philosophie religieuses* 69 (1989): 3–9; Amitai Etzioni, *The Moral Dimension* (New York: The Free Press, 1988); Louis Janssens, "Norms and Priorities in a Love Ethics," *Louvain Studies* 6 (1972): 207–38.

40. Jürgen Habermas, *Communication and the Evolution of Society* (Boston: Beacon Press, 1979), 80–93.

41. Pope, "The Order of Love and Recent Catholic Ethics," 257–62.

42. Midgley, *Beast and Man*, 134.

43. Singer, *The Expanding Circle*, 111.

44. Wolfe, *Whose Keeper?*, 94.

45. Ibid., 3.

46. Ibid., 6.

47. Immanuel Kant, *Foundations of the Metaphysics of Morals* (New York: Bobbs-Merrill Co., 1959), 47.

48. Basil Mitchell, *Morality: Religious and Secular* (Oxford: Clarendon Press, 1980), 31–32.

49. Gadamer, *Truth and Method*, 330; Robert Bellah, Richard Madsen, William M. Sullivan, Ann Swidler, and Steven Tipton, *Habits of the Heart* (Berkeley: University of California Press, 1985).

50. Wolfe, *Whose Keeper?*, 258.

51. Ibid.

52. George Gallup and Sarah Jones, *100 Questions and Answers: Religion in America* (Princeton, NJ: Princeton Research Center, 1989), 4.

53. Don Browning, *A Fundamental Practical Theology* (Minneapolis, MN: Fortress Press, 1991), 243–77.

54. John Fish, *Black Power/White Control* (Princeton, NJ: Princeton University Press, 1973); Charles Silberman, *Crisis in Black and White* (New York: Random House, 1964).

55. William Julius Wilson, *The Truly Disadvantaged* (Chicago: University of Chicago Press, 1987).

56. Ibid.

57. Judith Stacey, *Brave New Families* (New York: Basic Books, 1990), 268.

58. Browning, *A Fundamental Practical Theology*, 10–11, 171–207.

CHAPTER 6

Civic Virtue at Work: Unions as Seedbeds of the Civic Virtues

Thomas C. Kohler

The good citizen should know and have the capacity both to be ruled and to rule, and this very thing is the virtue of a citizen—knowledge of rule over free persons from both [points of view].[1]

* * *

The three great relations in private life are: 1) That of master and servant; . . . 2) That of husband and wife; . . . 3) That of parent and child.[2]

* * *

In democratic countries knowledge of how to combine is the mother of all other forms of knowledge; on its progress depends that of all the others. Among laws controlling human societies there is one more precise and clearer, it seems to me, than all the others. If men are to remain civilized or to become civilized, the art of association must develop and improve among them at the same speed as equality of conditions spreads.[3]

Home may be where the heart is, but, increasingly, Americans are likely to be found at work. For better or worse, men and women are tied to the market and the workplace in a way never before seen. The overall increase in labor force participation is one of the most striking social developments of the past 40 years.

A few statistics help to tell the story. Presently, 93 percent of adult men are in the labor force—a figure that has remained roughly constant for many decades.[4] Since 1950, however, women have increased their participation in the workforce by more than 200 percent.[5] Today, 74 percent of women 25 to 54 years old are employed,[6] the overwhelming proportion of them full-time.[7] Likewise, the majority of mothers are in the workforce. Their participation rates extend from 75 percent for women whose youngest child is of school age, to 52 percent for those with children under two.[8] In 1990, both spouses worked in nearly seven out of ten married-couple families.[9] Working hours for women have been increasing steadily during the past 20 years.[10] A recently published major study shows that after years of gradual decline, the normal American work week has increased to the point where the average employee now works the equivalent of an additional month more than was worked in 1970.[11] These figures burst with implications. Among them is this: the job has become a central part of most people's lives, and work increasingly is the place that people spend the major share of their waking hours.

The Changing Work World:
Implications for the Habits of the Citizenry

People make themselves to be what they are through the activities in which they habitually are engaged. Consequently, anyone interested in the sources of character and citizenship in American society must pay attention to those institutions that can serve to inculcate, sustain, and enhance the civic virtues in the workplace. Chief among such institutions are trade unions and the practice of collective bargaining.

This claim may jar some readers a bit or strike them as being at best naive. (Indeed, some of the less charitably inclined may see it as being the equivalent of nominating Boss Pendergast as citizen of the year.) In one respect, such reactions are not surprising. Once the subject of fervent controversy, unions represent one of the few things about which liberals and conservatives generally agree. And, as the new consensus has it, unions are relics of the past, inappropriate to an era of global economic competition and irrelevant, if not downright detrimental, to promoting the common good. An interest in unions tends to be treated as a species of antiquarianism even among academic employment law specialists, formerly called "labor lawyers," who increasingly have come to regard proposals for rethinking and reviving unions as being no less quixotic than a movement to bring back manned lighthouses.

The Conservative View of Unions

As conservatives typically understand them, unions are purely economic institutions. They represent no more than self-interested affiliations among otherwise unrelated economic actors, whose principal purpose is to extract higher wages for less work than a freely functioning market would otherwise permit. Unions achieve their goals by acting, or attempting to act, as monopolies. Through exerting control over employment terms—and in some industries, particularly the crafts, by their ability to limit the supply of labor—unions distort the outcomes of the market process in favor of their members. By trumping the market, many conservatives argue, unions decrease overall social welfare by imposing costs that everyone else must bear.

These costs take a number of forms. As their critics point out, unions are more prevalent in those sectors of the economy where income and productivity are naturally high. The impact of unions in the wage structure of industries in these sectors cause firms to limit their demand for workers. This results in unnaturally high numbers of people being employed in the lower-paid sectors of the economy where less-skilled service occupations tend to predominate. Consequently, the gains enjoyed by the "barons of labor" (who were relatively well-off to start with) come at the expense of the nonunionized, whose upward mobility is retarded by the presence in the market of organized workers. Thus, their critics frequently assert, unions create inequities in the distribution of income. Furthermore, union work rules and other restrictions of management discretion also lower the productivity of labor and capital. In short, as many conservatives portray it, unions leave everyone but their members worse-off by obstructing the efficient allocation and use of resources.

The degree to which this picture of the economic impact of unions is accurate remains a matter of debate among professional economists. Recent empirical work has called much of it into question. Several studies, for instance, demonstrate that unionized workers generally are more productive than their unorganized counterparts.[12] Recent evidence also indicates that, on balance, unions have the effect of decreasing the dispersion of labor earnings between highly and lesser-compensated workers. Similarly, the data show that unions have improved the economic status of black males relative to white males.[13] Despite this, the disapprobation of unions hardly is confined to conservatives and free-market advocates. Liberals themselves increasingly have come to regard unions as the detritus of a bygone age whose value (to the extent it existed) long since has disappeared.

The Liberal Critique of Unions

The standard liberal critique of unions proceeds not in economic terms but in the language of individual rights. It rests on the view that majorities cannot be trusted because they pose an ever-present threat to personal liberties and to the unfettered exercise of individual choice. As a result, many liberals regard unions with the same profound suspicion they exhibit toward legislatures and other institutions of majority will. From this perspective, individuals are freest and most secure when protected from the biases that almost invariably drive decision making in majoritarian institutions. Consequently, as many liberals see it, functions typically performed by unions can be discharged more reliably and equitably by some arm of the state.

Thus, for instance, disputes over employee dismissals—which in the unionized setting typically are adjusted through a private grievance-arbitration process that the employer and union jointly administer—are seen by many liberals as matters better adjudicated before a court or state administrative body. Likewise, liberals generally regard other aspects of the employment relationship as being more equitably, efficiently, and effectively established through uniform statutory standards rather than by the terms of a privately-negotiated collective bargaining agreement. In this view, fairness is a function of procedure, the regularity and formality of which the state can best guarantee. Thus, universal prescriptions are preferable to particular solutions developed at the local level by those directly affected. In fact, as many liberals see it, the union movement represents something like a historical stage in the evolution of the sovereign individual self whose progressive absolutization has occurred through the state's growing recognition of an ever more comprehensive body of personal liberties that majorities may not qualify or infringe.

The thoroughgoing distrust of majority rule that underlies many liberals' misgivings about unions also marks the point at which the views of Left and Right frequently converge. Many conservatives, especially those with a libertarian bent, also distrust majorities. The jointly-held suspicion about majoritarian institutions often leads liberals and conservatives alike to the same conclusion. Consequently, Left and Right condemn unions on the same basis that they often employ to argue that the judiciary's power to overturn legislation is necessary if individual rights are to be secure. Ordering carried out through nonrepresentative institutions, they agree, is more efficient and stable than reliance upon majority rule. What chiefly separates the two schools, of course, are the sorts of policies they think these nonrepresentative institutions should implement and what the character of these nonrepresentative institutions should be. An unrelieved skepticism about the ability of the average person to act intelligently, reasonably, and with self-restraint compels many on the Right and Left to the view that democracy is at best a utopian ideal. The state or the market are the alternatives they offer. But, in either case, the "iron cage" of technocratic orders and bureaucratic rationality are the results they ultimately suggest.

Unions in the Popular Mind

Unbeloved by elites, unions do not seem to fare well in the popular mind either. Not infrequently, the idea of unionism seems to be associated with Archie Bunker-like characters, cartoon versions of autocratic and possibly corrupt "boss" leadership, featherbedding work rules, and unnecessary contentiousness. Indeed, the less direct knowledge that individuals have of the collective bargaining process, the harsher their attitudes toward unions seem to be. Reporting on data collected by the National Longitudinal Survey, a recent study found that, among members of the labor force, current involvement in a union constituted by far the most significant factor in differentiating union supporters from opponents.[14] Opportunities for familiarization, however, are fast decreasing. Presently, only 11.9 percent of the private-sector workforce is organized.[15] In 1930, with the Depression in full swing and passage of the Wagner Act still five years away, the rate stood at 10.2 percent.[16] Some forecast that if current trends continue, unions will represent only about 7 percent of the private sector workforce by the end of the decade.[17]

Domestic Trends

Our currently prevailing views about unions, along with the apparent demise of collective bargaining in the United States, come at a strange time. During the past 25 years, the overall distribution of wages and earnings in the United States has become increasingly unequal, and there has been a pronounced erosion in the size of the nation's middle class.[18] Migration out of the middle class has occurred in both directions, and there has been growth in both the upper and lower classes. After 1980, however, the chances for movement out of the lower economic class lessened, with only the college educated demonstrating a higher than average probability of moving into the middle income group. During the same period, a smaller share of adults fell out of the upper class, but the chances of descending from the middle to the lower class significantly increased. A shift in the sources of total household income also has occurred. The portion derived from earnings fell while that attributable to capital investments increased. Likewise, growth occurred in the upper end, while lower-income households experienced a stagnation in real earnings. In fact, one recent study shows that average hourly wages have been declining for well over a decade and are 14 percent lower than they were in 1979.[19]

Along with these developments has come a significant loosening of the employment bond. So-called contingent employment arrangements—part-time, temporary, and contract arrangements—are on the rise, and many analysts expect the number of part-time employees to double in the next few years.[20] These "just-in-time" employees typically have at best highly restricted claims to pension, health, and other benefits incident to employment. In testimony before Congress, one well-known observer of labor market trends characterized contingent employment arrangements as representing "the utmost in fluidity and flexibility."[21] Such arrangements, she testified, increase productivity by permitting employers to expand or contract work-hours at will. Moreover, an employer "incurs no legal or moral obligation" to offer contingent workers "severance pay or layoff benefits, or rights to re-employment."[22] Similarly, employers "have no implied commitment to provide promotion opportunities, or to offer training and/or development" to members of the contingent workforce. Use of contingent workers, this observer stated, also enables employers to enhance the employment security of "core employees."[23] As American industry seeks to become more competitive, she predicted "all employment relationships are going to become more fluid."[24]

European Trends

Domestic trends aside, the collapse of collective bargaining in the United States also seems odd in light of comparative developments. In anticipation of its planned economic and monetary unification, the European Union (formerly the European Economic Community) adopted its Charter on the Fundamental Social Rights of Workers (the "Social Charter") in December 1989.[25] The Charter provides a comprehensive stipulation of twelve basic rights and policies that address the "social dimension" of the Union's internal market plan. These principles constitute an integral and organic part of the single-market scheme of European unity. Consequently, the Charter's preamble declares "solemnly that the implementation of the single European Act must take full account of the social dimension of the Community." It further states that "the same importance must be attached to the social aspects as the economic aspects" in establishing the single market, and it requires that these two dimensions "must be developed in a balanced manner."

Perhaps the most surprising things about the Social Charter from an American perspective are the way its principles were developed and the means suggested for their implementation. The principles set forth in the Social Charter grew directly out of an informal "social dialogue" between European-level trade union and employers' associations. The discussions between these "social partners" subsequently were supplemented and formalized by the European Commission and resulted in the promulgation of the present Charter.

Given its source, the fact that the Social Charter guarantees the right of employers and workers to organize trade organizations "for defense of their economic and social interests" hardly is startling. Much more remarkable, to an American's eyes at least, is the Charter's strong affirmation of collective bargaining as a social institution and the breadth with which it conceives of the process. Thus, the Charter not only sees collective bargaining as a means to adjust the economic aspects of the employment relationship. The Charter also provides for—and specifically encourages the use of—collective bargaining as a method for making law within the European Union. Moreover, the Social Charter regards collective bargaining as having a central role in the implementation and further elaboration of the fundamental rights and policies stated in the Charter. Indeed, the Social Charter's "Action Plan" specifically recognizes that implementation of the Charter's policies though the collective bargaining process makes "it possible to adapt to particular situations and enable[s] the two sides of industry to be actively involved."

The very terminology used in the Social Charter to describe collective bargaining demonstrates the markedly different attitude the European Union takes toward this social institution. Thus, unions and employers consistently are referred to as the "social partners" and collective bargaining is called "social dialogue." The Union's broad willingness, as reflected in the Charter's provisions, to rely on the "social dialogue" as a vital means for making law similarly stands in sharp contrast to the desiccated and overjuridified shell of what collective bargaining has become in the United States. Instead of normative "dialogue" between "social partners," it is much more typical in the United States to understand collective bargaining as a give-no-quarter adversarial contest between wholly self-interested parties which government seeks to contain and limit through complex and highly technical legal doctrines.

European politicians and scholars alike long have expressed a substantial interest in the United States' version of "free" collective bargaining—that is, a system characterized by a lack of state intervention in the substantive results of the bargaining process. It is one of history's strange little ironies that the United States seems intent on abandoning this homegrown institution at a time when Europe has begun to experiment with many of its central features. Scholars who engage in the comparative study of legal orders refer to the tendency of various systems of law to take on similar characteristics and to develop common approaches to solving problems as "convergence." When it comes to collective bargaining, something along the lines of a "transference" rather than a "convergence" seems at least potentially to be underway. Thus, the employment relationship in the United States is ever-increasingly being subjected to extensive (if piecemeal) state regulation while the stated desire of the Social Charter is to nudge the European community states in the opposite direction. The movement to "deregulate" the employment relationship swept the world during the past several years. Only in the United States, it seems, did that movement take the perverse form of government intruding more deeply into one of the most significant relationships of private life.

International Developments

Our contemporary attitudes toward unions also seem odd in light of the absolutely unprecedented international developments of the past few years. Although some tendency now exists to overlook this fact, the remarkable transformation of what used to be called the Eastern-bloc was spearheaded by an independent trade-union movement, which improbably survived despite the forces arrayed against it. Nor were the Poles left to go it alone. At a time when our

own government took a wait-and-see attitude, the AFL-CIO and
other unaffiliated American unions supported Solidarity from the
first with funds, equipment, and expertise. American unions also
lobbied Western governments on Solidarity's behalf and worked to
keep the Polish situation before the public's eye. This was hardly
an unaccustomed role for American unions, who have a long record
of supporting free trade unions and human rights movements
around the world. (It is no coincidence that the suppression of independent unions is one of the first steps taken by totalitarian governments of the Right or the Left.) In recognition of this record, the
conservative publication *Policy Review* recently named the late
George Meany, who served as president of the AFL-CIO from 1952
to 1979, as one of the "Cold War's Magnificent Seven."[26] (Others
so honored included Winston Churchill, Konrad Adenauer, and
Pope John Paul II.) The American union movement's resolute determination to remain truly autonomous and to set its own course
accounts for much of the enmity it has received from intellectuals,
particularly those with a leftist orientation.

There is also a pronounced tendency today to overlook, or to be
absolutely unaware of, the domestic contributions made by the
union movement. The support of unions, for example, was crucial
to the passage of the Civil Rights Act of 1964. Unions also have
been in the forefront of efforts to improve workplace safety, public
health, and to ensure pay equality for the sexes. Their interest in
these matters is long-standing. Equal pay for equal work was one
of the stated goals of the Knights of Labor in its 1878 constitution.
Similarly, the Knights by 1886 had 60,000 African-American
members, and when black delegates were refused accommodations
during a convention, white delegates walked out of the offending
hotel.[27] None of this is to suggest that the American union movement has anything like an unspotted history concerning racial or
sexual prejudice. It is merely to point out that its record is hardly
as one-sided as some unthinkingly presume. In fact, blacks are
more likely than whites to be union members, and blacks are much
more likely to support unionization than are whites.[28] Moreover, as
a group, women when surveyed are much more likely than men to
express support for unions.[29]

So, if unions are so wonderful, why aren't people flocking to join them? Accounting for the decline in union membership has become something of a cottage-industry among academics. Theories abound. Prominent among them are: structural changes in the economy,[30] peculiar characteristics of American labor law, combined with its weak or unsympathetic enforcement, and stiff but sophisticated employer opposition to employee self-organization.[31] Certainly, there is something to all these explanations. The appreciation in the exchange rate of the U.S. dollar during much of the 1980s, the deregulation of key industries like trucking, and a contraction of the domestic industrial base all have had a strong impact on sectors of the economy where unionization historically was strong. Likewise, since the beginning of this century, there have been a number of organized anti-union propagandizing efforts like the "open-shop" and "American Plan" drives led by organizations like the National Association of Manufacturers.[32] Their present-day descendants include the National Right to Work Committee (whose efforts are couched in the language of individual rights) and the loosely structured campaign for a "union-free environment." American labor law also has features that are found nowhere else in the industrialized world: An employer's unqualified right to "permanently replace" striking workers stands as a notable example.

Additionally, there exists the undoubted fact that the American union movement has done much to hurt itself. Incidents of corruption, mob influence, and wrongdoing by union officials, for example, have had a marked impact on our attitudes towards unions. The "McClellan Committee Hearings in the Spring of 1957," observes James Medoff, the author of the most extensive study yet conducted on the public's image of unions, "seem to have had an immediate and, it appears, lasting effect on the public's view of organized labor and its leaders."[33] Union members are nearly as likely as those without union ties to hold a negative view of labor leaders. Nor have unions done a good job of explaining—or, perhaps, of thinking about—the role they play in society and the contributions they can make to the common good. As Medoff concludes, the "public is aware of some of the good for all workers derived by trade unions." Nonetheless, "it still believes that unions primarily act as a special interest group concerned only with defending their higher rates of pay."[34]

All of the reasons offered to explain union decline have some force. Yet none of them, either singly or in combination, fully account for the long but steady fall in union membership that has occurred in the United States since the late 1950s. The real reasons for this decline lie further back and are part of a more complex and deeply imbedded set of issues that ever-increasingly bedevil our society. Americans are not anti-union. Rather, they might more accurately be characterized as being ambivalent about unions. The overall approval rating of unions has declined substantially over the past 25 years.[35] Indeed, the public has become more skeptical of nearly all social institutions during that period. Nevertheless, as Seymour Martin Lipset points out, extensive survey data repeatedly demonstrate that "the majority of Americans believe that unions are essential and do more good than harm, that without unions employers would maltreat workers."[36] A majority of Americans—6 in 10 in a recent poll[37]—also indicate that they "approve" of labor unions and an overwhelming proportion of the population believes that "workers should have the right to join unions."[38] However, as Lipset further observes, "Majority approval of the functions of unions . . . does not translate into willingness on the part of employed persons to vote for them."[39] In fact, when questioned, only about three in ten workforce participants indicated that they would join a union if one existed at their workplace.[40] In short, we think that unions are generally a fine idea—but for somebody else.

Rather than being an isolated phenomenon, it turns out that many of the reasons underlying our ambivalence toward unions are identical with our ambivalence toward associations and intermediate groups of all descriptions. In short, the declines in families, church and religious organizations, unions and voluntary associations of various types are tied together. The forces and habits of mind that erode one act to erode them all. Before discussing how unions and collective bargaining can act to enhance the civic virtues, it may be helpful to briefly outline the sources of destructive pressure that the various seedbeds commonly face.

Sources of Decline:
Why We Are Increasingly Ambivalent about Associations

Americans love to refer to Tocqueville's characterization of the United States as a nation of joiners. It fits with our image of ourselves as a self-reliant, can-do people to whom the world turns for lessons about democratic self-rule. This characterization also seems consistent with our political institutions and our social practices. After all, the First Amendment guarantees the freedom to associate, and few nations have higher rates of membership in voluntary associations than do Americans.[41]

Nevertheless, there is plenty of evidence to suggest that the deeply ambivalent attitudes we hold toward unions apply generally to our attitudes about communities and associations of whatever description. Recent survey data suggest that Americans remain eager participants in the activities of voluntary associations. Yet, the same data indicate that during the past 30 years, much of that participation has been limited to clipping a coupon in a magazine and returning it with a small financial contribution to an association like the Sierra Club, Common Cause, or the American Association of Retired Persons.[42]

The smaller, local bodies that concretely and directly mediate the relation between individuals and the large institutions of public life—and which consequently involve people in the often messy business of actually associating with one another—are faring less well. Statistics concerning the divorce rate and the number of children living in single-parent households speak for themselves. Other primary groups that tie people together through shared meanings are similarly frail. Neighborhoods, town or ward meetings, grass roots political clubs, and like institutions that characterized and grounded American democracy largely have disappeared. Service and fraternal organizations also have experienced steep drops in membership and their futures appear bleak. For example, the average age of a Lions Club member is 57, and two-thirds of this service group's membership is over 50.[43] Similarly, most mainline religious denominations have experienced a steady and significant decline in membership during the past 30 years.[44]

Scholars and commentators seem invariably to overlook the point. But the plain fact of the matter is that unions went into decline at roughly the same time that all other sorts of mediating institutions in our society began to unravel, and for strikingly similar reasons. We are deeply and increasingly ambivalent about association in almost any form. The decline of unions is but part of a much larger story.

The Case of Mainline Denominations

The steady withering of the mainline religious denominations provides a good illustration of the point. Americans are hardly an irreligious people. Well over 9 in 10 Americans believe in the existence of God,[45] and a huge proportion state that religion is "very important" (54 percent) or "fairly important" (31 percent) in their lives.[46] Likewise, about 6 in 10 Americans "believe that religion can answer all or most of today's problems."[47] Nevertheless, as George Gallup Jr. and Jim Castelli report, "while Americans attach great importance to religion, they do not equate religion with church membership or attendance."[48] They also found that a vast majority of Americans believe that one can be a good Christian or Jew without being part of a religious congregation.

A recently released major survey seems to support these observations.[49] It shows that only just over half (55.1 percent) of Americans are affiliated with Jewish or Christian religious congregations. It also reports that the unaffiliated account for more than half the population in much of the West (excluding Utah and much of New Mexico) and in substantial sections of Florida, Michigan, Ohio, Kentucky, West Virginia, Delaware, Maryland, Maine, New Hampshire, and Vermont.[50]

A recently published study of baby boomers who left mainline Protestantism[51] similarly reflects "a strong affirmation that you can be a good Christian without doing it in the context of the church."[52] This study concludes that those who left the churches in the 1970s and 1980s will not return. The study, however, does not show "the rejection of religion or even of the major Christian creeds, but a pulling away from the institutional church." For many baby boomers, the study reports, religious beliefs are purely a matter of individual choice. The value placed on the exercise of personal choice trumps denominational commitment. Nevertheless, those who left continue to believe that the church has an important function to perform in promoting a "moral code" for society. Moreover, nearly all who left the church want their children to receive some form of religious education. (Just how it is that the understandings of earlier generations can be preserved, enhanced, practiced, and passed on in the absence of institutions, however, was left unidentified.)

The notions of self-sovereignty and misgivings about reliance on a mediator of whatever character are pervasive. For example, 94 percent of Americans say that they pray.[53] Yet, Americans also state that they rely on themselves "rather than an outside power such as God, to resolve life's problems."[54] Similarly, although a substantial majority of Americans approve of the functions unions perform in society and think that unions are necessary to give employees a voice in the workplace, nearly the same number believe that they do not need a union to get fair treatment.[55] In short, we think that unions, churches, and the other institutions that compose civil society are great. But, whether it's the last things, the first things, or the mundane things of day-to-day living, we can make our own way, thanks. Perhaps it is not surprising that Gallup and Castelli report that "Americans are the loneliest people in the world" and that one of the things Americans most want of their churches is a "sense of community."[56]

The Forces of Erosion

Some of the reasons behind the decline in mediating groups lie fairly near the surface. With a greater proportion of the population actively participating in the workplace, there is simply less time to devote to nonwork activities, however important or meritorious they may be. Television (which drew people off their front stoops and away from communal entertainment and activities), the exodus from neighborhoods to the suburbs, and so forth, all have had their impact. As Michael Walzer so nicely summarizes, "four mobilities" characterize modern life.[57] These mobilities—geographic, social, political, and marital—provide an unstable and constantly shifting social foundation that undermines communal institutions of every description.

There are deeper sources of erosion at work as well. For the foreseeable future, we can expect a continued decline in mediating groups generally. This is so for at least two reasons. As a nation, we fast are losing the habit of participating in organizations that require more than dropping a check in the mail. Moreover, we increasingly no longer see the need for or the significance of these mediating bodies. They simply have lost their meaning for us. We won't make a commitment to things we don't begin to understand. And increasingly, we don't begin to understand what churches, Shriner's Clubs, unions, the Lower West Side Democratic Club, or even families have to do with anything.

What we characteristically do and the sorts of things we are open to understanding, indeed the very sorts of questions that occur to us, go hand-in-hand. Our habits and our knowings exist in a mutually conditioning relationship. As we have become less inclined to participate in mediating groups, we have strongly tended to think and speak about association in increasingly restricted ways. These in turn embody stilted and deeply impoverished notions about human character and the meaning of our personhood.

The Truncated Self and Associational Ambivalence

Briefly stated, we suffer from an odd sort of blindness: we can only see individuals. It is as if we claimed to know all about the various sorts of individual trees but were completely unaware of the forest whose interdependent series of ecosystems permit those trees to exist and flourish. We unthinkingly presume that what Walt Whitman celebrated as the "single, sole self" constitutes the absolute foundation of social reality and that every other institution of civil life is merely a derivative. We thus assume that families, churches, unions, and the like constitute no more than an aggregation of individual, monadic selves. We thereby implicitly adopt a sort of mechanical reductionism. We regard a machine as the sum of its parts, but overlook the fact that human community is far more. Humans are conditioned beings by virtue of the fact that we live and act only in communities. These communities give us our orientation and identity. They tell us what we are as humans and what the purpose and significance of our lives is. Although we often pretend otherwise, we do not know ourselves—or nearly anything else—immediately. Instead, what we come to know we learn only through the mediation of the communities and associations that ground us as people. Consequently, communities have a normative function, and well-functioning communities represent an irreducible human good. In this perspective, communities and associations exist *only for* the individual. Yet, the social good is prior to—stands at a higher level than—the individual good, because without it, the good for discrete individual persons could not exist. In short, perspective requires binocular vision.

As moderns, we are much more likely to be adherents of what Charles Taylor describes as the "clean slate" theory of life. For us, the past is never prologue, and association is primarily a function of individual consent. We assume that we can make and remake ourselves at will, regardless of the social setting or how we have constituted ourselves through our previous judgments and acts. With atomism ascendant, the link between act and consequence becomes increasingly opaque. We typically presume that individuals are sovereign beings invested with rights that exist independently and regardless of any societal arrangements. The notion of sovereignty suggests that people are self-enlightening, self-perfecting, and morally complete beings who can recognize truth—if any is to be found—without the help or mediation of others.

This perspective teaches us that we are selves apart from and prior to any relation with others. Consequently, human association of any description tends to be understood as artificial and instrumental alliances that are formed for the limited purpose of satisfying the self-directed wants of their otherwise unrelated members. These desires commonly are reduced to two categories: the desire for companionship (to enable self-fulfillment and self-expression) and the desire for economic or political power.

Since all forms of association with others is understood as being motivated essentially by some sort of self-seeking, our generalized distrust of groups is hardly surprising. The very way we speak about association instills an understandable ambivalence. The growing emphasis in our public discourse on absolute personal autonomy and the unrestricted freedom of individual choice exacerbates this ambivalence. This language suggests that subjective standards provide the only legitimate grounds for judging the content of our actions. Consequently, this language implies that individuals properly are unencumbered by any obligations unless they choose to accept them. This approach kills off the ideas of civic duty, public responsibilities, and political life altogether. Moreover, since everything is defined through its relation to the self, this framework suggests that meaningful association with others requires similarity in experience, taste, behavior, or physical appearance. In short, it implies that association represents an inward turning that rests on identity: the self and the group simply mirror and affirm one another. This understanding of association represents a peculiar variant of individualism, one which, to adapt a characterization made by Wilson Carey McWilliams, is "so sensitive that it cannot tolerate rule by others."[58] At its limits, it implies that any sort of community among persons of different ages, sexes, races, or religions is not possible.

These notions profitably can be compared with the sort of ideas reflected in the writings of Edmund Burke. As he describes it, society and the "little platoons" or intermediate associations in which society exists, constitute

> a partnership in all science; a partnership in all art; a partnership in every virtue and in all perfection. As the ends of such a partnership cannot be obtained in many generations, it becomes a partnership not only between those who are living, but between those who are living, those who are dead, and those who are to be born.[59]

In short, much of our ambivalence toward associations stems from the slim resources we typically have for understanding and describing their functions and potential. These limitations have helped both to undermine the sorts of habits that support self-rule and to denude us of the institutions that nurture the full development of human personality. The mutually conditioning relationship between weakening habits of association and narrowing ideas about human character combine to produce a cycle of decline that affects every aspect of civil life and threatens the existence of polity generally. Before turning to sources that may give us some aid in breaking this cycle, it is appropriate to discuss how unions can act as and support the existence of other seedbeds of civic virtues.

Unions as Seedbeds of the Civic Virtues

A word about the meaning of the term "civic virtues" seems in order before describing how unions and the institution of collective bargaining can act to promote them. Briefly stated, a virtue is a habit. It constitutes a consistent way of deliberating, choosing, and acting that is productive of an authentically flourishing human life. Thus, the essence of virtue is that it represents an operative habit. Acquiring the virtues results in a consistent disposition to perform well, particularly in one's relations with others. (Hence, our word ethics derives from the Greek word for habit—*ethos*.)

Its emphasis on operation and activity raises a point central to the virtues. This is the recognition that the most authentically and specifically human of activities typically involve actions in which the good intended inheres in the activity. In other words, the activity represents an irreducible good, an end in itself. Consequently, the whole point is to become engaged in the activity. In the classical viewpoint, for example, politics represents the fullest and most complete form of such an activity: participation in political activity actuates and enhances the sorts of intellectual and moral habits that citizens must acquire and continually practice if the common good is to be promoted and authentic self-rule to be achieved.[60] The good immanent in such activities, however, is not strictly confined to those directly involved in their practice. Rather, the existence of that good through its practice acts to set the concrete conditions for its ongoing recurrence. Briefly stated, politics represents a common effort to answer the question of how we are to live together. To the extent that it is so, a good community in its very performance devises institutional orders that recognize that the human good is at once both individual and social. Consequently, every virtue is in a sense a "civic" virtue. Their practice sets the conditions for the willing cooperation that sustains and promotes civic life, while their lack leads to distrust, withdrawal, and eventual social breakdown.[61] Unions and the practice of collective bargaining can serve as institutions that link authentic self-rule with the good of order necessary to sustain it. To understand how this is so, it is necessary to understand something about collective bargaining.

Collective Bargaining: A Private Law-Making System

There is a tendency to regard bargaining as an institution narrowly concerned with wage rates and benefits. While these matters are an important aspect of collective bargaining, they hardly constitute its essence. Collective bargaining can be best and most thoroughly understood as a private law-making system. In the Supreme Court's words, the collective bargaining agreement "is more than a contract; it is a generalized code" that represents "an effort to erect a system of industrial self-government" through which the entire employment relationship can be "governed by an agreed upon rule of law."[62]

The promulgation and administration of this law is the responsibility of the affected parties alone. Consequently, collective bargaining agreements typically erect a private adjudication system—the grievance arbitration process—that the union and employer jointly administer. These systems normally have jurisdiction over nearly every type of dispute that might arise concerning the employment relationship. The presence of an arbitration system generally precludes courts or other arms of the state from resolving matters that come within the parties' dispute-adjustment scheme. Briefly put, collective bargaining requires the parties to work out and maintain the order of their relationship themselves.

Whether and how people participate in decisions about the criteria for promotions, job training, health benefits, the discipline of a fellow employee, or the best way to handle a novel or difficult employment-relations question may seem trivial. But, it is a tremendous error to regard such matters as unworthy of serious attention. Individuals and societies alike become and remain self-governing only by repeatedly and regularly engaging in acts of self-government. It is the habit that sustains the condition. Consequently, a democracy encounters its greatest danger of becoming perverted when its people no longer have direct responsibility for making the day-to-day decisions about the order of their lives. This point represents an important aspect of the significance of collective bargaining as a social institution. For it is through their involvement in the collective bargaining process that average citizens can take part in deciding the law that most directly determines the details of their daily lives. Thus, unions and the practice of bargaining can serve as "schools for democracy," where the habits of self-governance and direct responsibility are instilled.

Collective Bargaining: A Conversational Activity

At its best, collective bargaining is a conversational activity. This fact constitutes its fullest significance and most characterizes its potential contributions. If they are to succeed, the actions a union undertakes must reflect the consensus of its members. Similarly, a collective bargaining agreement represents the achievement of a consensus between employer and employed about the order of their relationship. Consensus exists as the product of a discussion about what ought to be valued and why. This sort of discussion, in turn, is the most distinctively human of activities.

People are by nature social beings. This is borne out by the fact that most of our operating takes the form of cooperating with others.[63] Our innate sociality, however, is not unqualified. We are also intelligent beings. As such, we demand reasons for what we do. We will not undertake any activity or agree to any scheme until we have at least implicitly decided that it is in some way reasonable. Hence, whether and the degree to which we will subordinate ourselves and our personal desires to the rules of any sort of social order depends upon our judgment that the order makes sense. Machiavelli notwithstanding, force and fraud are never enough to sustain authentic authority.

Our capacity for speech grounds the specifically human characteristics of our natural sociality. As Aristotle observes in the *Politics*, unlike other animals whose utterances are limited to expressing pain and pleasure, the human voice manifests an apprehension of the desirable and the harmful, the just and the wrongful. Human community constitutes itself by and exists through a consensus over these issues. However obscurely, people appeal to notions about fairness and desirability whenever they attempt to achieve agreement by explaining and justifying to one another their conclusions and proposals. Since speech is the vehicle by which we reveal and test our understandings and judgments, speech is a normative activity, a good in itself. Our involvement in what the ancients referred to as the *civilis conversatio* literally actuates our capacity for self-rule. This fact enables Aristotle to observe that "in the case of human beings, what seems to count as living together is this sharing of conversation and thought, not sharing the same pasture, as in the case of grazing animals."[64]

Community, and the willing cooperation it engenders, represents a commonalty of understandings, judgments, and sentiments. Losing touch with one another puts that commonalty in jeopardy and ultimately calls the legitimacy of authority into question. By sustaining the relationship among people, webs of conversation maintain and revivify the commonalty and consensus that cooperation requires.

Conversations do not occur in a vacuum. Given the current situation, the workplace is a natural place for the "civil conversation" to occur, and the conditions of the employment relationship constitute a crucial topic for discussion. As Emile Durkheim so presciently understood, in contemporary society the workplace has become a (and for many perhaps the) primary source of common life for most adults. Work creates a moral environment, and its influence extends to nearly every sphere of one's life. Likewise, work is the chief (and again for many, the only) place outside the family where people directly are involved in a common undertaking.

Unions: A Forum For Self-Rule

These points not only call attention to the relationship between the day-to-day routines of the workplace and the civic virtues. They also highlight a key feature of unions and collective bargaining. Unions are autonomous bodies. They stand independently of the state and the organizations that employ their members. They come into being as a result of employee self-organization, and their health and continuing existence depends upon the ability of the members to maintain solidarity. Winner-take-all attitudes do not produce enduring relationships or democracies. Unions can provide a forum where people can learn to prevail on a point without triumphalism, to lose an argument without resentment, and most importantly of all, to practice the art of reasonable and responsible compromise. In short, unions and the institution of collective bargaining can act to reduce the sort of unreflective and ultimately enervating dependence on the state and the other large institutions of contemporary life that Tocqueville warned would erode the habits a democracy requires. By providing a forum for serious deliberation and self-directed action, collective bargaining can also reduce the fragmentation and isolation that dissolves community and undermines the possibility of authentic self-rule.

The potential impact of collective bargaining on personal habits reveals itself in the workplace. Thus, for example, recent studies show that unionized workplaces are more productive than others. Recent research also suggests that employee involvement programs and other workplace innovations perform best, and have the best chance for survival, where they are jointly administered with a union. Labor turnover is also lower among unionized workforces. But the potential effects of bargaining on personal habits radiates well-beyond the office, shopfloor, or the laboratory.

No single mediating body in society, whether in the form of families, religious congregations, political, civic or service organizations, or unions, is likely to survive in the absence of the others. All of these "seedbeds" require and can instill the same sorts of habits: decision, commitment, tolerance, mutual respect, and direct responsibility. No single institution alone can inculcate these habits. Consequently, the existence and decline of all of these bodies is mutually conditioning. The collapse or deformation of any of them threatens the rest. Because of the close to universal participation in the workforce, however, unions have a crucial role to play in supporting and sustaining the health of these other seedbeds. Habits left untended and unpracticed in one of life's central arenas will not magically reappear outside of it.

Collective bargaining provides the only alternative to the pervasive state regulation of one of life's primary relationships—employment. Indeed, it is no coincidence that piecemeal regulation of employment through legislatures and common-law courts has markedly increased as the practice of collective bargaining has declined. In a society dominated by large organizations, unions can also make an important contribution to the democratic process by giving an ordered and coherent voice to those who would otherwise be without it. The importance of such regularized and responsive channels of communication cannot be overlooked. Their absence not only leads to fragmentation and withdrawal but leaves employers and society alike vulnerable to spontaneous outbursts of discontent delivered through improvised bodies whose representative status is but self-proclaimed.

Unions can make other contributions to social and political stability as well. Democratic regimes, as Aristotle, Montesquieu, and Tocqueville all point out, require some rough sort of material and economic equality among their citizens if they are to survive as democracies. By moderating the dispersion of earnings and affecting the distribution of incomes, unions can assist in maintaining the sorts of material conditions necessary to democratic regimes. In periods of rapid technological change and structural shifts in the economic order, unions can also moderate the sorts of instrumental rationality that ultimately pits the market against the local and particular institutions that ground a democratic regime.

Reviving and reimagining the practice of collective bargaining presents no easy task. It requires rethinking what unions are and have the potential to be. It also compels a thoroughgoing reassessment of the patterns by which we presently constitute our institutional orders. Fortunately, we are not without sources for guiding our thinking on these matters, and it is to them that we now turn.

Sources of Restoration:
The Subsidiarity Principle and the Good of Order

The trouble with discussing any of the particular seedbeds is that at some point one has to consider them all. Each has a special set of functions to perform. Yet, those discrete sets of institutional operations are interrelated and ultimately only become intelligible in light of the whole. The real worth of unions, for example, lies in the contributions they can make in assisting the full development of human personality, the proper unfolding of which can only be determined through a set of values that are truly intelligible. To consider how we are to live together forces us to ask what it means to be a person.

Consequently, any attempt to rethink, reorient, and revivify the various seedbeds must proceed along a broad front. And, if we are to get beyond the iron cage that results from seeing the market or the state as the sole available choices, our efforts and the thought that guides them must be comprehensive. Because the human good is both individual and social, we need a standard for organizing our institutions that can take advantage of our natural sociality in a way that is consistent with our character as reasonable beings.[65] The subsidiarity principle supplies such guidance.

Simply stated, subsidiarity is an organizational norm. It teaches that social institutions of every description should be ordered so that decision making and the responsibility for acting remain at the lowest capable level. The principle insists that the state and all other forms of society exist exclusively for the individual. Consequently, social bodies should not assume what individuals can do, nor should larger groups take up what smaller associations can accomplish. Conversely, the state and other large institutions have the duty to undertake those functions that neither individuals nor smaller associations can perform. From this perspective, communities and social institutions exist to supply help (*subsidium*) to individuals in assuming self-responsibility. The subsidiary function of community thus rests not in displacing but in establishing the conditions for authentic self-determination.

The insights embodied in the subsidiarity principle stem from its practical yet nuanced understanding of human character. The principle emphasizes the primacy of humans as intelligent, reasonable, and responsible beings. It thus reflects the realization that deliberating, judging, and choosing are the most characteristically human activities, and that the desire to live reasonably is basic to humans.

The second aspect of the anthropology that informs the subsidiarity principle consists in its understanding of humans as situated beings. Subsidiarity recognizes that individuals, social institutions of every sort, and culture stand in a normative and mutually conditioning relationship. Consequently, over time, all rise and decline in concert, each influencing the other. Subsidiarity seeks to promote the full unfolding of human personality by giving individuals the fullest possible opportunity to reflect, choose, and act for themselves, and to take responsibility for the outcomes. The principle is in the best sense democratic. It opens the choices and rationale of institutions and individuals alike to the broadest possible examination and discussion. In so doing, the principle relies upon the normativity of speech as it engages people in a concrete exchange about what ought to be done here and now. This understanding of humans as conversational beings is the third element of the anthropology of the subsidiarity principle. Through its insistence on vesting authority at the lowest capable level and its emphasis on mediating bodies, subsidiarity seeks to engage both our natural sociality as well as our desire to live reasonably. Subsidiarity supplies guidance for devising well-constituted institutional orders of every type. The principle, however, is formal rather than substantive. Consistent with the view of the person that grounds it, subsidiarity depends on common sense and dialogue for its application. It is a heuristic device that guides deliberation but does not attempt to dictate the content of the outcomes. The principle is flexible, not dogmatic, and stresses practical insight over structural certainty and uniformity.

One journalist recently described subsidiarity as "an arcane theological principle." In reality, it is neither, although the principle does find its roots in Catholic social thought. Social Catholicism arose in Germany in the mid-19th century as a response to two developments: the severe social dislocations and urban poverty that accompanied the rise of industrialism, and the challenges posed by critical social philosophy, particularly that of Marx. Catholic social thought might be described as meliorist. It early on accepted markets and institutions like private property as being indispensable to an industrialized society. The teachings, however, go on to qualify modern liberal theory by characterizing the sorts of responsibilities that attach to the ownership of property and capital. From the first, the social teachings have been concerned with establishing the conditions requisite to authentic self-rule. As a result, the teachings consistently have called for self-help through labor unions, producers' cooperatives, and other self-organized associations, supported by a limited program of social legislation. Subsidiarity was integral to the first papal social encyclical, *Rerum Novarum*, which was issued in 1891. It was not until the 1931 encyclical, *Quadragesimo Anno*, that the principle received either its name or a comprehensive formulation. The principle since has been invoked in the social encyclicals of every pope.

Despite its provenance, however, subsidiarity properly has been characterized as "neither a theological nor even really a philosophical principle, but a piece of congealed historical wisdom."[66] Even Oswald von Nell-Breuning, who coined the term, called it an "ancient" principle. Its themes are consistent with the insights of Tocqueville and John Dewey, among others, concerning the types of social arrangements that enhance responsible self-rule and ongoing cooperation.

The subsidiarity principle lies at the core of the European Union's Social Charter, some of whose provisions were mentioned earlier. The principle illuminates much of the Charter's meaning, and it stands as a maxim for arranging the order of all types of social institutions within the Union. The principle has much to tell us as well. Sustaining the conditions for authentic self-rule is an ongoing project that requires comprehensive ways of acting and thinking. Subsidiarity supplies us with a method for proceeding in this work—one that is consistent with what we as humans are and have the potential to become.

Notes

1. Aristotle, *Politics*, bk. 3, ch. 4, trans. C. Lord (Chicago: University of Chicago Press, 1984), 1277 b-15, 92.

2. William Blackstone, *Commentaries on the Laws of England* (New York: Garland, 1978), 422.

3. Alexis de Tocqueville, *Democracy in America*, 13th ed., ed. J. P. Mayer, trans. George Lawrence (1850; reprint; Garden City, NY: Anchor Books, 1969), 517.

4. U.S. Department of Labor, Bureau of Labor Statistics, Bulletin 2385, *Working Women: A Chartbook* (Washington, DC: U.S. Government Printing Office, 1991), 48. (Labor force participation for persons 25–54 years of age.) Actual participation rates for men have declined slowly but steadily over the past three decades. In 1962, 96.8 percent of adult men were in the workforce. For one brief consideration of the decline among men in workforce participation, see Howard Hayghe and Steven Haugen, "A Profile of Husbands in Today's Labor Market," *Monthly Labor Review* 110 (Oct. 1987): 12.

5. Dana Priest, "Major Changes Seen in Female Labor Force; In 1990, 60% of Mothers With Young Went to Work," *The Washington Post*,

25 March 1992, p. A21. Also see, *Working Women: A Chartbook*, p. 48, Table A-16.

6. *Working Women: A Chartbook*, p. 48. In 1990, of nine industrialized nations (the United States, Australia, Canada, France, Italy, Japan, The Netherlands, Sweden, and the United Kingdom) only Sweden and Canada had greater female workforce participation than the U.S. Since 1970, the participation gap between Sweden and the U.S. narrowed while the rate for Canadian women grew rapidly and now narrowly surpasses the U.S. rate. Significant increases in workforce participation by women since 1970 also occurred in the United States, Australia, and the Netherlands. Italy's rate of 30 percent was the smallest proportion of the nations for which data was available. Id. p. 9–10.

7. Ibid., 13. The Bureau of Labor Statistics (BLS) figures show that 77 percent of employed adult women worked 35 or more hours weekly. Among unemployed women, 80 percent were seeking full-time work. Also see figures in Table A-16, p. 48.

8. Ibid., 35, and see figures in Table A-18, p. 50.

9. Priest, "Major Changes in Female Labor Force," A-21 (reporting results from a Government Accounting Office study issued March 24, 1992). See also *Working Women: A Chartbook*, 33. The BLS reports that since 1970, the proportion of children in two-parent families where both parents were in the labor force increased from 36 to 61 percent.

10. Thus, between 1970 and 1989, the proportion of women working on a full-time, year-round basis grew from 41 to 51 percent. *Working Women: A Chartbook*, 13.

11. Juliet B. Schor, *The Overworked American: The Unexpected Decline of Leisure* (New York: Basic Books, 1991), 17–43.

12. See Richard Freeman and James Medoff, *What Do Unions Do?* (New York: Basic Books, 1984), 162–81; Ronald Ehrenberg and Robert Smith, *Modern Labor Economics: Theory and Public Policy* (Glenview, IL: Scott, Foresman and Co., 1982), 360–62.

13. See Freeman and Medoff, *What Do Unions Do?*, 78–93; Ehrenberg and Smith, *Modern Labor Economics*, 356–580.

14. Stephen M. Hills, "The Attitudes of Union and Non-union Male Workers Toward Union Representation," *Labor Relations Review* 38 (1985): 179; also see the essay by Seymour Martin Lipset, "Labor Unions in the Public Mind," in *Unions in Transition: Entering the Second Century*, ed. Seymour Martin Lipset (San Francisco: Institute for Contemporary Studies Press, 1986), 287.

15. "Union Membership Unchanged at 16.1 percent of Employment in 1991," *Daily Labor Report* (BNA), 11 February 1992, A-A. Union

density has been steadily declining in the private sector in the United States since the mid-1950s. In 1958, 34 percent of private sector employees were unionized. By 1980, just 24 percent were—a decline unprecedented in American history. The free-fall in density continued throughout the 1980s. See, Michael Curme, Barry Hush, and David MacPherson, "Union Membership and Contract Coverage in the United States, 1983–1988," *Industrial & Labor Relations Review* 44 (1990): 5.

16. Irving Bernstein, *The New-Deal Collective Bargaining Policy* (Berkeley, CA: University of California Press, 1950), 2.

17. Leo Troy, "Convergence in Industrial Unionism, etc.: The Case of Canada and the U.S.A.," *British Journal Industrial Relations* 30 (1992): 1.

18. See U.S. Department of Commerce, Bureau of the Census, Econ. and Stats. Admin., Current Population Reports, Series P-60, No.177, *Trends in Relative Income: 1964–1989* (Washington, DC: U.S. Government Printing Office, 1991), 1–4 and accompanying tables; Paul Ryscavage and Peter Henle, "Earnings Inequality Accelerates in the 1980's," *Monthly Labor Review*, December (1990): 3; W. Norton Grubb and Robert H. Wilson, "Trends in Wage and Salary Inequality, 1967–88," *Monthly Labor Review*, June (1992): 23; Greg Duncan, Timothy Smeeding, and Willard Rodgers, "The Incredible Shrinking Middle Class," *American Demographics* (May 1992): 34–38 (Summary of study conducted by University of Michigan Survey Research Center). The difficulties in tracing these trends are well described in the Grubb and Wilson study.

19. See Lawrence Mishel and Jared Bernstein, *The State of Working America* (1992–93 ed.) (Armonk, NY: M.E. Sharpe, 1993); David R. Francis, "U.S. Workers on Job Longer for Less Pay," *The Christian Science Monitor*, 15 May 1992, 8.

20. Statistics also show a sharp increase in the number of people holding multiple jobs—an increase of 52 percent between 1985 and 1989. Women accounted for two-thirds of this increase. As of 1990, 72 million Americans held two or more jobs. See John F. Stenson, "Multiple Jobholding Up Sharply in the 1980's," *Monthly Labor Review* (July 1990): 3.

21. Statement of Audrey Freedman, Executive Director, Human Resources Program Group, The Conference Board, at a Hearing Before the Subcommittee on Employment and Housing, *Rising Use of Part-Time and Temporary Workers: Who Benefits and Who Loses?*, 100th Cong., 2nd Sess. (1988), 36.

22. Ibid., 38.

23. Ibid., 38–39.

24. Ibid., 36.

25. For a further discussion of these points, see Thomas C. Kohler, *Lessons from the Social Charter: State, Corporation and the Meaning of Subsidiarity* (University of Toronto L.J.), 43. (forthcoming).

26. Arnold Beichman, "George Meany: Worker of the World," *Policy Review* 59 (Winter 1992): 49. Meany, a highly controversial figure within and without organized labor, was President of the AFL from 1952 until its 1955 merger with the CIO, at which time he assumed the Presidency of the combined Federation.

27. See Milton Derber, *The American Idea of Industrial Democracy, 1865–1965* (Urbana, IL: University of Illinois Press, 1970), 95.

28. Hills, "The Attitudes of Union and Non-union Workers," 170; James L. Medoff, "Study for the AFL-CIO on Public's Image of Unions," *Daily Labor Report* (BNA), 24 December 1984: D-2.

29. Medoff, "Study for the AFL-CIO," D-2.

30. For example, see Troy, "Convergence in Industrial Unionism," 1.

31. For example, see Paul Weiler, "Promises to Keep: Securing Workers' Rights to Self-Organization under the NLRA," *Harvard Law Review* 96 (1983): 1769. Also see Henry J. Farber, "The Decline of Unionization in the United States: What Can Be Learned from Recent Experience," *Journal of Labor Economics* (1990), S-75.

32. On the rise of these campaigns, see Reinhard Bendix, *Work and Authority in Industry* (1956; reprint; Berkeley, CA: University of California, 1974), 254–74.

33. Medoff, "Study for the AFL-CIO," D-1.

34. Ibid., D-8.

35. In 1936, the first time the Gallup Organization surveyed Americans on this matter, 72 percent answered "approve" to the question "In general, do you approve or disprove of labor unions?" For a table tracking rates, see Lipset, *Unions in Transition*, 301.

36. Ibid., 299.

37. Gallup Organization, August 3, 1991 (telephone poll conducted July 18–21, 1991, of 1002 respondents). Thirty percent of those questioned disapproved of unions.

38. Eighty-one percent of the U.S. population. Medoff, "Study for the AFL-CIO," D-D.

39. Lipset, *Unions in Transition*, 302.

40. Medoff, "Study for the AFL-CIO," D-2.

41. David Horton Smith, "Voluntary Action and Voluntary Groups" in *Annual Review of Sociology* 1 (1975): 247; James Curtis, "Voluntary Association Joining: A Cross-National Comparative Note," *American Sociological Review* 36 (1971): 872.

42. Baumgartner and Walker, "Survey Research and Membership in Voluntary Associations," *American Journal of Political Science* 32 (1988): 908. The American Association of Retired Persons is now the largest voluntary association in the United States.

43. Flynn McRoberts, "Moose, Elk, Joining the Endangered," *Chicago Tribune*, 19 February 1991, Du Page Section, p. 1.

44. For figures and discussions, see Andrew M. Greeley, *Religious Change in America* (Cambridge, MA: Harvard University Press, 1989); George Gallup Jr. and Jim Castelli, *The People's Religion: American Faith in the '90's* (New York: Macmillan, 1989).

45. Greeley, *Religious Change in American*, 13–14.

46. Gallup and Castelli, *The People's Religion*, 37.

47. Ibid., 39.

48. Ibid., 45.

49. Association of Statisticians of American Religious Bodies, *Churches and Church Membership in the U.S.* (1992).

50. "55.1% of Americans Linked to Religious Groups, Survey Shows," *Los Angeles Times*, 11 July 1992, p. B-4. The study also shows that the unaffiliated outnumber the affiliated by a 3–1 margin in large sections of Colorado, California, Oregon, Washington, Nevada, Montana, Michigan, central Maine, and eastern Kentucky.

51. Dean R. Hoge, Benton Johnson, and Donald A. Luidens, *Vanishing Boundaries: The Religion of Protestant Baby-Boomers* (Louisville, KY: Westminster/John Knox Press, 1994).

52. "Protestant Baby-Boomers Not Returning to Church," *New York Times*, 7 June 1992, p. 28 (quoting Professor Donald Luidens).

53. Gallup and Castelli, *The People's Religion*, 45.

54. Ibid., 70–71.

55. Lipset, *Unions in Transition*, 302.

56. Gallup and Castelli, *The People's Religion*, 253. Polls show that 4 in 10 Americans "admit to frequent or occasional feelings of intense loneliness."

57. Michael Walzer, "The Communitarian Critique of Liberalism," *Political Theory* 18 (1990): 6.

58. See Wilson Carey McWilliams, *The Idea of Fraternity in America* (Berkeley: University of California Press, 1973), 40, for a discussion of identity in customary society and the erotic notion of the self that grounds the notion of the *gemeinschaft*.

59. Edmund Burke, *Reflections on the Revolution in France*, ed. Thomas Mahoney, Library of Liberal Arts (Indianapolis: Bobbs-Merrill, 1955), 110.

60. See Matthew Lamb, "Praxis," in *The New Dictionary of Theology*, ed. Joseph A. Komonchak, Mary Collins and Dermot A. Lane (Wilmington, DE: Michael Glazier, 1987), 784–87; Richard Bernstein, *Praxis and Action: Contemporary Philosophies of Human Activity* (Philadelphia: University of Pennsylvania Press, 1971).

61. See Bernard J. F. Lonergan, *Method in Theology* (Toronto: University of Toronto Press, 1992), 48.

62. *Steelworkers v Warrior & Gulf Navigation Co.*, 363 US 564, 580 (1964).

63. Lonergan, *Method in Theology*, 27–55.

64. *Nicomachean Ethics*, [1170] trans. Terrance Irwin, (Indianapolis, IN: Hackett Pub. Co., 1985), 10–15.

65. On these points, see Kohler, *Lessons from the Social Charter*.

66. John S. Coleman, S.J., "Development of Church Social Teaching" in *Readings in Moral Theology No. 5: Official Catholic Social Teaching*, ed. Charles Curran and Richard A. McCormick, S.J. (New York: Paulist Press, 1984), 169, 183.

CHAPTER 7

Social and Natural Ecologies: Similarities and Differences

Alan Wolfe

The Two Ecologies

For whatever reason—perhaps because it contains a grain of truth—the stereotype of a person who loves and respects animals but casts a cold eye on fellow human beings has become something of a cliche.[1] But cliche or not, the notion that things found in nature have a higher moral priority than those constructed by society plays itself out on a level far more important than individual idiosyncracies. For the fact is that at the very time when advanced industrial societies such as the United States have developed a concern for and an appreciation of the natural environment, they are allowing the social environments that make human development possible to deteriorate. We are becoming, as a society, the caricature of the animal rights activist writ large.

This relative bias in favor of the natural and against the social runs throughout just about every aspect of American society, from public policy down to popular consciousness. We require environmental impact statements before launching complex new technologies but there are no social impact statements required of innovations in health care delivery or day care. Our courts try to protect the environment in which species of wildlife flourish but, on the human side, are often more concerned with individual rights than the social conditions that allow humans to flourish. Everyone

knows a joke comparing lawyers to rats in which the latter come
out ahead. We like to think of nature as pristine and politics as
dirty. Pollution in the one realm is something to be cleaned up
while in the other it is considered the order of the day. Americans
are far more willing to recycle their garbage than their tax reve-
nues. Try to organize people around the protection of their neighborhoods against an incinerator or dump, and they will respond.
Try to interest them in the devastating effects of crime on inner city
neighborhoods, and they will look the other way.

Because of this general preference for the natural over the social,
we may be tempted, in thinking about society, to apply the insights
we have gained from the natural world. We have learned so much
about natural species—especially about the complicated relationship between any species and the larger environment in which it
finds itself—that surely there must be powerful conclusions about
the human condition to be drawn. Yet although this point may
seem obvious, it is a kind of "naturalistic fallacy." A closer look at
the natural and the social reveals ways in which the ecologies of
both are quite different as well as ways in which they are similar.
There *is* a complex social ecology that requires that far more attention be paid to how and why it functions as it does. But the ways it
works are not in all cases equivalent to the way the natural ecology
works. We ought to be as concerned with developing a model (or
many models) of the social ecology as the ones scientists have developed about natural phenomenon. But it cannot be the *same*
model, taken out of one context and applied to another.

Historians of ideas can cite one compelling reason why direct
comparisons between the social and the natural ought to be undertaken with caution. They have been tried before, and not always
with success.[2] In the 19th century both progressive and conservative opinion were fascinated by the relevance of nature to the
human condition. Herbert Spencer's borrowings from Darwinian
theory were believed to hold secrets directly applicable to such
human affairs as legislation and social reform.[3] "Nature" told us
that efforts to improve the working conditions of ordinary people
were doomed to fail because they would gum up the works of a
naturally evolving and self-regulating system of market exchange.
Although one still hears such arguments today—for example, in

theories which use sociobiology to explain what is wrong with feminism[4]—most forms of conservative rhetoric no longer base themselves on such explicit social Darwinist assumptions.[5]

Interestingly enough, opponents of Spencer's version of social
Darwinism also found solace in natural processes. From the point
of view of Victorian reformers, progress would come about because
governments were capable of encouraging the good genetic material and discouraging the bad. In contrast to the 20th-century way
of thinking about these things, in the 19th-century writers and
thinkers fascinated with genetic potentials were often on the Left,
leading the campaign for reform legislation, birth control, and attacks on poverty.[6] What is striking is that on both sides of the political spectrum—whether supporting social reform or attacking
it—so many writers appealed to nature for guidelines affecting the
social, as if there were insufficient insights provided by the social
sciences for understanding their own subject.

With the development of 20th-century social science, this effort
to seek grounding for human projects in the natural sciences withered away. Indeed, as Carl Degler argues, there was something of a
swing in the exact opposite direction, as culture became the explanation for just about everything.[7] Degler goes on to discuss a revival
of biological theories in the social sciences in very recent years.
To be sure, sociobiology, genetics, and other naturalistic ways of
thinking about such social topics as crime, inequality, and family
structure have begun to appear on the national agenda. My point
is not to take sides in the often furious debates about whether social
phenomenon have biological causes. It is rather to argue for a distinct social ecology because human beings have distinct characteristics.[8] If we merely want to preserve the social environment in
which human beings live, we might find help in the natural sciences. But if we want social institutions—including families, neighborhoods, workplaces, and political systems—not only to survive
but to contribute to the development of the character and competence of those who belong to them, we need to understand that
ecologies which have human beings at their center are fundamentally different than ecologies that are composed of non-thinking,
non-choosing organisms.

Similarities

The most obvious similarities between natural and social ecologies have to do with interdependence, fragility, adaptability, and the necessity of cultivation. Yet each area of similarity also contains within it aspects that point to the differences between nature and culture.

Interdependence

Surely one of the greatest accomplishments of contemporary ecology is the demonstration of how things are interrelated.[9] Alter a food chain, disturb an environment, introduce a new mutation—and before long the consequences will be as surprising as they are unpredictable. Because everything affects everything else, we ought to develop respect for interdependence before intervening too bluntly into natural patterns of reproduction.

Interdependence is also one of the most significant features of the social ecology that makes human culture possible. Although sociologists tend to specialize into different areas such as the family, crime, or education, what happens in one realm always has consequences for the others. If, for example, we want to strengthen schools, the most important thing we can do is not to spend more money on training teachers or buying computers, but instead to find ways to strengthen families. The one great truth we have about education is that parents matter more than anything else.[10] It can hardly be surprising that families and schools weaken together; the less time parents have to read to their children or to talk to them about fundamental values, the more difficult it will be for schools to teach math. When something goes wrong in a natural ecology, the result can be a vicious cycle; one species, losing its usual source of food, turns to a different prey, which then adversely affects another natural balance, and so on. The same kind of vicious cycle can be the result of the complex interdependence in social life. As families weaken, we ask the schools to carry out tasks once thought of as properly familial. The schools become responsible for teaching about sex and moral behavior. Or they assume day care activities after the formal school day ends. Or they take over the task of cultivating the political values of the young or even their attitudes toward the natural environment. Some writers laud these trends, viewing schools as the proper substitute for homes that are radi-cally changing.[11] But there is also the possibility that schools are not only assuming tasks for which they are ill-equipped but are also, in the process, further weakening the ability of the family to assume those tasks, thereby intensifying the resulting vicious cycle.

Under these conditions, there are some who, distrusting the schools entirely, want to break the vicious cycle by having the home carry out school functions rather than the school assuming the functions of home.[12] Homeschooling is a rapidly growing move-ment in the United States. Yet if the social ecology is interdepen-dent, it is as unsatisfactory a solution as its opposite. For if parents are the most important variable in whether schools work, commu-nity is the most important variable in whether every other aspect of society works. We need institutions that teach about obligations to others and practice such obligations as part of their daily busi-ness. It does not matter how many homeschoolers eventually attend Harvard. It does matter whether children come together with oth-ers with whom they share membership in a community that, while smaller than the nation-state, is larger than the individual family. Private solutions to public responsibilities such as education de-prive the latter of their ability to breathe.

There are, in short, important policy consequences that follow from the way in which the interdependence of the social ecology is similar to that of the national ecology. We need social impact statements when we contemplate major changes in policy. We should remind ourselves about the social consequences of economic changes so that we are aware that "positive" statistics in one area—say, economic growth—can have consequences in other areas that may not be positive. Our objective should be not merely to strengthen the family or the schools but to think about ways in which one can strengthen the other. The institutions that constitute the social ecology live or die together, which can be either a source of great strength or a potential weakness, depending on how we treat them.

Not all forms of interdependence are the same, however, and in thinking about the ways in which both nature and society link their parts together, we ought to keep in mind one difference. Interdependence in nature is the result of individual organisms fitting into predetermined patterns of harmony together with other individual organisms. We emphasize social interdependence, by contrast, not to praise social systems for acting "functionally" to reproduce any given social order but to further certain agreed upon values. The problem with all sociological theories from Durkheim to Parsons that emphasize such interdependence is that they can provide no external justification for the goodness or badness of a society but only its fitness.[13] Some standard of human purpose or meaning must be the objective of any morally appropriate social ecology, as I will argue later. Although establishing a standard is obviously well beyond the purview of this chapter, at a minimum it ought to be based on human capacities of character and competence and how they can be expanded and developed.

Fragility

Like the natural world, the institutions of the social world are incredibly fragile. Indeed they may, if anything, be far more fragile than natural phenomena, for although the man-made environment is constantly overrunning nature, the latter has ways of fighting back. There are many examples of nature retaking, so to speak, civilization, as weeds grow up around what were once thriving neighborhoods and communities. It is more remarkable when social institutions, once destroyed, begin to recover and thrive again. No one knows whether it will ever be possible to have cities in the United States that offer pleasant, safe, and efficient ways to live. And it is not just cities whose fragility is so pronounced. There are few institutions in the complex social ecology called civil society whose strength and survivability can be taken for granted. Schools, especially public schools, are in serious trouble. The voluntary activities so lauded by Tocqueville seem less robust than in the past. Once vibrant neighborhoods are decaying. This is not to lament the state of contemporary America; many critics of the critics have pointed to sources of resilience in American social life.[14] But it is to suggest that even when healthier than we sometimes imagine, the institutions of civil society are always fragile.

No other social institution has received more worried attention in this context than the family. When a quarter of all children under 18 live in single-parent families, the fragility of the two-parent family model becomes obvious.[15] One can properly debate whether weaker families are the price paid for progress, particularly for the greater empowerment and freedom of family members, especially women and children.[16] But that the family is fragile seems to be beyond debate, especially since a national consensus has begun to emerge around the need to strengthen the family as an institution. The increasing correlation between single-parent families and poverty, the psychological support for the notion that parents matter, and a sense that family instability lies behind many other forms of social instability all demonstrate why society has as much of an interest in strengthening its social institutions as it does in protecting its natural environment.

Yet how society does so is not simple. Like the natural world, destruction can take place as a by-product of other objectives, some of them necessary and important. While everyone wants to protect the environment, a blanket moral injunction to do so at any cost would have significant economic consequences that would disproportionately affect people dependent on jobs that are not especially high paying. The real question facing any discussion of nature's fragility is not whether everything in nature ought to be protected, but which things at what price. In a similar way, we can all agree that the social institutions of civil society need to be strengthened, while disagreeing not only about means, but also about the proper balance between contrasting objectives. Because the two-parent family is fragile no more means that we ought to restore the idealized family of the 1950s than the survival of the spotted owl means that we should immediately stop logging in Oregon. Nature is fragile, but it also changes. Social institutions are fragile, yet they must change as well.

If respect for nature teaches us simultaneously about fragility and change, the question one must always ask is not whether things change, but why they do. It is one thing to intervene in nature for purposes that rebound to human advantage, for then there are costs and benefits on both sides of the equation to be weighed. But to intervene in nature for essentially frivolous or wasteful reasons

Alan Wolfe

strikes most reasonable people as unacceptable. Motives also count when we consider the fragility of social institutions. Unlike markets and states, which have proven relatively durable, the institutions of civil society depend on trust, honesty, and long-term gratification to thrive, and these are all behaviors that are easily threatened by greed or self-interest. When a social institution's fragility is the result of avaricious behavior or narrow points of view, we are more likely to understand destruction as tragic than when it is viewed as the inevitable by-product of progress. Even good intentions, when applied naively or selectively, can have tragic consequences for social institutions. The destruction of Boston's once-thriving Jewish neighborhoods, which, despite their liveliness and positive rewards, were discovered to be quite fragile, strikes us as wasteful because banks made assumptions about race and ethnicity which created a vicious cycle that no one could stop.[17]

It is important that we be aware of the fragility of the social environment, even if recognition of this fragility cannot be the end of the story. Fragility is a quality that demands that we ask whether something is worth saving. The answer may in most cases be yes, but it cannot in all cases be yes. Nonetheless, if we were as sensitive to the potential for destruction in the social environment as we were in the natural, we would be better disposed to address our national needs than we are at present.

Adaptability

One of the reasons why the social Darwinists of the 19th century found in nature comforting metaphors for society was the remarkable adaptability found in the natural world. Ecological consciousness teaches respect for the multiple possibilities inherent in any limited number of initial conditions. Even if an ecological model simplifies reality down to the point where only two variables interact, the number of ways they can interact over large amounts of time produces a myriad of possible future outcomes.[18] The inevitable conclusion to be drawn from such endless variation is an inclination to let nature run its own course. If adaptability is taken as given, laissez-faire seems to follow.

There is no question but that some social processes manifest ex-

actly this same capacity to produce surprising and unexpected outcomes. The economy in particular is barely understood, for no
matter how complex the models, it is not uncommon for economists
to make incomplete, or even misleading, predictions. (Laissez-faire
usually means that government should not intervene; perhaps the
more appropriate lesson is that economists, especially those who
believe in laissez-faire, should not intervene.) If social phenomena
demonstrate as much adaptability as natural ones, the conclusion
that seems to follow is to leave them alone to find their own course
of development.

Interestingly enough, almost no one believes this, despite the current popularity of laissez-faire among conservatives. For the very
people who speak of leaving the economy alone to find its own
course very rarely would permit the family also to be left alone to
find its own course. Libertarians in economics are often statists in
morality, regulating one set of social institutions—and often in a
fairly heavy-handed way—while respecting the adaptability of others. On the other hand, many individuals on the Left, who argue
for state intervention to prevent job loss, redistribute income, or
plan for future growth, ask the state to keep its hands off decisions
involving abortion, religion, or family dynamics. Laissez-faire
seems to be the attitude toward things the other person cares about;
when it comes to the most closely held values, a belief in using
whatever means necessary to guide change seems the rule rather
than the exception.

To be sure, social institutions can adapt, and they often do so in
unexpected ways. We probably ought to respect the capacity of
social institutions, and the people within them, to participate in the
process by which new forms emerge. But it does not follow that
because social institutions can adapt, we ought to leave them alone.
It is particularly inappropriate to reach a laissez-faire conclusion,
moreover, by grounding social arguments on natural developments. For the fact is that despite the remarkable powers of adaptability found in nature, we no longer rely on nature to find its own
course either. We have learned that nature evolves best when
guided, lightly guided, perhaps, but guided nonetheless. Few things
are left to chance in this world, certainly not the development of
forests, oceans, and other examples of natural beauty.

Cultivation

Both nature and society require constant attention. In spite of a general preference for the natural over the social, these two aspects of modern experience are intertwined, and one of the most important things they have in common is that both require care. The very word culture comes, after all, from the Latin "to cultivate." Human inventions and skills, no matter how rarified and removed from the world of nature, will not persevere unless tended and nurtured.[19] The same thing works in reverse. Because there are no wilderness areas left, many of the natural habitats in which Americans seek refuge from the corruptions of society are themselves socially (and politically) created, our national parks being perhaps the best example. In the absence of cultivation, both the natural and the social ecologies will run wild, in neither case producing the balance and harmony generally necessary for a healthy existence.

The real question is not whether cultivation will take place but what kind of cultivation it will be. In contrast to the laissez-faire position that emerges out of a belief in adaptability, an emphasis on cultivation usually leads to an argument in favor of state intervention. Certainly those who believed in eugenics linked the need to cultivate human institutions together with an active program of government intervention. And in some models of the modern welfare state, government aid is provided to families for the same reason it is provided to police: to keep order among the potentially unruly. Although strict cultivationists are at the opposite end of the political spectrum from those who believe in laissez-faire, there are some similarities. Emphasizing adaptability, the hands-off advocates would let a thousand flowers blossom. Emphasizing cultivatability, the interventionists would cut the flowers with shears and regulate their growth with poisons. Each takes a metaphor that has a certain amount of truth—both natural and social institutions can and must adapt; both the natural and the culture require cultivation—and carries it to extremes. The result may not be the most appropriate lessons for human affairs. Strict cultivations, who use nature to justify the state just as laissez-faire used nature to justify the market, are not especially attractive to modern sensibilities. In the name of guiding people to attractive ends, they would use too many people, especially those viewed as less fit, as inappropriate means.

Although there are numerous similarities between the worlds of nature and society—no doubt more than I have listed here—even the similarities indicate a certain caution in generalizing from one realm to the other. No one can doubt that the social institutions of civil society are fragile. The need to protect them is obvious. Yet as we go about the task, we may find that as complicated as the natural ecology may be, the social ecology is far more complex and unpredictable. Natural ecological systems sometimes survive at the cost of the disappearance of particular organisms; indeed, one of the wonders of nature lies in the way animals sacrifice themselves for the good of evolutionary fitness.[20] Social ecologies that survived because the individuals who composed them would give up their lives strike us as less of a wonder. We want social institutions not only to be neutral with respect to the good life but to encourage individuals to be responsible and caring. For that reason alone, any ecology composed of people will be inherently different from an ecology composed of other types of organisms.

Differences

Just as one can draw certain similarities between natural and social ecologies, one can also point to the most significant differences between them. Without pretending that any such list will be exhaustive, the discussion here points toward rules, the state of scientific understanding, speed of change, and purpose as constituting the major sources of difference.

Rules

Complex ecological systems work despite their complexity because the behavior of the organisms that compose them is driven algorithmically. With the invention of the computer and the discovery of DNA, information processing models of behavior have become the dominant approach used in the information sciences.[21] Such models assumed that wholes could develop, even into complex forms, with parts doing little more than replicating each other imitatively. For even the smallest flaw in the replication at one point could, given enough moves over long stretches of time, produce enormous variation at another point. Such properties led to a fascination with algorithms; the rules, in a sense, became far more important than what was being ruled, irrespective of whether those rules were understood to be a code within a DNA molecule or a set of software instructions to a machine.

The single most significant difference between natural and social ecologies is that the components of the latter, people, have minds of their own. Because they do, mere replication is never enough to produce the variations that the human species has produced over what are, from a biological perspective, astonishingly short periods of time. Even sociobiologists like Richard Dawkins and Edward O. Wilson concede that, to understand humans, we need a theory of culture and, in some cases, of mind.[22] Capable of changing their minds, human beings cannot be understood algorithmically. From the standpoint of comprehending human behavior, what we lose in mathematical precision we gain in potentiality. Human beings do not, like computers, need a large bank of memory that can be accessed; nor do they, like primates, need long periods of time to learn new behaviors. They can instead govern the rules that in turn govern them.

This human capacity to alter rules is central to the question of how social ecologies work. To be sure, human beings have rules, ranging from the Ten Commandments to the laws that govern behavior in public places. But it has never been the case with human beings that simply telling them the rules guarantees their compliance with them. Strict adherents of law and order may be disappointed by this fact, but it is one of the secrets of how social ecologies work. Human adaptability is different from other forms of adaptability found in nature because people can take cues from their environment, recognize the distinctiveness of the situations in which they find themselves, and alter their behavior to account for particular conditions. Surely we know by now that a person of good character is not one who blindly follows the rules but is rather one capable of understanding how and why rules should be applied differently in different situations. That kind of character can only be exhibited by a being that possesses qualities of mind.

State of Scientific Understanding

A second reason to be cautious about applying ecological understandings directly to the social world is that, as poorly as we understand the dynamics of the former, we probably understand them better than we do the dynamics of the latter. Ecology and biology are both recent sciences, and each has made false starts. The theories that guide research into the affairs of other species, including sociobiology and ecology, are best viewed as theories in the making. Revised frequently to take account of new insights and new research, such theories are more like theories in the social sciences than they are like theories in physics. Indeed, it has been suggested that there can be no biological theory valid across all animal species, only theories for specific species.[23] Compared to physics, biology is far from a theoretically sophisticated science.

But as young as the biological sciences may be, they are far better grounded than any theories we have about culture, mind, agency, structure, and the other aspects of human behavior that bedevil sociologists. If biologists and ecologists had made as many mistakes in predicting the effect of various changes on the environment as social policy analysts made in predicting the effects of new programs on the ecology of families or communities, it is not clear that we would have a natural environment. We are in the very beginning stages of developing a distinct science for a distinct species; what we do not know about the social worlds around us is staggering. We ought to be acquiring knowledge about human institutions and practices before jumping to the conclusion that we can understand ourselves based on laws borrowed from the world of nature.

Speed of Change

Both natural and social ecologies evolve, but they evolve at different speeds. Because they do, efforts to rely on biological or naturalistic metaphors to understand the institutions that compose the social ecology often fall apart. This is especially true about how both conservatives and liberals have understood an institution such as the family.

Naturalistic ways of thinking often appeal to conservatives. If some practices, such as the nuclear family, can be considered "natural" while others—homosexuality for example—are considered unnatural, one is more easily justified than the other. (It is, however, a sign of our current confusion that the gay community is internally divided over the question of whether homosexuality is neurological, socially constructed, or both.) Analogies with nature further a political objective, for if something is natural, then efforts to change it will be futile. But natural metaphors can backfire on those who use them. If we understand families as part of a social ecology that resembles the natural ecology, then they will certainly change. The change may be slow, the consequences delayed, but there will be evolution, which means that any particular form existing at any particular time and place will be temporary. Defenders of social institutions as they are think of themselves as traditionalists, yet tradition is a very unnatural phenomenon; there are in fact few phenomena more sociological in nature than traditions.[24] Conservative defenders of social institutions ought to be arguing from sociological premises; when they shift to biology and nature, they undermine their own position.

Those who argue that families are not in decline, and may be in the process of a certain strengthening, by contrast tend to rely on sociological premises. All particular family forms, they argue, are socially constructed, the product of particular arrangements of power and discourse. Created this way, the family can be recreated that way. Humans are malleable and adaptable, so much so that their institutions are epiphenomenal and contingent.

But as important as such sociological language is in understanding rapidly changing family forms, a naturalistic set of images also comes into play among those sympathetic to family change. Sometimes these images are explicit; early radical feminism in particular absorbed, in Alison M. Jagger's account, "naturalistic assumptions about human biology," hoping to turn them in different directions than those inherent in conservative biological accounts.[25] More commonly, such metaphors are implicit and more directly ecological. Family forms are assumed to "evolve" from one historical stage to another, and this evolution, like the natural ecology, occurs so automatically as to take on an inevitable character. Because family forms evolve progressively, to go backwards, to reimpose the nuclear family and the subordinate position of women, would be as futile as trying to bring an extinct species back to life. "American families have repeatedly had to change in order to adopt to novel circumstances," two historians have written. It is therefore "futile" to worry about whether the family will survive, "nor do we need to worry obsessively about the increasing diversity of family arrangements, since ethnic, religious and economic diversity has always been a defining characteristic of American family life."[26] The ecological optimism of such passages, so reminiscent of the language of 19th-century Spencerian laissez-faire, raises the question of whether the assumption that nature is essentially tame and will find its own harmonious resolutions if left alone to follow its own evolutionary dynamics has simply shifted from the Right (and economics) in the 19th century to the Left (and social institutions) now.

Rather than basing either liberal or conservative values on inappropriate comparisons to natural patterns of evolution, we ought to recognize that the kinds of change that take place in nature and those that take place in cultural institutions vary widely with respect to the speed at which they change. Evolution happens "naturally" because the amount of time involved for such changes to take place is fantastically large, which means that the speed of change is remarkably slow. Human institutions, by contrast, have changed so much in the relatively short period of 2,500 years—let alone over the past 25—because the rate of change is so fast. Instead of this difference between nature and culture being an argument that the slowest forms of change are the best, it can also be an argument that because social change tends to take place so rapidly—who could have predicted two decades ago what the American family would look like today?—we need better ways of managing change than either traditionalism or evolutionary optimism permit.

Purpose

The use of naturalistic or ecological metaphors to analyze human institutions such as families is limited because it is a specifically human characteristic to live not just for reproduction but also for a purpose. We cannot understand social institutions such as the family without raising the question of what they are for—what larger purpose besides the reproduction of the species they are to serve. Naturalistic and ecological metaphors turn us away from such concerns. Except in a functional sense, we rarely ask what meaning the practices of other animal species serve. Darwinian theory encourages a perspective in which the answer to the question of purpose is contained already in the terms of the theory: animals develop particular behavioral patterns or physical features in order to help their species survive efficiently.

To the degree that social science models itself on natural sciences like biology, it usually adopts one or another form of such a functionalism; human practices are adopted or not adopted because of their socially reproductive consequences. From a functionalist perspective, nuclear families were explained by their mastery in contributing to successful social integration or by the way they seemed to "fit" the need for mobile wage labor in an industrial economy.[27] In either case, nuclear families were simply assumed to function best, with little attention paid to what values and capacities were being furthered by the family's reproduction. One of the limiting conditions of social theory borrowed from biology was its inability to evaluate institutions with respect to the specific human qualities of those who compose them. Because it could not take account of real people and their needs, especially women, functionalism predicted the continuation of one particular family form that was soon to lose its "inevitable" character. Understanding human families on terms borrowed from functionalist biology did not make for a good predictive science.

Functionalists are not the only ones, however, who fail to ask what families are for. The argument that families are social constructions has been enormously helpful to feminists, for it puts into question any "natural" division of labor within the family. But the argument for social construction can, in postmodern theory, be taken to some fairly extreme forms, from which it also becomes impossible to ask what a family ought to do. Not only are institutions understood as socially constructed, so are all conventions, all moralities, and all systems of ethical conduct, including—more than a few feminists have noticed—feminist values themselves.[28] When normative standards have no independent justification but represent the story told by the victor in a political struggle that has used discourse as the primary weapon, any discussion of purpose or meaning is irrelevant. Postmodern social theories turn to naturalistic and mechanical understandings of the world precisely to avoid concluding that human affairs are directed toward some purpose. To study an institution like the family from such a postmodern perspective is finally to come to the same conclusion that one would from a functionalist perspective; in both cases, families are what families do.

In contrast to such naturalistic metaphors, we should examine social institutions with concern for the purposes they ought properly to embody. It is obviously the case that humans will differ over the values they attach to such institutions. Because they differ—the 1992 election and its concern with family values is evidence enough of the passions these issues can arouse—it is always tempting to seek naturalistic grounding for one side of the argument or the other. But the unresolvability of value conflicts is not necessarily an argument for avoiding them. We can study nature with the tools of natural science because the things we study do not themselves live for a purpose. When we study organisms that do, we must develop a science that considers moral values one of its fundamental imperatives.

Conclusion

Whatever the differences between natural and social ecologies, we have to be impressed by the fact that both are threatened. In particular, the social institutions of civil society—cities, families, associations—have been human inventions for so long now that they appear to us as "natural," in the sense that life without them is as unimaginable as life without forests and oceans. Perhaps this is what Nathan Glazer means when he suggests that one fundamental task we face is "strengthening the natural social network."[29] Human beings are as thoroughly linked into social networks as trees and birds are linked into an ecological wonderland.

The question is not whether social ecologies exist nor whether they should be protected. They do and they must. The more crucial question is whether we can recognize what is distinct about social ecologies and, in the course of such recognition, whether we can develop policies and understandings appropriate to the human beings who constitute them. In the past half century Western industrial societies have been prey to a significant amount of abstract theorizing about public policy. The welfare state—or, in America, New Deal—programs were an experiment based on often optimistic assumptions about human nature. Allow people the room to be altruistic, and they will respond. A political atmosphere characterized by tax revolts and spending limitations now questions those assumptions. The best plans of the planners no longer seem to produce the good society they promised.

In reaction to the welfare state, laissez-faire and social Darwinist programs attracted support in the 1980s. These, too, were rooted in a theory of human nature, only this time the theory stressed how people would always pursue their self-interest. Moreover, such theories were as abstract and hypothetical as the assumptions that guided the welfare state. They were also based on the beliefs of planners and state officials who insisted that if more competition were introduced, better results would follow. Yet after more than a decade of such experiments, conservative notions about how the good society can be brought into being no longer have much acceptance either.

Perhaps the time has come to think about designing programs for people as they really are, not as our theories say they must be. Such programs would stress that it is not what the planners do that ultimately matters, but what people themselves do. We have come to realize that such human talents as character and competence are attached to the people whom policies govern, not to the policies that govern them. We will, in the next ideological and policy cycle, be developing programs that ask more of people in return for society doing more for them. If this is so, we need to know more about people: how they respond to alternatives; what beliefs motivate their actions; when they are selfish and when they are altruistic (for surely most people are both); and how they understand the contract they have as individuals with society at large. We will not learn what we need to know about people by developing models of society based on analogies with ants or birds. We will learn what we need to know about people when we recognize two things: First, because they live together with others, there is a social ecology from which they can never be apart; but, second, because they are individuals with minds of their own, that ecology can only be understood—and guided—when it is appreciated on its own terms.

Notes

1. Peter Singer, a leading animal rights theorist, even says that "no doubt there are some people of whom this is true." Peter Singer, *Animal Liberation: A New Ethics for Our Treatment of Animals* (New York: Avon Books, 1975), 234.

2. For an analysis of the overlaps between biology and social theory, see Howard L. Kaye, *The Social Meaning of Modern Biology: From Social Darwinism to Sociobiology* (New Haven, CT: Yale University Press, 1986).

3. The classic work remains Richard Hofstader, *Social Darwinism in American Thought, 1860–1915* (Philadelphia: University of Pennsylvania Press, 1945).

4. See George Gilder, *Men and Marriage* (London: Pelican, 1986) and Stephen Goldberg, *The Inevitability of Patriarchy* (New York: Norton, 1973).

5. Albert O. Hirschman's recent book on conservative rhetoric, *The Rhetoric of Reaction: Perversity, Futility, Jeopardy* (Cambridge, MA: Belknap Press of Harvard University Press, 1991), barely mentions analogies with nature. A recent partial exception is Charles Murray and Richard Herrnstein, *The Bell Curve* (New York: Free Press, 1994).

6. See Greta Jones, *Social Darwinism and English Thought: The Interaction Between Biological and Social Theory* (Sussex: Harvester Press, 1980). On birth control, see Ellen Chesler, *Woman of Valor: Margaret Sanger and the Birth Control Movement in America* (New York: Simon and Schuster, 1992), 216.

7. Carl N. Degler, *In Search of Human Nature: The Decline and Revival of Darwinism in American Social Thought* (New York: Oxford University Press, 1991). See also, Robert Wright, *The Moral Animal: Evolutionary Psychology and Everyday Life* (New York: Pantheon, 1994).

8. This is the theme in Alan Wolfe, *The Human Difference: Animals,*

Computers, and the Necessity of Social Science (Berkeley and Los Angeles: University of California Press, 1993). A few paragraphs in this chapter have been borrowed from the book.

9. For a stimulating intellectual history of ecology, see Donald Worster, *Nature's Economy: The Roots of Ecology* (San Francisco: Sierra Club Books, 1977).

10. James Coleman and Thomas Hoffer, *Public and Private High Schools: The Impact of Community* (New York: Basic Books, 1965).

11. Jane Roland Martin, *The School Home: Rethinking Schools for Changing Families* (Cambridge, MA: Harvard University Press, 1992).

12. David Guterson, *Family Matters: Why Homeschooling Makes Sense* (New York: Harcourt Brace Jovanovich, 1992).

13. On this point see Derek L. Phillips, *Toward a Just Social Order* (Princeton, NJ: Princeton University Press, 1986).

14. One who does so effectively is Claude Fischer, *To Dwell Among Friends* (Chicago: University of Chicago Press, 1982).

15. The pressures placed on the contemporary family, and its declining ability to respond to them, are the themes of David Popenoe, *Disturbing the Nest: Family Change and Decline in Modern Societies* (New York: Aldine de Gruyter, 1988), and Sylvia Ann Hewlett, *When the Bough Breaks: The Cost of Neglecting Our Children* (New York: Basic Books, 1991).

16. For a recent argument along these lines, see Arlene Skolnick, *Embattled Paradise: The American Family in an Age of Uncertainty* (New York: Basic Books, 1991), 101–24.

17. Hillel Levine and Lawrence Harmon, *The Death of an American Jewish Community: A Tragedy of Good Intentions* (New York: Free Press, 1992).

18. This is the theme of James Lovelock, *Gaia: A New Look at Life on Earth* (New York: Oxford, 1979).

19. Hannah Arendt, *Between Past and Future: Eight Exercises in Political Thought*, 2d ed. (New York: Viking Books, 1968), 211.

20. R. L. Trivers, "The Evolution of Reciprocal Altruism," *Quarterly Review of Biology* 46 (March 1991): 35–57.

21. The case for a unified science that would use the principles of information theory to reach conclusions about a wide variety of different kinds of organisms is advanced in Herbert Simon, *Sciences of the Artificial* (Cambridge, MA: MIT Press, 1969).

22. Dawkins emphasizes the importance of cultural change driven by what he calls "memes," which, over time, become more important than genes. See Richard Dawkins, *The Selfish Gene* (New York: Oxford Univer-

sity Press, 1976). Lumsden and Wilson develop a theory of mind to account for gene-culture coevolution in Charles J. Lumsden and Edward O. Wilson, *Genes, Mind, and Culture: The Coevolutionary Process* (Cambridge, MA: Harvard University Press, 1981).

23. N. Blurton Jones and Melvin J. Konner, "!Kung Knowledge of Animal Behavior," in *Kalahari Hunter Gatherers*, ed. R. B. Lee and I. DeVore (Cambridge, MA: Harvard University Press, 1976), 347; and cited in Richard A. Shweder, *Thinking Through Cultures: Expeditions in Cultural Psychology* (Cambridge, MA: Harvard University Press, 1991), 311.

24. Edward Shils, *Tradition* (Chicago: University of Chicago Press, 1981).

25. Alison M. Jagger, *Feminist Politics and Human Nature* (Totowa, NJ: Rowman and Allanheld, 1983), 106.

26. Stephen Mintz and Susan Kellogg, *Domestic Revolutions: A Social History of American Family Life* (New York: Free Press, 1988), 243.

27. Talcott Parsons, "The American Family: Its Relation to Personality and to the Social Structure," in Talcott Parsons and Robert F. Bales, *Family, Socialization and Interaction* (New York: Free Press, 1955), 3–33; and William J. Goode, *World Revolution and Family Patterns* (New York: Free Press, 1963).

28. The overlaps and differences between feminism and postmodernism are explored in Linda Nicholson, ed., *Feminism/Postmodernism* (New York: Routledge, 1990).

29. Nathan Glazer, *The Limits of Social Policy* (Cambridge, MA: Harvard University Press, 1988), 112.

CHAPTER 8

Reinstitutionalizing Virtue in Civil Society

William M. Sullivan

The Historical Irony of the Topic

To speak today in the United States of the need to recover the meaning of civic virtue and to nurture its sources may seem odd or quaint to many. These are themes which much contemporary opinion thinks obsolete. Yet, in the longer historical passage it is this situation which is the real irony. The world-transforming career of the modern West was in major part launched by a historically unprecedented explosion of virtue. Modern virtue has been deeply ambiguous, inculcating self-transcendence for very different reasons, sometimes heroic and violent, at other times patient and constructive.

The modern career of civic virtue in particular began in the Christian revival of the 16th and 17th centuries, a movement deeply interrelated with the civic upsurge which produced the new nation-states of the same era. Behind the modern West's climb to planetary dominance lay not only extraordinary military ferocity but a novel ascetic capacity to discipline individual energies for regular work and social cooperation. Those capacities were first sought because they were thought to be necessary to restore humanity to its proper stature, for religious, philosophical, or even political reasons. The result was the mobilization of enormous human energies, for both good and ill. Even when unrecognized, virtue remains a key ingredient in the attitudes we now call modern, and nowhere has this been more true than in the first "new nation," the United States.

The Protestant Reformation brought to European Christendom heightened demands for an ascetic discipline previously known only to the cloister. This new ascesis, however, was applied to everyday life, to worldly vocation and the duties of the subject, if not the citizen. It transformed the spirit of the institutional order, from the family and education to economic and political life. While the new spirit enhanced the freedom of individuals to enter contracts, it also gave to these something of the moral weight of the Biblical covenant which stood at the center of the Reformed religion. At the center of the new Protestant moral order lay a notion of religious virtue as conversion. Cooperation with grace was manifest in the individual's development of a conviction of vocation, a calling to a specific sphere of worldly activity which could harmonize all aspects of one's life to serve the restoration of the Kingdom of God.

The resulting sense of spiritual purpose and moral energy found its echoes throughout contemporary Europe, so that the new concern with virtue came to speak in Catholic and humanist accents as well. The builders of the new states of Europe, both Catholic and Protestant, took over from the humanist scholars of the Renaissance the exalted and newly attractive examples of the Greek and Roman classics. There they found not only a celebration of citizenship and service to the commonweal but what they saw as potential programs for transforming their own subjects into new kinds of men and women, citizens in a sense not seen for over a millennium. The idea of civic virtue stood at the core of the emerging political order of early modern Europe. Civic humanism also taught a conversion, arguing that individual fulfillment—and public happiness—would spring from the pursuit of excellence, especially through the integrity of one's contribution to the common good, and this above all in offices of service to the civic body.

As European societies began to develop into recognizably modern states, led by the Netherlands, Britain, and France, the Christian and classical sources of virtue vied and struggled, but in practice they not infrequently reinforced each other. While the question of the compatibility between the Biblical and the classical traditions was opened sharply once again by the Reformation, the idea of their synthesis, a continuing legacy of medieval Christendom, found expression in the tradition of natural law. This too would develop in new ways under the impetus of the times. In English North America, especially in the Calvinist diaspora of New England, these currents coalesced powerfully in the religious and civic culture of the Puritans. Even today the vestigial moral images of that lost New England continue to haunt the American imagination as the "city upon a hill."

The American republican founding of the late 18th century drew upon the religious as well as secular forms of virtue to create a modern state based upon individual liberty of conscience and contract. Public virtue was thought by the nation's founders to depend in top-down fashion upon stimulus from a virtuous leadership class. George Washington was fondly and sincerely celebrated as a new Cincinnatus. As Alexis de Tocqueville noted, the American republican order found its most powerful stay in religious belief and practice. By contrast, the French revolutionaries, operating in the atomized society of the Old Regime, sought less successfully to mold a divided people into a modern Sparta. In both cases, however, the foundation of a truly modern society was assumed to be an intensified civic virtue. Without this, the Enlightenment followed the ancients in believing; civil liberty could not long survive the downward pull toward anarchy and tyranny.

The 18th-century Enlightenment gave to these long-term developments a compelling, novel, and in certain ways misleading interpretation. This interpretation was to become familiar as philosophic liberalism. Its most novel and attractive idea was the notion that human beings were by nature endowed with certain rights, existing within a realm of private property, free contract, and opinion that was independent of the control of ecclesiastical or state authority. This was the notion of civil society as set forth by John Locke. For Locke, this natural order of civil society was emphatically part of a larger Christian moral cosmos that shared many features with medieval natural law. But the idea of civil society, as both stimulus and response to a changing society, was soon developed in a different direction. The British thinkers David Hume and Adam Smith, along with Montesquieu in France, developed the thesis that commerce civilizes. Identifying the evident strength of the United Kingdom with its promotion of commerce, these thinkers emphasized the freedom of the individual within the bonds of a civil society linked by freedom of contract. Freedom came to be separated in theory from civic virtue.

This separation remains one of the roots of modern philosophic liberalism, in the form of both the social contract theory of government and the utilitarian theory familiar in modern economics and political science. The implications of the liberal idea have, of course, been many and have not formed a single, coherent doctrine. Liberal ideas have contributed greatly to making modern life more humane. But philosophic liberalism has also given rise to a confusion which worked to eclipse the notion of virtue, civic as well as religious, which has had important effects upon the development of modern societies everywhere.

The seductive idea at the heart of the liberal project has been the notion that increased individual freedom—and its institutional premise, the expansion of free exchange relations in a market society—automatically brings about general social betterment. It is today still a source of unending debate within Western nations as to whether this thesis of "commercial humanism," that the progress of commerce means both the growth of opulence and the refinement of manners, should guide social policy. But it has been as a doctrine for export, in the wake of Western global dominance during the past century, that classic liberalism has revealed its insufficiency.

Today, the enormous difficulty of quickly "transplanting" the liberal institutional order to societies which did not share the formative Western experience has become evident once again. This is especially clear in the nations newly liberated from Soviet tyranny. There the banner of "civil society" has been raised, as in Western Europe a century and a half ago, in the hope of thus rapidly reinventing nations so as to enjoy a Western form of life. Today, as then in Germany and Middle Europe, the "transition" has suddenly been revealed as far more arduous and lengthy than anyone would wish. And again, nationalism has emerged as a kind of short cut to mobilizing societal energies, and not always beneficently.

What liberal ideologues typically overlook is that Western liberalism was made possible by the portentous—and often violent—development of new habits of virtue, especially collective self-discipline and cooperation, within the most dynamic nations of the West. This was both the hidden source of the awesome power of those nations, often enough vented outward on less-organized others, and also the social gyroscope that gave the atoms at play throughout civil society the stability to sustain cooperation.

As historian Theodore Von Laue has described the point, "The key idea of liberalism was freedom naively abstracted from its underpinnings and universalized. . . . Paradoxically, the peoples most highly disciplined individually and collectively for social cooperation considered themselves the freest, unaware of the restraints bred into their freedoms and critical of all forms of external compulsion observed in less fortunate countries, which they incited to compete with them."[1] The historical irony of today's rediscovery of civic virtue is a reminder of the perils of accidental success. The most important, if unexpected, offspring of Western civic virtue, philosophic liberalism, has obscured the social and moral roots of its own viability. Today, it is the increasingly evident failure of the simplistic liberal creed to sustain the conditions of its own possibility within the societies that gave it birth that has given rise to a renewed search for the sources of the social viability of free institutions. That search has brought us to rediscover civic virtue. The discovery of a "need for virtue" is, however, a long way from either fully understanding or effectively addressing the issue.

The Scope of the Contemporary Challenge

Because of their historically unique dynamism, modern societies have a strongly intentional quality. What in other civilizations could most often be entrusted to ancestral custom, modernity had to convert into articulated values and purposes. The sources of this dynamism are still debated. Besides the cultural revitalization sparked by the development of ecclesiastical and political communities of cooperative virtue, however, it is clear that the other central force has been the unprecedented expansion of instrumental and technical rationality. This process was described by Max

Weber as "rationalization." At the heart of Western modernity Weber discerned the rapid growth of calculative, instrumental thinking applied to human affairs to organize social relationships for power and effectiveness. These processes seemed to Weber increasingly self-generating, cut free from the traditional constraints of custom and from the religious morality which had helped set them in motion.

As Weber saw it, rationalization has meant the relentless tendency to organize activity in pursuit of ever more efficient means, thereby pushing questions of ends to the margins of cultural life even as it tied modern societies ever more closely into a functional unity. But Weber was not alone in seeing the two-sided quality of these modern energies, nor was he unique in pointing out that these tendencies had propelled humanity into a situation without historical precedent. The economist Joseph Schumpeter, for example, provided a view of the capitalist market economy as such a world-changing, ambivalent force, a picture strongly at odds with the 18th century's notion of benign commerce. As Schumpeter described it, the market is enormously creative of new wealth, technologies, and forms of social organization. Yet this growth comes at a high human cost: new developments always mean the obsolescence of traditional capacities and the destruction of established ways of life. This process of "creative destruction" does, as the 18th century had hoped, vastly improve material life as it binds regions, nations, and peoples ever more completely into patterns of global interdependence. But it is a conflict-filled, unequal interdependence in which some suffer while others prosper as the cycles of creative destruction play relentlessly on.

Another 20th-century thinker, Graham Wallas, caught the two-sided character of the modern challenge in his notion of the "Great Society." By this Wallas meant the "invisible environment" formed by communication and commerce which linked the globe ever more tightly but was evolving far faster than human abilities to grasp much less to manage it. As Wallas saw things early in the present century, the growth of technology and economic interdependence posed a severe challenge to humanity's survival even as it engendered vast new powers for raising the quality of life. The challenge of the Great Society could only be met by a great enlargement of the intellectual grasp of the new environment, complemented by the growth of a moral imagination able to bend those anarchic forces into the service of human society.

In other words, the challenge of modernity, whether seen as rationalization, creative destruction, or the emergence of the Great Society, poses inescapably the nurture of civic virtue as the central practical problem facing contemporary societies. Theodore Von Laue has described this challenge as the need for a citizenship, which can include the local but extend as far as the global level. All genuine citizenship, according to Von Laue, illustrates the "paradox of socialization," the willingness to submit to a collective self-discipline "for the sake of enlarged self-affirmation."

To be effective, Von Laue argues, this social discipline must be "anchored in the core of our psyche." It presumes the learning of self-cultivation, "a challenge traditionally faced most effectively in religious practices that offer their own rewards." Virtue, understood this way, does not entail submission to unjust social orders nor the suppression of artistic freedom of expression. Rather, the cultural skills embodied in self-transcending virtue "promote a liberating submission to the necessities of peaceful cooperation, the guaranty of civilized life and its creative potential." So, "fortunate are those societies which can rely on the routine (and nonpolitical) practice of these spiritual skills."[2] Fortunate, too, are those individuals who learn to appreciate and master these capacities.

A Theory of Civic Virtue: The Public Sphere

Von Laue's insistence upon the primacy of virtue as spiritual discipline should not be misinterpreted as a purely inner, personal transformation, though of course it is that as well. Von Laue speaks of the need for political and cultural leadership that is willing and able to engage in "consensus-building interaction" toward developing the needed new habits of mind.[3] The allusion is to the notion of the public sphere, an interpretation of civil society more political in the classical sense than economic. The public sphere as conceived by thinkers such as Kant, Mill, Tocqueville, Dewey, and most recently, Jürgen Habermas, refers to the legally-secured sphere in which ideas and opinions circulate freely and in which individuals can develop through voluntary, non-coercive participation in purposes beyond the economic and private. The public sphere is conceived as the conscience and enlightener of the state, as the rightful place of religious life after ecclesiastical disestablishment, and the forum for debate and the formation of public purposes and consensus. It is the natural source of enlightened civic virtue.

The viability of a democratic society is directly tied to the health of its public sphere. An effective public sphere, like civic virtue itself, depends upon a society's particular kind of institutional order. No habits of mind and heart can be cultivated unless the institutions of a society support and "teach" these capacities. Good institutions are the crucial matrix of any effective virtues, while poor or badly functioning institutions are the source of prevalent vice. In its core sense an institution is a sanctioned set of social practices which actualize certain human capacities in a reasonably stable way. An institution provides individuals with significant challenges, normative guidance in the pursuit of certain purposes, and recognition of themselves as responsible agents.[4] Thus, institutions are a name for the basic forms of life. The general character of people in any society will bear the marks of the moral pedagogy fostered by that society's institutional order, the round of life it makes available and, to varying degrees, obligatory.

Much of this argument about the challenges and demands of modernity was anticipated in remarkably prescient form by G. W. F. Hegel in the early 19th century. Hegel anticipated Weber, Schumpeter, and Wallas in his description of civil society as a "system of needs."[5] In his conception of "ethical life," Hegel sketched a theory of a public sphere which could redeem the promise of modernity through an enlarged and reflective civic virtue based in vital institutions. Both analyses provide useful correctives to much of the partial and confused theorizing characteristic of this era of historical discontinuity. In this sense, Hegel's theory of modernity can provide a heuristic to guide the recovery of a theory of civic virtue, as it served in different ways for significant thinkers over the past century, notably T. H. Green, Benedetto Croce, Josiah Royce, and John Dewey.[6]

Hegel recognized the positive dynamism of the modern commercial economy. It conferred unprecedented freedom upon individuals to realize their unique abilities, to achieve a unique identity, and to be recognized as such. This growth of "abstract right" represents a historical advance, a further unfolding of human capacities, a stimulation of personal agency and individual responsibility. This positive aspect of civil society, however, remains unstably institutionalized. Individual identity, interpreted by utilitarian individualism, remains precarious because it is competitively achieved. Further, the relations among individuals remain external; within a competitive economy each can be for the other primarily a means to personal ends because there is no common aim at shared goods, little sense of living a larger life. Hegel's description of the aggregate effects of market relations anticipated Marx and Schumpeter's analyses. The negative effects are social pathologies, class and international conflict.

In short, civil society as constituted by free contract alone, is not and cannot be a complete or humanly satisfying realm. First of all, it cannot be self-sustaining. Civil society depends upon the noncompetitive and noncontractual matrix of family life for its members. In its full expansion, civil society must be stabilized and in a real sense integrated into a larger context, which Hegel calls "ethical life." As the family, ethical life is the natural basis of the partial yet dynamic realm of abstract right, while as the constitution of the state that encompasses the family as well as civil society, this larger life provides the redemption and completion of individual striving. Civil society provides the conditions of differentiation and individuation. But these processes, left to themselves, are finally self-destructive unless they receive a deeper meaning by being reintegrated into ethical life. The institutional vehicles of this larger life Hegel saw as three: the family, the state, and vocational associations. They remind the individual of the possibility of a wider identity and a deeper significance while they provide practical training in civic virtue.

Hegel dramatically linked the origins of the family to those of the state in the pattern of settled, agricultural life. He noted that "the real beginning" of states is rightly linked to the "introduction of agriculture along with marriage," because agriculture brings with it "the formation of the land" and also the "tranquility of private rights and the assured satisfaction of needs." In parallel with these developments, sexual love becomes concretized in marriage, while needs expand "into care for a family, and personal possessions into family goods. Security, consolidation, lasting satisfaction of needs . . . the most obvious recommendations of both marriage and agriculture—are nothing but forms of universality, modes in which rationality, the final end and aim, asserts itself in these spheres."[7] In both family and state, though at different levels of social complexity and ethical consciousness, individuals have the experience of individual agency through cultivation of a common life in which each can find significance and self-transcendence. The common theme, which ties them both to their origins in agricultural life, is the idea of settled cultivation: of land, relationships, and character.

The experience of the goods of settled cultivation in the ethical life of the family was for Hegel the indispensable basis for a secure individual identity amid the adventures and storms of civil society. Participation in vocational associations, Hegel's version of the "mediating institutions" of the public sphere, was to be the other "root" of ethical life planted in civil society. In its end as in its beginning, individual existence must finally reach beyond the adolescent virtues of autonomy and self-reliance to find an enduring significance and satisfaction. For Hegel, these goods could only be secured by the effort to transcend narrow self-concern to live within the larger, mediated ethical life brought to focus in the state. All this, of course, becomes highly problematical as the Great Society sweeps away the settled conditions of agricultural life, intensifies the rhythms of creative destruction, and through economic necessity and the universalizing of the possibilities of active selfhood, propels women as well as men to seek recognition in the system of needs that is civil society.

One need not indulge in the currently fashionable nostalgia for the working family farm to grasp the applicability of the Hegelian argument. Under modern conditions, the family, the forms of recognition and opportunities for expression made possible by civil society, and the possibilities for community and shared meaning identified with the state and the public sphere are all in dynamic movement. The hope of the good life, the expansion of democratic possibilities mediated by an enlarged sense of mutual responsibility, rests upon our collective ability to grasp the larger purposes that can structure the changing elements into meaningful social patterns.

What Hegel actually urged for his time was to continue the notion of politics set forth by Plato in the Laws. There, whatever one may think of the specific arrangements, Plato argued that the key political task is to direct the development of the common form of life so as to realize the fullest development of human capacities consistent with the constraints of time and place. This meant a focus upon laws understood as the scripts of institutional choreography, with the pedagogic effects of institutional life foremost in mind. In Plato's conception, as in Hegel's, ethics is finally the internalizing of the capacity to contribute responsibly to the realization of institutional purposes in ways appropriate to one's concrete situation. In Plato, this meant the fixed forms of a rigid and hierarchical division of labor in which only the few are able to judge and guide. For Hegel, religious and social evolution had opened the way to a much more fluid division of labor and a far more egalitarian sense of community in which the collective choreography provides the themes on which individuals are invited to develop variations. The basic aim, however, remains the same: the good life of human fulfillment lies in the settled cultivation of a coherent ethical life, only the task is made more complex, if not more rewarding, by modernity's opening of new possibilities for the enrichment and broadening of that life.

Imagining a New Public Philosophy: The Virtue of Settlement

To tie the hopes for a modern civic virtue and a revitalized public sphere to the themes of settled cultivation and an integrated collective form of life might seem so unlikely as to appear utopian, if not absurd. Certainly, this has been the reigning opinion among both orthodox liberals and Marxists until quite recently. Today, however, this consensus seems to be changing, as the loss of the cold war enemy makes the need for continual ideological mobilization

less obvious everywhere. As we collectively step back from Armageddon, the Weberian vision of modernity in its several forms and
successors—the iron cage of instrumental reason, the world domi-
nation of technology, the disciplinary practices of a carceral society,
or the (no longer so metaphorical) warfare of unmediated value
pluralism—provides a terrifyingly real anticipation of a disinte-
grated modernity. In response to these dystopian possibilities, the
themes of integration and meaningful interconnection have once
more appeared on the cultural agenda. With this shift in agenda,
civic virtue in a revived public sphere may be finding its voice and
a constituency.

Look at just two examples. In the West, and increasingly elsewhere, the awareness that the biosphere must be thought of as a
whole, as an organic entity in which processes are also functions
sustaining a complex entity, has begun to modify the mechanistic,
reductionistic thinking dominant for three centuries. In the social
sciences as well as popular culture, metaphors of social and cultural
ecology have begun to provide alternative points of view to the
more familiar ruling images of engineering and strategic interaction. In the former Eastern Bloc, something similar is afoot; there,
such ideas reach highly developed expression in the works of states-
man-intellectuals such as Adam Michnick and Vaclav Havel.

There the ideas of cultivation and settlement are finding a new
resonance in the struggle to rebuild public spheres devastated by
totalitarian oppression. Not only the family but also the relations
of state to civil society are being rethought. Against the doctrinaire
free-market liberals, who would reduce the public sphere to the
marketplace, Havel has recently defended the essential role of the
state as a moral agency. "If we wish," writes Havel, "to create
a good and humane society, capable of making a contribution to
humanity's 'coming to its senses,' we must create a good and humane state." Such a state, he continues, will necessarily have a
strong ethical dimension, so that it will "no longer suppress, humil-
iate, and deny the free human being, but will serve all the dimensions of that being."[8]

What form might these tendencies be taking in the more fortunate, though still problematic, conditions of the United States?
Here the appearance of new concerns for the viability of the family

is a generally positive sign and one that should be linked to the spreading concern about the fraying of all kinds of social bonds. The way toward resolving these needs is surely through the revitalizing of civic concern and the restructuring of our institutional arrangements to facilitate such a stronger civic pedagogy. In a democratic society, however, all these developments will be to some extent contentious. Persuasion toward developing the kind of social movement and political will necessary to work in this direction will require a convincing and coherent vision of not only how but why such institutional reconstruction should be undertaken. Such a vision will be needed to give the themes of cultivation and settlement a new cogency and importance.

Intentional efforts to support the cultivation of civic virtue in family life, education, religion, but also the world of work, will require important reshaping of the dominant institutional order. In a democratic society, a public philosophy is a key part of such a massive process. A public philosophy interprets institutions and projects by giving an articulation of their purposes and the values they aim to sustain.[9] By making purposes and ends explicit, a public philosophy does not just idealize or celebrate those purposes. It also generates discussion and debate about them. In this way, public philosophies serve to frame social discourse, creating common ground for discussion and places where consensus can be developed. What, then, might a public philosophy of cultivation and settlement look like? Are there examples on hand?

There are a number of such possibilities, which are discussed at length in *The Good Society*. Here, however, it seems helpful to call attention to one, the developing concern with settlement and place itself as a focus of moral concern. This is a theme that may represent an inchoate public philosophy that resonates with both current ecological and social concerns. Decades ago, Lewis Mumford, one of the important American public intellectuals of mid-century, wrote about the contrast in American, and in all modern cultures, between the urge toward "exploitation" of resources, human and natural, and the imperative of "cultivation." Mumford pointed out that much of American development had been bought at considerable price in natural devastation and cultural impoverishment. Once the possibilities of profitable exploitation had been exhausted, the American pioneer moved on, leaving "rack and ruin" behind. But Mumford insisted that no civilization can exist on this "unstable and nomadic basis: it requires a settled life, based on the possibility of continuously cultivating the environment, replacing in one form what one takes away in another."[10]

If we were to apply this insight to the problems of the collapsing social fabric of our cities—and our suburban or exurban "edge cities"—what would immediately catch the eye is the need to "replace in one form what one takes away in another." Thus, if family members must work more outside the home, ways must be found to ensure time together and adequate provision to support family practices such as common meals, recreation, and the like. The same might be argued for education: schools can become anchors and generators of community bonds in places where they are weak, if administrators, staff, and parents come to understand their common dependence upon one another.

Mumford's themes have recently been given new and powerful expression in a work by Tony Hiss, *The Experience of Place*. Hiss draws upon one of Mumford's co-workers of the 1930s, regional planner Benton MacKaye, creator of the Appalachian Trail. MacKaye believed that a major source of modern moral disorientation has been the loss of spatial connectedness with the larger environment. Establishing landscape connectedness, MacKaye thought, could help "halt the headlong, panicked flight from blight; and, at the same time, reinvolve all modern Americans in patterns of kinship and partnership and neighborly and intellectual connections."[11] Building on MacKaye's notion that reestablishing people's physical maps is a key toward changing their mental maps, Hiss describes new developments around land-use planning going on under the impetus of state governments in New England.

What is emerging there, Hiss believes, is a "new approach to community development" which is also the creation of a new politics of responsible interdependence. As a planning professional involved in these projects commented, this new approach "asks people to think about the long-term needs of a place and of all its residents. We're in the process of building local institutions that take over the job of looking after public value on a volunteer basis, and we're learning how to reinvest in areas so that they'll be more valuable to the next generation than they are to ours." This planner concluded with the observation: "I think we can now show that stewardship springs from connectedness—it gives people back a sense of thinking responsibly on behalf of the whole community."[12]

By bringing together economic development, social justice, and concern for the natural environment, the new, participatory approach to planning that Hiss describes, like some current experiments in urban revitalization, suggests that the problem of creative destruction may be manageable in well-organized polities that have been able and willing to assist the growth of strong cities and regions. This theme converges with the claims advanced by a number of economists and social theorists that in the new global economy even economic success depends upon constructing a "healthy civic infrastructure and shared goals."[13] This amounts to a pragmatic, economic argument for the indispensability of a strong public sphere. Civic virtue, that is, can be shown to pay. Yet, it only does so, as Hiss enables us to see, because people have become persuaded that the cultivation of relationships and places are worthy ends in themselves.

While these trends and arguments do not amount to a full-blown public philosophy, nor even to a full-scale social movement, they are surely more than mere straws in the wind.[14] Here, perhaps, is one hopeful source for the revival and reinstitutionalization of an enlightened civic virtue.

Notes

1. Theodore H. Von Laue, *The World Revolution of Westernization: The Twentieth Century in Global Perspective* (New York: Oxford University Press, 1987), 37, 49.

2. Ibid., 363.

3. Ibid., 354.

4. This concept of institution follows that developed in Robert N. Bellah, Richard Madsen, William M. Sullivan, Ann Swidler, and Steven M. Tipton, *The Good Society* (New York: Alfred Knopf, 1991), 4–12 and passim.

5. This and the following discussion of Hegel depends upon *Hegel's*

Philosophy of Right, trans. T. M. Knox (New York: Oxford University Press, 1952). For civil society as the system of needs, see part III.II.a.

6. I am indebted to a variety of philosophers and political theorists who have interpreted Hegel in this way, especially to Charles Taylor's *Hegel* (Cambridge and London: Cambridge University Press, 1975).

7. *Hegel's Philosophy of Right*, III.II.a (para.203).

8. Vaclav Havel, *Summer Meditations*, trans. Paul Wilson (New York: Vintage, 1993), 121.

9. The use of public philosophy here draws upon earlier work. See William M. Sullivan, *Reconstructing Public Philosophy* (Berkeley and Los Angeles: University of California Press, 1982), esp. 9–10.

10. David L. Miller, ed., *The Lewis Mumford Reader* (New York: Pantheon Books, 1986), 213.

11. Tony Hiss, *The Experience of Place: A Completely New Way of Looking At and Dealing With Our Radically Changing Cities and Countryside* (New York: Alfred Knopf, 1990), 189.

12. Ibid., 207–8.

13. See Wallace Katz, "Response: Letting Go of Liberalism," *Tikkun* (September/October, 1992): 73.

14. The new resonance of journals such as *The Responsive Community* strongly suggests this. See Amitai Etzioni, "A Communitarian Campaign," *The Responsive Community* 2, no. 4 (Fall 1992).

CHAPTER 9

The Difference of Virtue and the Difference It Makes: Courage Exemplified

Stanley Hauerwas

Why All Virtue Theories Are Not Created Equal

The current enthusiasm for a recovery of an ethic of virtue is often thought to be a "good thing" for religious communities in the United States. For the emphasis on virtue seems to suggest that churches, which have become increasingly irrelevant to the public issues before our polity, can now contribute to that polity by being the kind of communities that can produce people of virtue. I will argue, however, that those who wish to return the church to public prominence through making us serve the public weal by being communities of virtue are making a decisive mistake.

By so arguing, I certainly do not mean to deny that I think issues concerning virtue are not important for political practice and/or theory. Indeed, I have long argued against the predominant forms of moral theory produced by liberal society exactly because they have, by necessity, been based on a law-like paradigm that ignores the significance of the virtues. In short, it has been the project of liberal political and ethical theory to create societies that could be just without people that constitute those societies being just. Thus the attempt to create social institutions and/or discover moral principles that would insure cooperation between people who share no common goods or virtues. The examples of this project are legion but perhaps it is nowhere better exemplified than in John Rawls's *A Theory of Justice*, whose elegance of argument is undeniable. Of course Rawls does not exclude considerations of virtue, but he assumes, like most modern political and ethical theorists, that any account of virtue is secondary to principles and institutions that are more determinative than virtue itself.

So it would seem that I should take heart in the rediscovery of the importance of virtue by "communitarians" and those concerned with a recovery of the republican tradition in America. Yet such a celebration of virtue fails to acknowledge the difference between virtue theories and the difference that that makes. Moreover that difference is political, as different polities will produce different accounts of virtue. By focusing on the virtue of courage I hope to show why all accounts of virtue are not created equal.

For example, Jean Bethke Elshtain, in response to the calls for civic virtue made by the authors of *Habits of the Heart*, notes that "the problem with the tradition of civic virtue can be stated succinctly: that virtue is *armed*."[1] That virtue tends to come armed should not be surprising since, as she observes, for the Greeks, war was a natural state of affairs and the basis of society. This presumption was continued by the great civil republicans such as Machiavelli and Rousseau.[2] Thus the first duty of Machiavelli's prince is to be a soldier and create an army of citizens. Note the task is not simply to create an army to protect citizens but to make citizens an army. Napoleon in this respect is but the full realization of Machiavelli, and interestingly enough democratic order is based on the arming of citizens.

Hegel, perhaps, best understood this as he saw, without war, bourgeois life would be a "bog" in which the citizens of the liberal state would lack the means to rise above their own self-interest. For Hegel, without war the state cannot become the embodiment of the universal.

Elshtain, however, argues that Rousseau is the great prophet of armed civic virtue since it is Rousseau who saw most clearly that for modern societies a vision of total civic virtue is required. For the chief process that drew people out of their provincial loyalties and made them conscious of belonging to a wider community—a national community—was military conscription. Thus the "*national* identity that we assume, or yearn for, is historically inseparable from war. The nation-state, including our own, rests on mounds of bodies." In fact, the United States is a society that in particular is constituted by war. For, as Elshtain observes, a nation-state can exist on paper long before it exists in fact. But "a *united* United States is a historical construction that most visibly comes into being as cause and consequence of American involvement in the Great War. Prior to the nationalistic enthusiasm of that era, America was a loosely united federation with strong and regional identities."[3]

Elshtain's observations are particularly important for my argument since I will suggest that the virtue of courage is usually exemplified by soldiers facing death in battle. There are good reasons for this since courage is thought to involve a disposition toward death that pervades many aspects of our life but is paradigmatically displayed by the courage of soldiers. Yet I shall argue that for Christians such an account of courage cannot be normative. In fact, from a Christian point of view such courage may not be courage at all but rather can only be a semblance of courage or even may be demonic.

Why that is the case requires some discussion of what may appear to be "technical" issues in any theory of virtue. For example, questions of the unity of the virtues are involved in order to understand why someone who appears courageous may in fact not be so.[4] Moreover, to understand why Christians have maintained that the virtues of the pagan are but splendid vices, we will need to explore the Christian presumption that charity, in Aquinas's words, is the form of all the virtues. In order to investigate these issues, I will compare Aristotle's account of the virtue of courage to that of Aquinas. I will show what difference it makes for a display of the virtues, insofar as Aquinas thought that martyrdom, a quite different death in a quite different battle, is the exemplary form of courage for Christians.

Aristotle on Courage

Aristotle's account of the virtue of courage occurs in Book III of the *Nicomachean Ethics*. Courage is really the first virtue he treats in detail as he develops his analysis of courage, along with temperance, as part of his account of voluntary and involuntary action. Courage and temperance are virtues necessary to the right formation of our desires which enable us to act in such a way that these actions in turn make it possible to form the habits necessary for us to be virtuous. We therefore see the circular nature of Aristotle's account of the virtues, since one can only become virtuous just to the extent that one's actions are displayed in the manner that a virtuous person would do them.[5]

For Aristotle, as well as Aquinas, any account of the virtues requires that virtues be exemplified in concrete lives. We become just by copying the deeds of just people, but "copy" is not some mechanical imitation, though that may not be a bad place to start, but rather it involves having the same feelings, emotions, and desires that the virtuous person has when she acts. Aristotle observes that it is a hard task to be good:

> [F]or instance, not everyone can find the middle of a circle, but only a man who has the proper knowledge. Similarly, anyone can get angry—that is easy—or can give away money or spend it; but to do all this to the right person, to the right extent, at the right time, for the right reason, and in the right way is no longer something easy that anyone can do. It is for this reason that good conduct is rare, praiseworthy, and noble.[6]

The virtues, for Aristotle, involve not only disposition for appropriate action, but also an "attitude" that embodies the appropriate emotions and desires. Thus we must be trained in order to become virtuous, as we become what we are only through the gradual buildup of the appropriate characteristics. Aristotle observes that "we control only the beginning of our characteristics: the particular steps in their development are imperceptible, just as they are in the spread of disease; yet since the power to behave or not to behave in a given way was ours in the first place, our characteristics are voluntary."[7]

Courage is crucial to all the virtues becoming "voluntary" for Aristotle because courage is the mean between fear and confidence. Aristotle thought courage and temperance particularly important to acquiring any virtue since courage and temperance are the virtues that form what he assumed were our most basic desires—fear and pleasure. The purpose of the virtues for Aristotle is not to repress such desires but to form our desires to fear rightly. As we shall see a person without fear—the reckless—cannot be a person of courage exactly because they lack fear. A "reckless" person may do what a courageous person does but that person is not courageous as he or she lacks the proper "feeling."[8]

The importance of this cannot be overlooked if we are to understand why it is so important for Aristotle to be able to distinguish true courage from its counterfeit. For some may well appear to be courageous exactly because they no longer are afraid of death. He observes:

> [I]t is true that we fear all evils, e.g., disrepute, poverty, disease, friendlessness, death. But it does not seem that a courageous man is concerned with all of these. There are some evils, such as disrepute, which are proper and right for him to fear and wrong not to fear: a man who fears disrepute is decent and has a sense of shame, a man who does not fear it is shameless. Still, some people describe a man who fears no disrepute as courageous in a metaphorical sense, for he resembles a courageous man in that a courageous man, too, is fearless. Perhaps one should not fear poverty or disease or generally any evil that does not spring from vice or is not due to oneself. However, it is not the man who has no fear of these things who is courageous. But we call him so because of his resemblance to the courageous man. For some people who are cowards on the battlefield are generous and face the loss of money cheerfully. On the other hand, a man is not a coward if he fears insult to his wife and children, or if he fears envy or the like; nor is he courageous if he is of good cheer when he is about to be flogged.[9]

Aristotle is thus led to ask what kinds of fears characterize the courageous man. He suggests they must no doubt be those of the greatest moment. Since the most fearful thing is death, then it would seem that courage is the virtue that rightly schools us to face death. But even death does not show the courage of a man in all circumstances.

> For example, death by drowning or by disease does not. What kind
> of death, then, does bring out courage? Doubtless the noblest kind,
> and that is death in battle, for in battle a man is faced by the greatest
> and most noble of dangers. This is corroborated by the honors which
> states as well as monarchs bestow upon courage. Properly speaking,
> therefore, we might define as courageous a man who fearlessly faces
> a noble death and any situations that bring a sudden death. Such
> eventualities are usually brought about by war. But of course a cou-
> rageous man is also fearless at sea and in illness, though not in the
> same way as sailors are. Because of their experience, the sailors are
> optimistic, while the courageous man has given up hope of saving
> his life but finds the thought of such an (inglorious) death revolting.
> Furthermore, circumstances which bring out courage are those in
> which a man can show his prowess or where he can die a noble
> death, neither of which is true of death by drowning or illness.[10]

That the paradigm case of courage for Aristotle is facing death in battle is not surprising since his ethics are but the preface to his politics. All virtues are political virtues exactly because they reflect the common good as well as constitute the content of the common good. The virtues are therefore inescapably conventional as they depend on practices that are generally agreed to be good. To call them conventional is not to call them into question but rather to indicate that any account of the virtues for any community requires the display of behavior that is generally agreed to be good.

For example, in his wonderful book *Mencius and Aquinas: Theories of Virtue and Conceptions of Courage*, Lee Yearley notes that for Mencius propriety is a virtue that seems most foreign to Western accounts of virtue. Propriety covers such activities as solemn religious occasions—funerals, for instance—as well as what we call etiquette. The latter are reasonable and humanly learned conventions we associate with rituals such as saying "excuse me" after a sneeze. Yearley notes that Mencius links these because he assumes they both foster a behavior that manifests distinctly human activities rather than instinctive reactions.

Mencius believes these emotional reactions require conventional rules for their expression; they can find expression only through the ritual forms a society possesses. The rules or forms, in fact, are what allows people to achieve the good found in expressing and cultivating these reactions. For example, I cannot easily, or even adequately, show my respect for a cook, a host, or an elderly person unless social forms exist that allow me to express such attitudes. Furthermore, both I and others must know what those forms are and what they express. I need to know, for instance, that a slight bow and somewhat servile smile express respect not irony or rancor. The attitude of respect toward others, Mencius thinks, must express itself in a disposition to follow the conventional rules of propriety. A person observes these rules as an expression of reverence for people, their roles, and even the social-organism that they embody and help preserve.[11]

While no doubt Yearley is right that Mencius's understanding of propriety has no exact parallel in most accounts of virtue associated with the Greeks and Christians, the essential structure has parallels insofar as accounts of the virtues depend on a close interrelation of the virtue with the forms of its expression. Thus facing death in battle becomes the central paradigm of courage for Aristotle not simply as an example but as the actual expression of what constitutes courage. In other words, without the possibility of war courage would lack the necessary occasion for its expression.

That such is the case is why, as we saw above, virtue theory cannot escape the problem of the semblance of the virtues. For virtue cannot exist without agreed upon forms of expression that make particular virtues possible. But, at the same time, those very forms threaten to undermine virtue itself since the form can be mistaken for the person actually having the virtue. So it is not surprising that Aristotle must work to distinguish genuine courage from that which is only the semblance of courage.

Of course genuine courage is possible only for the person who possesses all the virtues. Only the man of practical wisdom is capable of being courageous in a manner characteristic of a person who is also just, temperate, generous, and magnanimous—which are, of course, only some of the virtues requisite for a person of complete virtue in Aristotle's sense. For Aristotle the completely virtuous person must not only do the right thing rightly, she must feel right about that which she does.

For example, Aristotle notes that while there is no name for a man who exceeds in lack of fear, such a man, while he may appear courageous in certain circumstances, is in fact only reckless. Not to feel fear is to lose exactly the state necessary to be courageous.[12] It is equally the case that the man who exceeds in fear is a coward since such a man fears all the wrong things in a wrong manner.

Aristotle lists five types of persons who are called brave because they appear to be so, who in fact act bravely yet lack the virtue of courage. Aquinas, who remains one of the best commentators on Aristotle's ethics, provides a summary by noting that such a semblance of virtue may happen in three ways:

> First, because they tend to that which is difficult as though it were not difficult: and this again happens in three ways, for sometimes this is owing to ignorance, through not perceiving the greatness of the danger; sometimes it is owing to the fact that one is hopeful of overcoming dangers—when, for instance, one has often experienced escape from danger; and sometimes this is owing to a certain science and art, as in the case of soldiers who through skill and practice in the use of arms, think little of the dangers of battle, as they reckon themselves capable of defending themselves against them; thus Vegetius says "No man fears to do what he is confident of having learned to do well." Secondly, a man performs an act of fortitude without having the virtue, through the impulse of a passion, whether of sorrow that he wishes to cast off, or again of anger. Thirdly, through choice, not indeed of a due end, but of some temporal advantage to be obtained, such as honor, pleasure, or gain, or of some disadvantage to be avoided, such as blame, pain, or loss.[13]

Aristotle's treatment of these matters is filled with insight and wisdom. He is, for example, well aware that a person with a spirited temper may appear courageous, because courageous people are in fact spirited. Yet unless choice and purpose are added to such spirit it can as easily lead to immorality as nobility. Perhaps most interesting is Aristotle's observation that optimists are not courageous for they have gained their confidence from having won many victories over people. Aristotle concedes that they can certainly look like the courageous, "but when things turn out contrary to their expectation they run away. On the other hand, a courageous man is characterized by the fact that he endures what is fearful to man and what seems fearful to him, because to do so is noble and to do otherwise is base."[14]

Particularly fascinating is Aristotle's sense that a man who no longer is frightened of battle cannot be considered courageous. For example, Yearley quotes a General Skobeleff:

> I believe that my bravery is simply the passion and at the same time the contempt of danger. The risk of life fills me with an exaggerated rapture. The fewer there are to share it, the more I like it. The participation of my body in the event is required to furnish me an adequate excitement. Everything intellectual appears to me to be reflex; but a meeting of man to man, a duel, a danger into which I can throw myself headforemost, attracts me, moves me, intoxicates me. I am crazy for it, I love it, I adore it. I run after danger as one runs after women; I wish it never to stop.[15]

From Aristotle's perspective General Skobeleff is not a courageous man exactly because absent are the virtues necessary to give him the wisdom to subject his daring to the appropriate purposes.

Yet Aristotle's judgment about people like General Skobeleff does not mean that he thinks that the life of courage is without pleasure. Certainly the courageous are called such because of their ability to endure pain. That is why courage is praised since it is more difficult to endure what is painful than abstain from what is pleasant. Yet it is still the case that that at which courage aims is pleasant though it may be obscured by the immediate pain. Just as those who engage in painful athletic events do so for the pleasure of the resulting honor, the same is true of courage.

> Death and wounds will be painful for a courageous man and he will suffer them unwillingly, but he will endure them because it is noble to do so or base to do otherwise. And the closer a man is to having virtue or excellence in its entirety and the happier he is, the more pain will death bring to him. Life is more worth living for such a man than for anyone else, and he stands to lose the greatest goods, and realizes that fact, and that is painful. But he is no less courageous for that, and perhaps rather more so, since he chooses noble deeds in war in return for suffering pain. Accordingly, only insofar

as it attains its end is it true to say of every virtue that it is pleasant when practiced.[16]

Aristotle's account of courage is obviously profound, and I suspect it makes sense to many of us.[17] It is, of course, hard to appreciate Aristotle's description of courage absent a full treatment of his account of the life of *eudamonia*. Yet I hope enough has been said to suggest that Aristotle is acutely aware of how difficult it is to know if we are genuinely courageous. It is not sufficient that we act rightly in battle, but the dispositions that form those activities must also characterize our entire life. Accordingly the forms of courage, without which we have no way to even know what courage might look like, may also protect us from learning what it means to be courageous in contexts where the expectations of battle are not so clearly delineated (e.g., when we must tell hard truths to a friend that may endanger the friendship itself). As we shall see, these issues become no less difficult when we turn to Aquinas's account.

Aquinas on Courage

It is well known that Aquinas extensively drew on Aristotle's philosophy in his *Summa Theologica*. Yet he uses Aristotle's account of the virtues in a manner that essentially transforms the structure as well as the content of those virtues.[18] For example, Aquinas's distinction between the natural and theological virtues can give the impression that all Aquinas is doing is "topping" Aristotle's virtues with faith, hope, and charity. Such an account, however, fails to do justice to Aquinas's claim that charity is the form of all the virtues. As Aquinas says:

> In morals the form of an act is taken chiefly from the end. The reason for this is that the principle of moral acts is the will, whose object and form, so to speak, are the end. Now the form of an act always follows from a form of the agent. Now it is evident that it is charity which directs the acts of all other virtues to the last end, and which, consequently, also gives the form to all other acts of virtue; and it is precisely in this sense that charity is called the form of the virtues, for these are called virtues in relation to "formed" acts.[19]

Aquinas, therefore, maintains that no true virtue is possible without charity. He notes that if we speak of virtue as that which is ordered to some particular end, then there may be a virtue where there is no charity, but such virtue remains a "false likeness" to genuine virtue. Indeed, Aquinas follows Augustine, contending that the "actions which an unbeliever performs as an unbeliever, are always sinful, even when he clothes the naked, or does any like thing, and directs it to his unbelief as end."[20] Therefore, the virtues of Aristotle are only vices when they are separated from the charity through which God makes us his friends.[21]

Charity, moreover, is not a virtue that we can acquire but rather one which must be "infused." "Infusion" is Aquinas's language to remind us that for Christians our life comes as a gift from God and thus cannot be earned.

> [C]harity is friendship of man for God, founded upon the fellowship of everlasting happiness. Now this fellowship is in respect not of natural, but of gratuitous gifts, for, according to *Romans* 6:23, the grace of God is life everlasting. Therefore charity itself surpasses our natural powers. Now that which surpasses the power of nature cannot be natural or acquired by the natural powers, since a natural effect does not transcend its cause. Therefore charity can be in us neither naturally, nor through acquisition by the natural powers, but by the infusion of the Holy Ghost, Who is the love of the Father and the Son, and the participation of Whom in us is caused charity.[22]

The "natural virtues" or the "acquired virtues" are, therefore, not simply "topped" by the supernatural virtues in Aquinas. As Yearley observes, Aquinas compares and contrasts the virtues so that every virtue is at once a semblance of another virtue and yet remains a standard against which some other virtue is measured as a semblance.

> For instance, acquired virtues are semblances of virtue if we use infused virtues as the standard of measurement. But any specific, acquired virtue will resemble more or less closely the integral form of that virtue. Acquired courage always is a semblance of infused courage and yet a particular instance of acquired courage will be only a semblance of real acquired courage. Indeed, he can identify the

"same" phenomenon (e.g., giving up one's life for one's country) both as a semblance and as a standard. That identification depends on which criteria of value or sort of explanation he uses and thus on which hierarchies he employs.[23]

Accordingly, Aquinas's account of courage is at once remarkably similar and significantly different from Aristotle's. Like Aristotle he thinks courage is necessary for forming practical reason, thereby ensuring that our actions are voluntary and not subject to the difficulties which contending appetites produce. Also, like Aristotle, he assumes that courage is a mean between fear and confidence. Yet as Yearley points out, fear and confidence represent different states of character and thus relate in distinct ways to practical reason.[24] Thus Aquinas notes:

[I]t belongs to the virtue of fortitude to remove any obstacle that withdraws the will from following the reason. Now to be withdrawn from something difficult belongs to the notion of fear, which denotes withdrawal from an evil that entails difficulty. Hence fortitude is chiefly about fear of difficult things, which can withdraw the will from following the reason. And it behooves one not only firmly to bear the assault of these difficulties by restraining fear, but also moderately to withstand them, when, to it, it is necessary to dispel them altogether in order to free oneself there from for the future, which seems to come under the notion of daring. Therefore fortitude is about fear and daring, as curbing fear and moderating daring.[25]

But the very meaning of fear and daring have now changed in Aquinas since that which we fear and that in which we ought to have confidence are now schooled by charity. Yearley notes that Aquinas believes prudential concern for our future should always inform a person's judgment. Thus Aquinas argues that "take no thought of the morrow" only involves those dangers that arise in preoccupying oneself with future ills. However, it is spiritual goods that are truly virtuous people's first concern. Thus hope in providence should modify our fears about loss of temporal goods.

Aquinas never claims that Christ teaches that temporal goods will appear if spiritual goods are sought. He does claim, however, that spiritual goods should be people's major concern, and they should hope (not presume) that temporal goods will appear. The higher perspective of "a view to the final good for the whole of life" allows people to understand the crucial issue of what really ought to be feared. The major fear courage ultimately should deal with is the fear of not possessing fully the spiritual goods virtuous people pursue and manifest, as Christ's teachings on providence both underline and illuminate.[26]

Like Aristotle, Aquinas assumes that courage involves an orientation if not a willingness to die.

It belongs to the notion of virtue that it should regard something extreme: and the most fearful of all bodily evils is death, since it does away with all bodily goods. Wherefore Augustine says (De Morib. Eccl. XXII) "that the soul is shaken by its fellow body, with fear of toil and pain, lest the body be stricken and harassed with fear of death lest it be done away and destroyed." Therefore the virtue of fortitude is about the fear of dangers of death.[27]

Yet exactly because the kind of death we should fear is now transformed by being made part of God's economy of salvation, the very character of courage is also changed. As Yearley observes, for Aquinas endurance and not attack is the most prominent characteristic of courage.[28] For example, Aquinas does not deny that courage may have to do with death in battle, but adds, "a brave man behaves well in face of danger of any other kind of death; especially since man may be in danger of any kind of death on account of virtue: thus may a man not fail to attend on a sick friend through fear of deadly infection, or not refuse to undertake a journey with some godly object in view through fear of shipwreck or robbers."[29] Aquinas is not simply taking Aristotle's account of courage and applying it to new ends, but the very character of courage is now transformed since "endurance," steadfastness, and constancy characterize the courageous.

Perhaps nothing makes this clearer than the emphasis that Aquinas puts on patience and perseverance as integral to the very meaning of courage. This emphasis is but a correlative of Aquinas's view that the moral life is a journey to God during which we must learn

to endure much.[30] Patience and perseverance are required if we are
to live courageously. Again Yearley provides a concise account of
Aquinas's position: "Perseverance, with its opposed vices of obsti-
nacy and softness (a too easy yielding to pleasure), concerns the
need to adhere to the good sought. Patience concerns the need to
overcome the sorrow brought by the inevitable loss of some
goods."[31]

Obviously, the importance of perseverance and patience in Aquinas are correlative to his understanding of courage as a form of
endurance. Endurance can be justified on Aristotelian grounds as
the part of courage needed for accomplishing difficult purposes.
But much more important for Aquinas is his understanding of the
dangers that the very kind of life being a Christian creates. It is
generally true that the world of the courageous person is different
from the world of the coward for the very courage the courageous
possess makes the world more dangerous. But Aquinas well understood that the kind of world that Christian courage makes is quite
different from the world, for example, of Aristotle's high-minded
and courageous man.

As we have seen, Aquinas refers to Aristotle's sense that courage
is exemplified by facing death in battle though he does not make
much of it. The reason is quite simple: martyrdom stands over all
of Aquinas's thinking about courage. He thus has a completely different paradigm and example that was unavailable to Aristotle. Accordingly, Christians are required to patiently persevere in the face
of persecution since they have the confidence that enduring wrong
is a gift of charity. Aristotle's correlation of courage and facing
death in battle is transformed by Aquinas:

> [I]t belongs to fortitude to strengthen man in the good of virtue,
> especially against dangers, and chiefly against dangers of death, and
> most of all against those that occur in battle. Now it is evident that
> in martyrdom man is firmly strengthened in the good of virtue, since
> he cleaves to faith and justice not withstanding the threatening dan-
> ger of death, the imminence of which is moreover due to a kind of
> particular contest with his persecutors. Hence Cyprian says in a ser-
> mon: "The crowd of onlookers wondered to see an unearthly battle,
> and Christ's servants fighting erect, undaunted in speech, with souls

unmoved, and strength divine." Wherefore it is evident that martyr-dom is an act of fortitude; for which reason the Church reads in the office of Martyrs: They "became valiant in battle."[32]

The prominence of martyrdom in Aquinas's account of courage confirms that true courage, as opposed to all semblances of cour-age, is a gift of the Holy Spirit. Thus the patience characteristic of Christians is that which displays the joy of being of service to God.[33] Such joy is possible because patience is formed by charity. In like manner, courage as a gift of the spirit protects the martyr from the "dread of dangers" in a distinctive manner:

> The Holy Spirit moves the human mind further [than the steadfast-ness of normal courage], in order that one may reach the end of any work begun and avoid threatening dangers of any kind. This transcends human nature, for sometimes it does not lie within human power to attain the end of one's work, or to escape evils or dangers, since these sometimes press in upon us to the point of death. But the Holy Spirit achieves this in us when he leads us to eternal life, which is the end of all good works and the escape from all dan-gers. And he pours into our mind a certain confidence that this will be, refusing to admit the opposing fear.[34]

Those formed in charity literally do not fear the fears of Aristot-le's courageous man. Courage, as a virtue, "perfects the mind in the endurance of all perils whatever; but it does not go so far as to give confidence of overcoming all dangers: this belongs to the forti-tude that is a gift of the Holy Spirit."[35] Yearley suggests rightly that such "confidence includes more than just an assurance about what will happen in the future. They [the courageous] also feel assurance about the meaning of those signs that ensure them the Holy Spirit moves them and that they are participating in the relationship of friendship with God that characterizes charity."[36]

Courage: Christian or American?

It may well be asked where this analysis and comparison of Aris-totle's and Aquinas's understanding of courage has gotten us. At the very least, it should now be clear that there is no virtue theory in general. Rather the characterizations of the virtues, their content, how they interrelate, will differ from one community and tradition to another.[37] This diversity is often obscured by the fact that the virtues have the same name and may in fact seem structurally similar. Thus, courage for Aristotle and Aquinas obviously deals with fear and confidence, as those attitudes are structured by our stance toward death. But as we have seen "death" represents quite a different reality for Aquinas than for Aristotle. Moreover, the contrast between the confronting of death in battle and that of martyrdom obviously makes *all* the difference for how they understand courage.

This last contrast in fact brings us back to the issues raised at the beginning of this essay. For if liberal societies, and in particular America, deduce their moral intelligibility from the sacrifices derived from their wars, then it seems obvious that there will be a conflict between the kind of courage that should be produced by Christian practices and that which is in service to the nation-state. I am well aware, of course, that Aquinas justified, on just-war grounds, Christian participation in war. Indeed, as we have seen, he knew that there were some analogies between the kind of courage required to face death in battle and that characteristic of martyrdom. But a people shaped by the stance of endurance and patience, derived from the example of the martyrs, are the kind of people that Aquinas thought capable of employing just-war reasoning. I think it fair to say that such people are clearly not the kind that constitute the American republic. It is not even clear that they are capable of the kind of courage depicted by Aristotle, since they have not been formed to fear the right things rightly.

I should, of course, be candid and acknowledge that I am an advocate of Christian nonviolence. I assume, therefore, that Christians will always find themselves in tension with those accounts of virtue and courage that derive their intelligibility from war. Yet I have displayed Aquinas's account of courage exactly because it makes clear that one who does not share my nonviolent convictions still gives an account of courage quite different from that based on war.

In truth, I have used courage to exhibit what I take to be the necessary tension between the two political communities—one called "the nation" and the other called "the church." I have done so to dispel the presumption that a renewed appreciation for the importance of the formation of virtuous citizens will also help us recover the importance of the church as politically significant. Such presumption is based on the idea that virtue-forming institutions must exist somewhere, and the church seems a likely candidate. Christians, it is assumed, are trained to be honest and truthful, and such virtues surely are important for the working of good social orders. But as we have seen from Aquinas's point of view, such "virtues" cannot but be the semblance of virtue, lacking as they do the form of charity. Christian virtues, and courage in particular, formed by charity may just as easily become subversive to the political order as they are of service to such order.

Christian courage will more likely deter, if not subvert, the political order based on courage that derives its intelligibility from the practice of war. That is why Rousseau rightly thought that the Christians as much as possible should be suppressed. If Aquinas's account of courage comprises what Christians should think about courage, I think there can be little doubt that Rousseau was right in his suspicion of Christians' relation to the kind of social order he thought desirable.

The usual reply to such a suggestion is that democracy has surely solved this set of problems. Freedom of religion means that the wider political order encourages dissenting voices. Indeed, democracies grow stronger just to the extent that they are challenged by strong voices such as the church. So if Christian courage in some ways challenges the understanding of courage shared by the wider society, so much the better.

Such a response, however, will not work. It will not work because inherent in such an account of the church's relation to democracy is the distinction between the public and the private.[38] That distinction has been the agent of the destruction of any coherent account of civic virtue in liberal societies. More importantly, it will not work because courage as understood by Aquinas necessarily is in substantive conflict with the semblance of virtue found in liberal social orders.

Of course, it may be the case that a semblance of virtue is better than no virtue at all. There is great power in such a response, not only from the perspective of liberal political orders but also from the perspective of the church. For Aquinas rightly thought that those formed by the courage necessary to face death well might, at least, begin to be led to the fuller account of courage he thought characteristic of Christians. The difficulty with such a suggestion is just to the extent such growth is possible the church must make clear that virtue constituted by the civic order is, at best, only a pale reflection of what we are called to be. I suspect few polities wish to be so challenged.

Notes

1. Jean Bethke Elshtain, "Citizenship and Armed Civic Virtue: Some Critical Questions on the Commitment to Public Life," in *Community in America: The Challenge of Habits of the Heart*, ed. Charles H. Reynolds and Ralph V. Norman (Berkeley: University of California Press, 1988), 47–55.

2. I do not mean to imply that "war" meant the same thing for Aristotle as it did for Machiavelli and Rousseau. For example, see Stanley Hauerwas, "Can a Pacifist Think About War" (forthcoming).

3. Elshtain, "Citizenship and Armed Virtue," 51.

4. I will not be able to treat the complexity of this issue in this chapter since it involves the development of a full account of the virtues. No better discussion can be found than that provided by Alasdair MacIntyre in *After Virtue* (Notre Dame: University of Notre Dame Press, 1984), 163–64 and 178–80.

5. For an attempt to show that such circularity is not vicious, see Stanley Hauerwas, "Happiness, the Life of Virtue, and Friendship: Theological Reflections on Aristotelian Themes," *Asbury Theological Journal* 45, no. 1 (Spring 1990): 5–48.

6. Aristotle, *Nicomachean Ethics*, trans. Martin Ostwald (Indianapolis: Bobbs-Merrill, 1962), 1109a25–30.

7. Aristotle, *Nicomachean Ethics*, 1115a1–3.

8. Thus Aristotle and Aquinas assume that the descriptions of actions are inseparable from the character of the agent. See MacIntyre, *After Virtue*, 149–52.

9. Aristotle, *Nicomachean Ethics*, 1115a10–24.

10. Aristotle, *Nicomachean Ethics*, 1115a 28–1115b5.

11. Lee H. Yearley, *Mencius and Aquinas: Theories of Virtue and Conceptions of Courage* (Albany: State University of New York, 1990), 37.

12. Aristotle, *Nicomachean Ethics*, 1115a25–35.

13. Thomas Aquinas, *Summa Theologica*, trans. Fathers of the English Dominican Province (Westminster, Maryland: Christian Classics, 1948), II, ii, q. 123, a. 1, a. 2.

14. Aristotle, *Nicomachean Ethics*, 1117a15–20.

15. Yearley, *Mencius and Aquinas*, 18.

16. Aristotle, *Nicomachean Ethics*, 1117b7–15.

17. By "us" all I mean to suggest is the widespread assumption shared by many that courage is exemplified in contexts of physical threat.

18. MacIntyre rightly observes that Aquinas's appropriation of Aristotle involved the fitting together of the inheritance from heroic cultures with the Christian but also the problem of specifically biblical virtues (*After Virtue*, 177). See also, Stanley Hauerwas, *The Peaceable Kingdom* (Notre Dame, IN: University of Notre Dame Press, 1983).

19. Aquinas, *Summa*, II, ii, q. 23, a. 8.

20. Aquinas, *Summa*, II, ii, q. 23, a. 7, a. 1.

21. Aquinas, *Summa*, II, ii, q. 23, a. 1. See also, Paul Wadel, *Friends of God: Virtues and Gifts in Aquinas* (New York: Peter Lang, 1991) for the importance of Aquinas's account of friendship and the virtues.

22. Aquinas, *Summa*, II, ii, q. 24, a. 2.

23. Yearley, *Mencius and Aquinas*, 33.

24. Yearley, *Mencius and Aquinas*, 121.

25. Aquinas, *Summa*, II, ii, q. 123, a. 3.

26. Yearley, *Mencius and Aquinas*, 129.

27. Aquinas, *Summa*, II, ii, q. 123, a. 4.

28. Yearley, *Mencius and Aquinas*, 130.

29. Aquinas, *Summa*, II, ii, q. 123, a. 5.

30. See MacIntyre, *After Virtue*, 176.

31. Yearley, *Mencius and Aquinas*, 130.

32. Aquinas, *Summa*, II, ii, q. 124, a. 2. It would probably be a mistake to make much of the change of language in the Dominican translation of the *Summa* from courage to fortitude, but fortitude surely comes closer to the resonance of Aquinas's account of what Aristotle called courage. I have simply used courage and fortitude interchangeably.

33. Aquinas, *Summa*, II, ii, q. 136, a. 3.

34. Quoted in Yearley, *Mencius and Aquinas*, 141.

35. Aquinas, *Summa*, II, ii, q. 139, a. 1.

36. Yearley, *Mencius and Aquinas*, 141.

37. For an astute discussion of the political significance of moral vo-

cabularies, see Ronald Beiner, *What's The Matter With Liberalism?* (Berkeley: University of California Press, 1992), 49.

38. The public/private split works in many different ways in American society, but in general it makes it difficult for any institution in America to engage in the kind of training to produce people of virtue. A recent controversy in the high school in Chapel Hill, North Carolina, nicely illustrates this dilemma. A guidance counselor, John Cardarelli, it seems had been encouraging students not to enlist in the military. This occasioned the following editorial in *The Chapel Hill Herald* (Wednesday, 17 June 1992, p. 4):

> John Cardarelli the individual has a right to his own opinions about the military. But John Cardarelli the Chapel Hill High School guidance counselor should keep them to himself. . . .
>
> Pacifism is a noble philosophy, and we would defend anyone's right to practice this belief. But Cardarelli's professional obligation to the school system is to provide balanced, objective information about career choices, not promulgate his own convictions. . . .

What is remarkable about such an editorial is how nicely it embodies the liberal assumption that our most substantive convictions must be relegated to the "private" exactly because they are substantive. This, of course, is the necessary price for sustaining the illusion that public education is possible in a society that shares no goods in common. "Objectivity" through "choice" becomes the ideology necessary to prevent any serious debate. For a further discussion of these issues, see Stanley Hauerwas, *After Christendom?* (Nashville: Abingdon Press, 1991), 23–31.

CHAPTER 10

Ordinary Virtue as Heroism

J. Brian Benestad

The concept of ordinary virtue is most fruitfully understood as the character everyone needs to live an ordered life. "Ordinary" is actually derived from the Latin word *ordo*, whose meanings include order and regularity. Of course, the meaning of order in one's life is subject to a fair amount of disagreement today. The issues dividing various groups surely create obstacles to recognizing points of agreement. Few would doubt, however, that the practice of ordinary virtue, however understood, is extremely difficult, requiring insight and courage.

I rely on two works of literature here in order to present a vision of ordinary virtue: Jane Austen's *Persuasion* (1818) and Alessandro Manzoni's *I Promessi Sposi* (1840), or *The Betrothed*.[1] Although the latter book is well known in Europe and one of the Harvard Classics, it is still relatively unknown in the United States. I do not expect to do justice to Austen and Manzoni but do hope to draw enough from these works in order to advance the discussion on virtue. While presenting the vision of Austen and Manzoni, I will offer reflections that will link the two novelists to the tradition of Christian thought on virtue.

Then I will focus on one of the main obstacles to the understanding and practice of ordinary virtue, namely, the decay of religion. Religion is decaying for basically two reasons: unwise accommodation to the culture and religious ignorance. Religious communities uncritically yield to the pressure of the *Zeitgeist* and fail to pass on the knowledge of faith to their members.

Persuasion

A helpful way to approach Jane Austen's *Persuasion* is to examine the two crucial scenes in the novel where the outcome depends on the willingness to be persuaded. The first scene depicts a decisive moment that took place eight years before the events being narrated in the story. At the age of 19, Anne Elliot falls in love with Frederick Wentworth, an intelligent, spirited, charming naval officer. Anne, says Jane Austen, was "an extremely pretty girl, with gentleness, modesty, taste and feeling. Half the sum of attraction, on either side, might have been enough, for he had nothing to do, and she had hardly anybody to love" (55). Anne's father, Sir Walter Elliot, opposed the marriage because Frederick was not wealthy and had no connections to insure his advancement in the navy. Anne's friend, Lady Russell, also opposed the marriage because of her low opinion of Frederick. In her mind, he was brilliant, headstrong, and poor, with no certain prospect of attaining the requisite affluence for marriage. She advised Anne to break off the engagement. Since the death of her mother five years before, Anne had come to rely on the judgment of the well-meaning Lady Russell. In response to her godmother's tender, confident advice "she was persuaded to believe the engagement a wrong thing—indiscreet, improper, hardly capable of success, and not deserving it" (56). Jane Austen notes that Anne was not motivated by "selfish caution" but saw her painful self-denial as contributing to Frederick's true interest. Frederick is bitterly disappointed, leaves the country, and harbors resentment against Anne.

The other scene occurs eight years later, when Anne is 27. Frederick, still unmarried, returns to Anne's neighborhood because of family ties. He develops an interest in Louisa Musgrove, to whom he explains his view of good character, which Anne inadvertently overhears without Frederick's knowledge. After Louisa explains that she is never easily persuaded, Frederick praises Louisa for her firmness and says, "It is the worst evil of too yielding and indecisive character, that no influence over it can be depended on. You are never sure of a good impression being durable. Everybody may sway it; let those who would be happy be firm" (110). Frederick has obviously drawn a very clear lesson from his experience with Anne's change of mind.

Shortly after his impassioned defense of firmness, Frederick, Louisa, Anne, and others are out for a walk near the seashore. Louisa insists on jumping down to the pavement from a height. She jumps once and insists upon doing so again. In vain Frederick attempts to dissuade Louisa. She smiles and says, "I am determined I will" (129). Frederick holds out his hands; Louisa jumps but trips and falls on the pavement, unconscious. In the face of general consternation Anne keeps her composure and suggests what should be done to care for Louisa and then attends to her distraught friends, including Captain Wentworth. After proper care is arranged, Jane Austen gives us a glimpse of Anne's thoughts about Frederick's opinion of a good character:

> Anne wondered whether it ever occurred to him now to question the justness of his own previous opinion as to the universal felicity and advantage of firmness of character, and whether it might strike him, that, like all other qualities of the mind, it should have its proportions and limits. She thought it would scarcely escape him to feel that a persuadable temper might sometimes be as much in favor of happiness as a very resolute character. (136)

During her convalescence, Louisa falls in love with a Captain Benwick. Frederick and Anne eventually get back together and decide to marry. Anne then casually explains her decision to Frederick not to marry him eight years before. While both are admiring green lawn plants, Anne says:

> I have been thinking over the past and trying impartially to judge of the right and wrong, I mean with regard to myself, and I must believe that I was right, much as I suffered from it, that I was perfectly right in being guided by the friend whom you will love better than you do now. To me she was in the place of a parent. Do not mistake me, however, I am not saying that she did not err in her advice. It was perhaps one of those cases in which advice is good or bad only as the event decides; and for myself, I certainly never should, in any

circumstance of tolerable similarity, give such advice. But I mean
that I was right in submitting to her, and that if I had done otherwise
I should have suffered more in continuing the engagement than I did
even in giving it up, because I should have suffered in my conscience.
I have now, as far as such a sentiment is allowable in human nature,
nothing to reproach myself with; and if I mistake not, a strong sense
of duty is no bad part of a woman's portion.(248)

Student reaction to Anne's explanation is generally quite negative.
My students contend that Anne was weak because she followed
Lady Russell's advice. That, of course, was Frederick's judgment
at the time, too.

Jane Austen's literary presentation of persuasion brings to mind
classical and Christian understandings of prudence. For example,
Augustine, according to Aquinas, describes prudence as "the
knowledge of what to seek and what to avoid" and as "love discerning aright that which helps from that which hinders us in tending to God." Aquinas says, "Love is said to discern because it
moves the reason to discern." In fact, prudence is "in the reason"
and may be properly characterized as right reason applied to action. Otherwise stated, it is the function of prudence to apply right
reason to action with the help of an ordered appetite. In applying
reason to action, prudence does not appoint the ends of the moral
virtues but chooses the means appropriate for realizing these ends.[2]

In order for people to achieve right reason, they must take counsel and then make a judgment. Applying right reason to action
requires the act of command which is the chief act of the practical
reason. The act of commanding, says Aquinas, "consists in applying to action the things counselled and judged."[3] Counsel and judgment are necessary because the exercise of prudence requires not
only knowledge of universal principles but also familiarity with a
host of "singulars" or the relevant factors in a situation. It belongs
to counsel to discern the pertinent singulars from the great number
present to a person's mind.

"The pre-eminence of prudence," says Joseph Pieper, "means
that realization of the good presupposes knowledge of reality. He
alone can do good who knows what things are like and what his
situation is. The pre-eminence of prudence means that so-called

'good intention' and so-called 'meaning well' by no means suffice."[4] We take counsel or advice in order to grasp what needs to be known about a particular situation. This ability to see is enhanced by long experience and the possession of various qualities designated by Aquinas as the quasi-integral parts of prudence. *Experience* helps us discover "what is true in a majority of cases." Since "experience is the result of many memories . . . memory is fittingly accounted a part of prudence."[5] *Docility* is another aspect of prudence since we have a "very great need of being taught by others, especially by old folk who have acquired a sound understanding of the ends in practical matters."[6] It is docility which makes us open-minded and thus disposed to learn from others. *Shrewdness*, says Aquinas, is the disposition "to acquire a right estimate by oneself."[7] The quality of *foresight* enables us to take contingent future events into account.[8] Still other parts of prudence mentioned by Aquinas are understanding, the ability to use reason well, circumspection, and caution. All these qualities enable us to come into contact with reality.

As is well-known, Jane Austen believes that a person needs good judgment in order to do the right thing. The young need to listen attentively to parents and other adults in order to become ever better observers of people and situations. Because they are subject to various and sundry disordered passions, such as pride, vanity, and immoderate love of money and pleasure, young men and women may not heed wise counsel. Jane Austen would have readily understood a bishop's statement to Monica that her son, the future St. Augustine, was not yet willing to heed wise counsel. Various passions and mistaken religious opinions held sway over him. Even well-meaning, good adults may not always be wise counselors. While Lady Russell usually gave Anne and her family good advice, she wrongly discouraged Anne from marrying Frederick because of prejudices on her part. Lady Russell did not appreciate Frederick's "sanguine temper and fearlessness of mind" nor his intelligence. Jane Austen seems to imply that even the most teachable young person can be misguided by imprudent adults. She also implies that humans cannot grow up well in communities and families where good advice is not forthcoming.

I would add that all young people must learn how to see reality and all need guidance, especially from family members and close friends and even authoritative traditions that are very much alive, at least in the church, if not in the culture. To choose between a "persuadable temper" and a "resolute character" is an ongoing task. Youth is a time when docility to authoritative guidance is especially necessary. In this time of misplaced compassion, choice without requisite information and an exaggerated sense of independence, Jane Austen's vision of persuasion in a community is an appealing alternative. There are things common to all human lives that must and can be understood before choices are made. Not will but understanding is primary in Jane Austen's world.

Being open to persuasion is a mark of good judgment which is an abiding characteristic of Anne Elliot. To her own chagrin, Anne recognizes that her father, Sir Walter, was extremely vain about his appearance, a spendthrift, a lover of rank, unaffectionate, and not respectful of her opinions. Jane Austen is very critical of Sir Walter's attitude toward his daughter. "Anne, with an elegance of mind and sweetness of character, which must have placed her high with any people of real understanding, was nobody with either father or sister [i.e., her older sister Elizabeth]" (37). Anne perceives her situation but neither complains nor grows bitter. She seems to understand intuitively that being resentful or bearing grudges is harmful to one's character.

Anne also displays unerring judgment about the character of people in her surroundings. She knows that Mrs. Clay, the companion of her sister Elizabeth, says what pleases and is probably scheming to become Sir Walter's wife. Anne is perfect in her judgment about the worth of her suitors. At the age of 22, contrary to the advice of Lady Russell, she rejects a marriage offer from Charles Musgrove "whose landed property and general importance were second in that county, only to Sir Walter's" (57). Lady Russell wanted Anne to marry Charles not only to benefit from Charles's money and importance but also to secure a respectable removal "from the partialities and injustice of her father's house, and settled so permanently near herself" (57). Although Charles was a pleasant fellow and patient with the whining of Mary, the sister of Anne, whom he eventually marries, he is lazy and boring. Jane Austen sums up his life by saying that "he did nothing with much zeal but sport and his time was otherwise trifled away, without benefit from books or anything else" (70).

At the age of 27, Anne comes to the judgment that her cousin, William Elliot, would not make a suitable marriage partner. While not prying into the details of his disreputable past—which she eventually discovers—Anne, nevertheless, picks up from conversation that at one period of his life he had been "careless on all serious matters" (173). Although he was agreeable and expressed good opinions, Anne remained skeptical.

> Mr. Elliot was rational, discreet, polished—but he was not open. There was never any burst of feeling, any warmth of indignation or delight, at the evil or good of others. This, to Anne, was a decided imperfection. Her early impressions were incurable. She prized the frank, the open hearted, the eager character beyond all others. Warmth and enthusiasm did captivate her still. She felt that she could so much more depend upon the sincerity of those who sometimes looked or said a careless or a hasty thing, than of those whose presence of mind never varied, whose tongue never slipped.(173)

Another aspect of Anne's character and Jane Austen's vision of a good person is revealed in the encounters between Anne and Mrs. Smith, the former Miss Hamilton. Anne accidently discovered that her former schoolmate was living nearby, "who had the two strong claims on her attention, of past kindness and present suffering" (106). During the course of a year, Miss Hamilton had graciously softened Anne's grief over the premature loss of her mother. Now 13 years later, Mrs. Smith was a widow, poor, sickly and "almost excluded from society" (165). Against the judgment of her father and sister, Elizabeth, Anne visits and consoles her old friend in a section of town where Sir Walter would never be seen. Anne discovers a woman displaying a patience in the face of suffering that is truly extraordinary.

> . . . Neither sickness nor sorrow seemed to have closed her heart or ruined her spirits . . . . A submissive spirit might be patient, a strong understanding would supply resolution, but here was something more: here was that elasticity of mind, that disposition to be comforted, that power of turning readily to good, and of finding employ-

ment which carried her out of herself, which was from Nature alone. It was the choicest gift of heaven. (166–67)

It is, of course, not surprising to find that Anne appreciates the beauty of patient endurance. She herself was patient, despite suffering from her separation from Frederick Wentworth on account of Lady Russell's mistaken advice. She bore with equanimity slights from her father and sister Elizabeth. She put up with the constant complaints of her sister Mary and even responded with kindness both to her and her children. Anne rallied her spirits by gladly embracing the duties available in her state of life. She genuinely showed love to her family and acquaintances, and—Jane Austen notes in passing—she regularly distributed alms to the poor.

The importance of patient endurance is developed both in Scripture and in the writings of such major theologians as St. Ambrose, St. Gregory the Great, St. Augustine, and St. Thomas Aquinas. Ambrose begins his *De Officiis* by counseling his readers to learn silence in the face of verbal abuse and equanimity in response to wrongs inflicted on them. Ambrose, in number 23 of Book One, even calls the patience of keeping silence one of the most important foundations of virtue. St. Gregory the Great goes so far as to affirm that charity cannot exist without patience. He further says, "The less patient a man proves to be, the less instructed does he show himself to be; and he cannot truly impart by instruction what is good, if in his own way of life he does not know how to bear with equanimity the evils that others do."[9] Aquinas says patience safeguards "the good of reason against sorrow lest reason give way to sorrow."[10] The moderation of sorrow is important both to obviate the temptations to such vices as anger and hatred, and to prevent loss of enthusiasm for the practice of virtue. According to Scripture, " . . . because wickedness is multiplied, the love of many will grow cold" (Matt. 24:12). Giving way to sorrow because of personal suffering or societal injustice not only takes up valuable time, but also decreases zeal for accomplishing whatever good is possible.

Not surprisingly, Aquinas argues that patience is caused by charity, which no one attains without the help of grace. A strong desire to love God and neighbor gives the strength to bear adversity and everyday difficulties. As Augustine says in *De Patientia*, "the strength of desire helps a man to bear toil and pain; and no one willingly undertakes to bear what is painful save for the sake of that which gives pleasure."[11]

Anne's patient endurance in the face of personal sufferings protects her from the debilitating effects of sadness and self-pity. Anne maintains her enthusiasm for life and is kind to her family and acquaintances, even when they do not respond. Anne's good judgment enables her to love wisely (e.g., by giving good counsel to her father and sister Elizabeth). While Anne's prudence and patient endurance are the most striking aspects of her character, no less noteworthy is her temperance. The function of this virtue, says St. Augustine, is to restrain and still the passions which cause us to crave the things that turn us away from the laws of God and the enjoyment of His goodness. As examples of these passions, Augustine mentions covetousness, bodily pleasures, desire for human glory, and desire of vain knowledge.[12] Unlike her father and sister Elizabeth, Anne is not inordinately fond of money, rank, personal appearance, or the good opinion of "important" people. If attached to the opinion of those in her father's social circle, she could never have shown gratitude and friendship to Mrs. Smith. Desire for property and security probably would have led Anne to accept Charles Musgrove's proposal of marriage. Anne's detachment from inordinate desires also removed temptation to any kind of hypocrisy. Anne was never angling for recognition or money. She was always straightforward and candid.

It is interesting to note how Anne's life displays the connection among the virtues so often discussed by theologians. Anne's prudence, patience, and temperance all facilitate the practice of charity or beneficence toward others. Jane Austen makes clear that real kindness toward others depends on the virtues Anne possesses.

The Betrothed

Alessandro Manzoni's *The Betrothed* is a historical novel set in the 17th century in what is now northern Italy. Manzoni's scenes and characters nicely reveal the meaning of virtue as well as the dependence of the common good on the practice of virtue. The novel opens 7 November 1628, when two bravos of a local nobleman, by the name of Don Rodrigo, order Don Abbondio, a simple parish priest, not to marry two peasants named Renzo Tramaglino and Lucia Mondello. Don Rodrigo wanted Lucia for himself. Don Abbondio is thoroughly intimidated, complies with the order and thereby sets in motion the subsequent events.

Don Abbondio had not become a priest for religious reasons. Seeing himself as an "earthenware jar . . . in the company of many iron pots," Don Abbondio willingly followed his parents' command to enter the priesthood. "To win the means of living with some degree of comfort, and to join the ranks of a revered and powerful class seemed to him more than sufficient motive for such a course" (38). Manzoni briefly sums up the years of Abbondio's priesthood. He got along by not taking sides in the frequent conflicts "between clergy and lay authorities, between military and civilians, between noble and noble—right down to quarrels between two peasants arising from a hasty word, and settled with fists or knives" (38). If forced to take sides, Don Abbondio "always sided with the stronger of two contendants" in such a way as to avoid offending the weaker party. "He kept away from bullies when he could, he pretended not to notice passing, capricious acts of arrogance, and greeted those that arose from a serious and deliberate intention with total submission. . . . But above all he used to declaim against those of his colleagues who took the risk of supporting the weak and the oppressed against a powerful bully" (38–39).

In response to the difficult situation caused by Don Abbondio's cowardly behavior, Lucia decides to ask for help from Father Cristoforo, a Capuchin priest, "a man of great authority, both within the monastery and outside of it." Before becoming a Capuchin friar, Father Cristoforo's name was Lodovico. As the son of a rich merchant, he used his resources "to set himself up as a protector of the down-trodden and a righter of wrongs" (79). On one occasion Lodovico, accompanied by his servant Cristoforo, lets himself be provoked into a quarrel with a tyrannical nobleman. Manzoni's narrative shows that the pride and blazing temper of Lodovico suck him into a useless sword fight, thereby, unjustifiably putting both himself and Cristoforo at risk of being harmed and of inflicting harm on others. As things turn out, Cristoforo dies trying to protect his master and Lodovico kills the nobleman. To make amends for his deed, Lodovico gives all his property to Cristoforo's wife and eight children and resolves to become a Capuchin and to take the name of his servant, Cristoforo. He then humbles himself before the relatives of the man he killed and actually frees them from their anger and hatred toward him. As a Capuchin friar "his two official duties were those of preaching and of tending the dying which he carried out willingly and conscientiously, but he never missed a chance of performing two other duties, which he had set himself— the composing of quarrels and the protection of the oppressed" (90). He tries to save people from immoderate anger and finds ways of protecting the oppressed without doing anything unjust himself.

Given his mission in life, Father Cristoforo willingly agrees to help Lucia and Renzo. He goes to Don Rodrigo and offers a face-saving way to let the two young people marry. When Don Rodrigo refuses, Father Cristoforo opposes him to his face and then arranges safe passage for Renzo and Lucia to another part of the country. Cristoforo acts to save the young peasants from Don Rodrigo's anger and desire and acts to save Renzo from his own anger against Don Rodrigo. Cristoforo consequently suffers a transfer to another locale for his courageous deed because Don Rodrigo is well connected with the Capuchin authorities. Manzoni indicates that Rodrigo has no trouble manipulating the Capuchins, who were possibly innocent as doves but not wise as serpents. Like many of his Capuchin confreres, Cristoforo volunteers to take care of plague victims and eventually dies from the plague. Before succumbing Cristoforo looks after the dying Don Rodrigo, another victim of the plague, and succeeds in persuading Renzo to give up his hatred for Don Rodrigo and even to forgive him.

At a convent in Monza where Lucia takes refuge, Manzoni introduces the reader to Gertrude, also known as the Signora or the nun of Monza. Upon first meeting Lucia, Gertrude importunately asks the young girl whether Don Rodrigo was indeed a "hateful persecutor." When pressed to give an answer, Lucia reluctantly says that she would "rather die than fall into his clutches" (173–74). She also says of Renzo, "I chose him for my husband of my own free will" (173). Lucia's invocation of free choice sets the stage for the presentation of this young woman who tyrannizes over herself and others in response to the tyranny of her father. Freedom is the leit-motif of the two chapters Manzoni devotes to the nun of Monza.

Along with a number of other girls, Gertrude was placed in the convent at the age of six to receive an education. Most left at the age of 14 to take their place in the world. Early in her life, Gertrude knew that she was expected to become a sister when she turned 14. During her eight-year residence in the convent as a lay person, Gertrude would often tell her companions how she would freely decide to become a nun or to get married. She desperately wanted to live in the world but could not bear the thought of opposing the will of her father. Manzoni says she lost all sense of real religion and became subject to an unreal image of religion.

> Then poor Gertrude would be overcome by confused terrors and op-pressed by confused ideas of duty until she imagined that her repug-nance toward the cloistered life and her resistance to the subtle influence of her elders in the matter of a future choice constituted a sin, which she would resolve to expiate by voluntarily taking the veil.(180)

She submits an application to become a nun but according to Church law she must wait a year and then be examined by a priest known as the vicar of nuns. His duty is to make certain that her decision to enter the convent is "of her own free choice." At the end of the year Gertrude decides not to enter the convent and in-forms her father by letter. After suffering verbal abuse from her father and imprisonment in her own home, Gertrude again changes her mind and agrees to enter the convent. When undergoing the requisite questioning by the vicar of nuns, she makes up her mind to deceive the priest and succeeds. Unable to break free of the tyr-anny in her life, Gertrude serves 12 months as a novice and then takes her final vows.

Manzoni's comment on Gertrude's final decision is a reflection on the power of the Christian religion to offer help in any circum-stance.

> If there is a remedy for what is past, she prescribes it and gives us the vision and strength to carry it out, whatever the cost. If there is

no remedy, she shows us how to make a literal reality of the prover-
bial expression "to make a virtue of necessity". She teaches us to
continue wisely in the course we entered upon out of frivolity. She
chastens our heart to accept gladly that which is imposed on us by
tyranny, she gives a reckless but irrevocable choice, all the sanctity,
all the wisdom, all the—let us say,—all the joyful happiness of true
vocation. (203–04)

Gertrude does not try to become religious but instead tortures the
young pupils placed in her charge out of envious revenge for the
happiness they will one day enjoy outside the convent. She begins
an affair with Egidio, a low-level criminal living near the convent,
who works for a powerful criminal whom Manzoni calls the Unnamed. Gertrude even becomes an accomplice in the murder of a
lay sister because of her threat to tell the authorities about Gertrude's relationship with Egidio. Lucia appears on her doorstep a
year after the murder.

Manzoni reports that Gertrude suffered great interior torments
because of her way of life such that even her physical appearance
manifested the pain and disorder in her soul. Her situation
worsened when the Unnamed gave Egidio the order to kidnap
Lucia and bring her to his castle for delivery to Don Rodrigo. Gertrude took pleasure in Lucia's company and helping her was even
an act of expiation for her sins. She did not want to sacrifice an
innocent girl but, as usual, acting against her better judgment,
complied with Egidio's demand for help in carrying out the crime.
Complicity in kidnapping was of a piece with her acceptance of
bloodshed and other crimes. As Manzoni writes, "Crime is a rigid,
unbending master, against whom no one can be strong except by
total rebellion. Gertrude did not make up her mind to this—and so
she did what she was told" (372).

Manzoni introduces the Unnamed to his readers just before the
kidnapping of Lucia takes place. He is a man who "had outdis-
tanced the ordinary crowd of evil doers and left them far behind."
Around the age of 60 he begins to feel "not remorse but a sort of
disquiet at the thought of his past crimes." The numerous offenses
which had piled up in his memory, if not on his conscience, seemed
to come to life again whenever he committed a new one" (369).

Manzoni reports that feelings of repugnance first arose when he initially embarked on a life of crime. He was able to overcome the pangs of conscience with thoughts of his own strength and the long future ahead of him, as well as by the excitement of his life. "In earlier times," writes Manzoni, "the non-stop spectacle of violence, revenge and murder had filled him with a ferocious competitive spirit and also served as a sort of counterweight to his conscience" (370). But now the thought of a God to whom he was responsible kept intruding into his consciousness—"AND YET I AM" (370). He was still laboring to expel thoughts of repentance when Nibbio brings Lucia to his castle and, totally out of character, talks to the Unnamed about the feeling of compassion he felt for Lucia. The frightened girl pleads with him and says, "God will forgive so many things, for a single act of mercy" (386). He begins to wonder why he ever agreed to help Don Rodrigo kidnap this girl but cannot come up with an answer. At this point, Manzoni offers an interpretation of the Unnamed's motivation: "His willingness to take that action had not been the fruit of a deliberate decision, but rather the instantaneous response of a mind trained to follow long-standing, habitual ideas—the consequences of a thousand previous events" (393–94). The Unnamed was just acting in character according to his settled habits. Upon further self-examination, the Unnamed begins to realize the enormity of his crimes, "an enormity which the passions had previously concealed" (394).

Manzoni's reference to the blinding effect of passions calls to mind the longstanding Christian tradition on this theme. Freely-willed personal sin causes a lack of self-knowledge and an inability to appreciate the attractiveness of virtue. In *The Confessions*, St. Augustine eloquently describes his self-willed ignorance. He accuses himself of not wanting to know the truth about God and himself. Commenting on his tendency to ask questions with the wrong attitude, Augustine writes, "I sought an answer to the question 'Whence is evil?' but, I sought it in an evil way, and did not see the evil in my search."[13] In Book Eight, Augustine explains at length how bad habits voluntarily assumed become a despot and a burden. For example, he says, "For in truth lust is made out of a perverse will, and when lust is served it becomes habit, and when habit is not resisted, it becomes necessity."[14] The Unnamed's habit of crime had become a necessity in his life. Augustine also explains how God's grace gave him the opportunity to see his mistake and the strength to change course. As the Unnamed begins to see the horror of his life, he first feels despair and even contemplates suicide, but then finds some relief in Lucia's words "heard more than once, only a few hours before, 'God will forgive so many things, for an act of mercy' " (395). The final stage of the Unnamed's conversion takes place in front of a man as famous for his virtue as the Unnamed was notorious for his vice. He is Cardinal Federigo Borromeo, the Archbishop of Milan.

Upon first meeting Cardinal Borromeo, the Unnamed does not speak.

> The Unnamed had been driven there by the compelling force of a mysterious inner tempest, rather than led there by a reasoned decision; and it was the same force that made him stand there, tormented by two contrary passions—on the one hand, a powerful longing and a confused hope of finding relief from his internal torture, and on the other, wrath and shame at the idea of coming like a penitent, an underling, a vulgar wretch, to admit himself in the wrong, and implore the help of a fellow man.(413)

In a few moving pages, Manzoni reports the conversation between the two "great" men and conveys the emotions felt by both. Manzoni clearly shows that the Cardinal's insight into the soul of the Unnamed, as well as his virtue, especially humility, facilitate the last stages of the Unnamed's conversion. The Unnamed once again understands the depth of his iniquities but this time is able to say: ". . . and yet I feel a comfort, a joy . . . yes, yes . . . a joy such as I have never known during all this repugnant life of mine" (418).

The Cardinal's interpretation of the joy felt by the Unnamed echoes perennial Christian wisdom. He says, "That is a foretaste of joys to come . . . which God gives you to make you love his service, and to hearten you to enter resolutely into the new life in which you will have so much evil to undo, so many acts of reparation to perform, so many tears to shed" (418). The Unnamed responds to the Cardinal by telling him about the outrage to which Lucia had been subject. Then both the Unnamed and the Cardinal set about to restore Lucia to her former way of life.

Manzoni's description of Federigo Borromeo gives still additional angles on virtue. "He was one of those few men—rare in any age—who devote the resources of an exceptional intellect, of vast wealth, and of a privileged position in society in an unbroken effort to seek out and practice the means of making the world a better place" (401). As a young boy Borromeo was able to accept the constant teaching of his religious tradition on humility, the vanity of pleasure, and the injustices of pride even though diametrically opposed teachings were often professed and lived by the very people who taught the authentic Christian doctrine. He came to believe that everyone has a duty to perform so that life is not "a treadmill for the majority and unending holidays for the few" (401). He had no interest in having a superior position so that he might enjoy superiority over others. He was content to do his duty as a simple priest and only accepted to become Archbishop of Milan "at the express command of the Pope" (403).

While Archbishop, Borromeo was frugal in the use of resources for himself, but very generous toward others. He used his great personal wealth both to help the poor and to support learning. He did the latter on a grand scale by establishing the Ambrosian Library and paying a salary to nine scholars to work in theology, history, literature, and oriental languages. Manzoni reports that Borromeo continued his patronage of the library and scholars despite hearing criticism. When a plague was ravaging Milan, Cardinal Borromeo resisted pressure to leave the city, but stayed on, motivating his priests to offer their lives in the care of the sick.

Cardinal Borromeo's conversation with Don Abbondio shows pastoral care and an appreciation for the possibility and obligation of overcoming moral weakness. As Abbondio's bishop, Borromeo reproaches him for failing to carry out his priestly duty to marry Renzo and Lucia. But then he helps the parish priest to overcome his fear of threats, to appreciate the sufferings of the betrothed, and to grow in love for them. The bishop tells the parish priest that he should have prepared himself for his duties by asking God for the requisite courage. This exhortation reminds me of Augustine's reflection on the accountability of the soul in number 218 of Book Three of *On the Free Choice of the Will*: "It must be held to account for what it has not tried to know, and for what it has not taken proper care in preparing itself to perform rightly." Don Abbondio clearly did not prepare himself to carry out the duties of the priest-hood. In fact, he never tried to understand the meaning of being a priest.

A remarkable trait possessed by Cardinal Borromeo was his in-dependence from the opinions of others. After describing an un-usual act of kindness by Borromeo, Manzoni writes, "we would like to see more examples of a virtue so free from influence by the reign-ing opinions of the day—for every period has its own . . ." (408). Despite criticism Borromeo had given a young girl a suitable dowry so that she would not be forced into a nunnery by her father.

Manzoni makes clear that Borromeo's virtues were quite extraor-dinary, even for a good bishop. Despite the pressures of the culture and corruption within the church, Borromeo was able to avoid un-wise accommodation to the spirit of the age. He lived out, in truly remarkable fashion, the Biblical teaching that all men and women should find ways to live for the common good. "Like good stewards of the manifold grace of God serve one another with whatever gift each of you has received" (1 Peter 4:10).

Manzoni is such a realistic storyteller, with an eye for revealing details, that his readers cannot but see more clearly into the per-sonal and social consequences of passions and virtues. The story of Cristoforo shows that zeal for justice requires equal attentiveness to one's own vices and imperfections as well; Gertrude's life makes the reader *feel* that freedom is a necessary condition of genuine virtue; the conversion of the Unnamed reveals how the attainment of self-knowledge requires a person to overcome the blinding effect of passions. The description of Borromeo suggests the possibility of learning to live the Christian faith even when religious leaders inculcate Christian and non-Christian teachings at the same time. His story also shows that the attainment of the common good de-pends on the practice of virtue by individuals, especially leaders.

On the last page of his novel, Manzoni himself expresses agree-ment with the reflections of Lucia and Renzo on the meaning of the events in their lives. After being married for some indeterminate period of time, they both come to this conclusion:

". . . troubles may come because we have asked for them; but that the most prudent and innocent of conduct is not necessarily enough to keep them away; also that when they come, through our fault or otherwise, trust in God goes far to take away their sting, and makes them a useful preparation for a better life." (720)

Why Ordinary Virtue Is Heroic: The Decay of Religion

There are two general reasons why the understanding and practice of the virtues just described are especially difficult these days: the influence of American culture and the decay of religion. The troublesome aspects of American culture could be variously formulated. My formulation would address topics such as the following: the eclipse of duties by rights talk, the absence of public discussion about virtue, individualism (as described by Tocqueville) and subservience to public opinions, the exaggerated emphasis on autonomy in ethics and extreme notions of privacy in the law, the affirmation of what is right and good in terms of subjectively held "values," the removal or attenuation of moral norms by misplaced compassion, the incidence of divorce, the reasons offered to justify abortion and euthanasia, "values clarification" in the schools, the influence of the entertainment media (MTV, etc.), the randomness of genuine liberal education in the universities, materialism, subservience to the "money culture," the disappearance of the public good, especially in the minds and hearts of college students, and the lack of real attention to the problems of the underclass.

Religion, of course, could also be viewed as an aspect of culture. It is more helpful, in my judgment, to look at religion as the other major influence on the minds and the hearts of people *and* as a critic of culture. Still any treatment of religion's decay will necessarily touch on negative cultural influences.

In any era the prevailing culture will pose more or less serious obstacles to the practice of religion. Consequently, even religious communities with an anchor in an uncorrupted religious tradition will experience difficulty in educating all their members. Today the hold of many churches in America on their anchor is, at best, tenuous because of two factors: religious ignorance within every community and various levels of accommodation to the *Zeitgeist*. Let us focus on these two factors in general and then seek to discern their influence in the Catholic Church.

The Prevalence of Ignorance

For a long time polls have indicated that Americans consistently identify themselves as religious, much more religious than the rest of the industrialized world. How then is religion decaying? One helpful way to begin answering the question is to look at the old Herberg thesis. Back in 1955 Will Herberg drew attention to the problem of religion in America in his justly famous book, *Protestant, Catholic, Jew*. Herberg wrote, "America seems to be at once the most religious and the most secular of nations."[15] At the time Herberg was writing, Americans described themselves as religious, flocked to church, regarded the Bible as the revealed word of God, bought Bibles and distributed them. Yet, a 1950 Gallup poll revealed that 53 percent of Americans couldn't name one of the four Gospels. In 1954 *Time* reported the responses of 30 outstanding Americans who were asked "to rate the hundred most significant events in history." Herberg's summary of the results makes an impression: ". . . first place was given to Columbus' discovery of America, while Christ, His birth or crucifixion, came fourteenth, tied with the discovery of x-rays and the Wright brothers' first plane flight."[16] After thoroughly analyzing the evidence, Herberg came to the following conclusion in the last chapter of his book: ". . . the new religiosity pervading America seems to be largely the religious validation of the social patterns and cultural values associated with the American way of life."[17] Americans readily admit, Herberg further explained, that religion "has little to do with their politics or business affairs, except to provide an additional sanction and drive. Most of the other activities of life—education, science, entertainment—could be added to the list."[18] Herberg described this way of looking at things as secularism. ". . . [F]or what is secularism but the practice of the absence of God in the affairs of life. The secularism characteristic of the American mind is implicit and is not felt to be at all inconsistent with the most sincere attachment to religion."[19]

In short, Herberg came to the conclusion that religion in America was a watered-down version of Protestant, Catholic, or Jewish faith. Religion made Americans feel good about themselves and their culture instead of moving them to repent of their sins and to recognize the imperfections and downside of the American way.

Two recent books draw attention to the problems of religion in America today: Robert Wuthnow's *Act of Compassion: Caring for Others and Helping Ourselves* and E. J. Dionne's *Why Americans Hate Politics*. Wuthnow, a sociologist at Princeton University, attempted to discern the influence of religious faith as a possible explanation for acts of compassion. He discovered that regular church attendance and a felt experience of God's love motivated people to engage in charitable activities. "People who said they feel it is important to develop their own religious beliefs independently of any church were also less likely to value caring for the needy than people who took issue with this popular form of religious individualism."[20] Wuthnow's data also revealed that some people made sense of their compassionate behavior in the light of the Good Samaritan story. So, Biblical teachings have, indeed, influenced the way they live. In general, though, Wuthnow found that Americans have little knowledge of the Bible, theology, or religious ethics, and cannot usually relate religious teachings to compassion. In addition, religion is having less and less real impact on people's lives.

Departing from the role of the neutral observer, Wuthnow argues that the decline of religious practice will have an adverse effect on the common good. "If fewer and fewer people participate regularly in religious organizations, then the impact of the Good Samaritan story is bound to diminish."[21] As it is, according to Wuthnow, the young are already decidedly less familiar with the story of the Good Samaritan than older people. The preservation of this story in the minds and hearts of young and old is a very important antidote to the negative effects of American individualism. "For us, the story of the Good Samaritan is fundamentally about the possibility of human kindness in a society of strangers."[22] It further shows "that even somebody not 'in' can make a contribution to society."[23]

If the Good Samaritan story, as well as other Biblical stories, continue to fade from people's consciousness, the possibility of keeping alive the tradition of religious virtue, as well as the meaning of individual virtue, will decline proportionately. My own experience teaching mostly Catholics bears out Wuthnow's observations about the decline of religious knowledge. Upon walking into theology class, few students can name a virtue and most are hard pressed to explain such terms as revelation, the Incarnation, or the Redemption. Furthermore many are not embarrassed about their ignorance nor do they have a strong desire to learn something about the faith in which they have been reared. The exceptions to the general rule prove to be interesting. After reading one of Avery Dulles's books on the Church, one student recently told me that she decided to renew the practice of her faith. She wondered why no one ever told her about many of the things Christians believe.

In analyzing the acts of real compassion, Wuthnow discovered that individualistic Americans have great difficulty giving a justification for their compassion. Wuthnow's most compelling explanation of this embarrassing fact is the absence of appropriate language in American public life. He says that with all the emphasis on self-fulfillment and feeling good about one's self "the language of sacrifice has dropped out of our vocabulary."[24] Even more to the heart of the matter is Wuthnow's endorsement of a view advanced by the well-known sociologist Robert N. Bellah. "Bellah argues," writes Wuthnow, "that many of the things we cherish deeply—family, virtue, religious freedom—have come to be defended as matters of personal preference. We have, he suggests, lost our capacity to defend these values in terms of any higher-order principles or universalistic claims."[25] In other words, people believe they create their own values by an act of will rather than discover objective right or wrong by using their mind or relying on their religious faith. Thus, without a widely accepted agreement on the meaning of the good and of virtue, individualistic Americans just do not have the categories to explain their behavior except in terms of personal choice. My own experience in the classroom generally bears out the contention of Wuthnow and Bellah that people usually do not appeal to objective moral norms based on faith or reason. In response to the question, "Why do you respect people's rights?" students most often respond, "So that other people will respect mine" or "because it's the law." Rarely will a student ever say because it is the right thing to do. In all my years of teaching mostly Catholic students, no one has even alluded to virtue as a

seems to be assuming the colors of its environment, but the result is that it loses its identity, which depends on just that distinction between the sacred and the profane, and in the conflict that can and often must exist between them.[28]

Christianity shows fear of modernity when it compromises its teaching for the sake of being accepted. As examples of Christian compromises, Kolakowski mentions cooperation with so-called "sexual liberation," approval of concupiscence, and praise of violence. Kolakowski's judgment on these tendencies goes right to the point: "There are enough forces in the world to do all these things without the aid of Christianity."[29]

The problem of religion is basically the same today—only intensified—as it was in 1950. Religious ignorance and accommodation to the culture inhibit religions from maintaining their identity. The ignorance and accommodation is so pervasive and deep that many religious leaders and their followers have no idea that they are slipping away from genuine faith. Secularism within the churches is proving to be a much more formidable opponent than any Enlightenment attacks on the religion.

Accommodation and Ignorance within the Catholic Church

The Catholic Church in the United States, often ridiculed—more rarely praised—for its opposition to the spirit of the age, has also been affected both by the ignorance of its adherents and by unwise accommodation to cultural trends. William Galston, a political theorist and observer of Catholicism from the outside, believes the Catholic Church in the United States has made significant accommodations to the liberal public culture.

Witness the extraordinary recent meeting in the Vatican between U.S. Catholic bishops and representatives of the Pope: The Roman prelates inveighed against what they saw as the laxity of the American Church. American bishops responded with a fascinating disquisition in which they pointed out, *inter alia*, that liberal political culture encourages rational criticism of all forms of authority, a tendency the American Church is not free to disregard. The notion of unquestioned authority . . . is almost unintelligible to U. S. Catholics.[30]

Galston means, I think, that Catholics tend to look at authoritative teachings on faith and morals through the prism of such concepts as autonomy, choice, rights, subjectively held values, and personal preference. There are many illustrations of Galston's point but one close to home readily comes to mind.

Last spring the student newspaper at the Jesuit University where I teach ran an editorial arguing that the spread of AIDS cannot be controlled unless people use condoms "when they choose to engage in sexual activity." In response to this fact, the editorial continues, the university has two choices: stubbornly reiterate Catholic teaching on premarital sex and the use of condoms "even at the expense of student lives" or "attempt to carry out the Jesuit mission of holistic education." Holistic education, as understood by the student editors, does not explicitly condone premarital sex but explains and advocates the use of condoms for the sexually active student. The editorial presents holistic education as the mean between simple "stubborn adherence to church doctrine" and neglect of doctrine altogether.

There are several presuppositions to this new doctrine of the mean. Students are so taken by sexual pleasure that education to the virtue of moderation is impossible. People cannot or will not refrain from casual sex, and churches are unable to teach the mystery of sex and marriage as depicted, for example, by Paul in the Epistle to the Ephesians (5:21-32). Still another presupposition is that students will not effectively learn "safe" sex practices unless the university contributes to the instruction.

There is more to the student editorial than disregard for church teaching in the name of autonomy. Students can obviously get condoms and instruction without help from the university. Their editorial then must be a plea for understanding, compassion, and even some kind of approval for their sexual mores. They do not want to feel ashamed. Students will undoubtedly feel better about themselves if society, the university, the church, and parents encourage them to practice "safe" sex. Making the young feel good is the primary goal of many educators and caregivers—who also want to feel good about themselves. The idea of nurturing an Augustinian restless heart in the young is Greek to many in the helping professions. In the name of realism, caring people too often rush to press condoms on the young instead of laboring to give reasons for giving up shameless, destructive behavior.

The concept of holistic education in the Jesuit tradition can mean many things when interpreted in the light of the malleable concepts such as historical consciousness, historicism, and culture-bound contexts. Albeit an elementary student of *The Spiritual Exercises*, I am quite sure that St. Ignatius—even if he were living in our culture—would not accept advocacy of condom use as part of Jesuit education. The students who offered an interpretation of Jesuit education in tune with the contemporary *Zeitgeist* could have supported their argument by an explicit reliance on the new theories of interpretation that prevail in secular and religious circles. These theories allow readers to reinterpret or dismiss texts that oppose or raise serious questions about accommodation to prevailing cultural trends.

A candid abandonment of one's faith is no longer necessary given the possibilities offered by reinterpretation of texts and longstanding teachings. In my judgment, churches could more easily deal with avowed atheism and agnosticism than with their own members who "reinterpret" teachings that seem wrong, outdated, or embarrassing.

The argument from the perspective of ordinary virtue against the typical "compassionate" response to student sexual behavior would run like this. Engaging in promiscuous sexual activity is not really safe even with condoms. Condoms sometimes fail to prevent the transmission of the AIDS virus. Even when condoms do preserve the life of the sexually active person, they do not save anyone from serious spiritual harm. Promiscuity rips apart present friendships and endangers future marriage commitments because it leads men and women to treat each other as objects of gratification, not as humans made in God's image. Learning to appreciate the wonderful gift of life inclines students to render thanks to God by not harming themselves or their friends through premarital sexual activity.

The habits of "hooking up" and of persistent, excessive drinking pose an insurmountable obstacle to serious education at any university. What Socrates said in another cultural context is, nevertheless, still pertinent: ". . . We surely know that when someone's desires incline strongly to some one thing, they are therefore weaker with respect to the rest, like a stream that has been channelled off in that other direction."[31] Being absorbed in the pursuit of pleasure is not only an obstacle to the attainment of personal excellence, such as the education of the mind, but also diminishes the energy and inclination to address problems pertaining to the common good.

The easy acceptance of casual sexual relations has certainly been influenced by the new thinking on shame. In a recent book-review essay on the subject of shame, Christopher Lasch writes: ". . . Formerly, shame was the fate of those whose conduct fell short of cherished ideals. Now that ideals are suspect, it refers only to a loss of self-esteem." In other words, "shame these days, refers to whatever prevents us from 'feeling good about ourselves,' "[32] such as attempting to live according to the expectations of parents, church, or society. In *The Laws* of Plato, the Athenian describes shame as fearing the opinion of others "when we think we will be considered evil if we say or do something that is not noble."[33] The Athenian claims that this fear saves people from cowardice and self-indulgence. To some extent a sense of shame, according to the Athenian, fills a void caused by the absence of the virtue of courage and moderation. Plato's text reminded students in my class of what some young people on campus designate as "the walk of shame." This is an early morning return to the dormitory of a student who has spent the night elsewhere. (Other students in the class quipped that such a return was "the walk of triumph.")

That students can still speak of "the walk of shame" shows that the old notion of shame is not yet extinct, despite the efforts of many professionals. In his review of the literature on shame, Lasch reports that students of shame, including enlightened ministers and rabbis, recommend "the deflation of ideals as the prescription for mental health." In other words, he says, they want "to cure shame with shamelessness."[34] Lasch derides the attempt to manufacture self-respect for people by removing any obligation to measure up to impersonal standards. This kind of compassion, argues Lasch, is "the human face of contempt" because it reveals a low view of human beings. Lasch concludes his review by suggesting that real religion may be able to do something for people who suffer from "an inner conviction of 'absolute unlovability.' "[35]

At this time Catholicism has an opportunity to make an important contribution to the ordinary lives of Americans and even to the ennobling of democracy. But to do so effectively, it must frankly address its internal problems. Neither the Bible, the teachings of Jesus, nor Church teachings are simply authoritative for many Catholics, especially for younger adults. It is, of course, commonplace for young Catholics to have little interest in what the Church teaches. They will often say that the Bible makes unrealistic demands on people or, more rarely, that Jesus was mistaken about a few things he taught.

Catholic rejection of authoritative teaching is, however, mitigated by ignorance. As mentioned, many younger Catholics have only a passing knowledge of their faith. At least since the 1960s, religious education programs have not been successful in educating the minds of Catholics regarding essential Catholic teachings on faith and morals. In fact, the formal religious education of most Catholics stops in the eighth grade after the reception of Confirmation. Even what religious knowledge they receive up to that point is usually not well presented.

The kind of instruction Catholics receive during Sunday mass does not seem to make up for the deficiencies of CCD. Many priests these days receive neither a fine liberal education nor a thorough grounding in philosophy, theology, or Biblical languages. Because of their deficient education even well-meaning priests may not be capable of offering much insight into the Scripture readings. Rarely have I seen any priests go back to Aquinas, Augustine, or other church fathers, to understand either Scripture or Church teaching.

Even hardworking, dedicated priests are unwittingly influenced by the non-Christian aspects of the culture. The education of many, if not most, priests will be influenced at some time by what James Hunter calls cultural progressivism. Progressivists, Hunter correctly notes, have "a strong tendency to translate the moral ideals of a religious tradition so that they conform to and legitimate the contemporary *Zeitgeist*. In other words, what all *progressivist* worldviews share in common *is the tendency to resymbolize historic faiths according to the prevailing assumptions of contemporary life.*"[36]

The accommodation of Catholic preaching to the culture is usually not egregious. Parish priests will rarely express dissenting theological opinions from the pulpit. They are much more likely to pass over in silence unpopular Christian moral teachings, especially on sex and property. Priests are also prone to avoid an in-depth explanation of Christian doctrines such as an article of the Apostles' Creed. Insufficient or inadequate commentary on the doctrine of the Catholic faith is an accommodation to the pragmatic bent of the American mind. As Tocqueville said, "In the present age the human mind must be coerced into theoretical studies."[37] Finally, when imbued with the categories of compassion, values, rights, affirmation, and empowerment, priests will tend to omit or soften the language of virtue, sacrifice, and opposition to the prevailing culture.

One educated woman in my neighborhood recently told me that a priest in a local parish talked about chastity from the pulpit at a morning mass. She was so delighted that she congratulated him and offered encouragement to repeat his remarks at a special evening mass for the youth of the parish. She was amazed when the priest failed to do so. That same priest told me that he doesn't like to talk about religious teachings not likely to be warmly received by the young in his audience.

The Catholic bishops in the United States have not taken sufficient steps as a conference either to overcome the religious ignorance of Catholics or to stem the tide of gradual accommodation to the culture. None of the bishops' major statements over the past 25 years has specifically addressed these problems. The U.S. bishops have, of course, *indirectly* addressed the religious ignorance and their practice of accommodation through various statements and actions. The bishops of the world, in collaboration with Vatican authorities, have succeeded in producing a new catechism entitled *Cathechism of the Catholic Church*. Whether it will be effectively used in the United States remains to be seen. (What individual bishops have done in their capacity as diocesan ordinaries is beyond the scope of this paper.)

A look at the record will show that American bishops have spent an inordinate amount of time on politics to the detriment of the religious mission of the Catholic Church. Recently the Catholic bishops published a four-volume collection of their letters and statements.[38] In his foreword to *Volume 4*, Cardinal Bernardin of Chicago says that social justice is the most frequently addressed subject between 1975 and 1983. The bishops' focus on social justice has taken them beyond the realm of principle deep into that of policy. In their social justice statements, the bishops spend little time explaining the principles of Catholic social teaching that would be acceptable to Catholics of all political persuasions. For example, they do not explain why the public good depends on the practice of virtue by individual citizens. Instead, they concentrate on delivering their own political opinions, with which Catholics may legitimately disagree.

Although the bishops have admitted advocacy of debatable political opinions (see their 1983 pastoral letter on war and peace), they have occasionally denied involvement in partisan politics, that is, lobbying like any other interest group. For example, Bishop James Malone, as President of the NCCB/USCC, said, shortly before the 1984 presidential election, that the USCC takes positions on public policy issues but does not endorse political candidates. "The point needs emphasizing," said Malone, "lest in the present political context, even what we say about issues be perceived as an expression of political partisanship."[39] Malone implied that only the episcopal endorsement of political candidates would properly be called partisanship.

It is certainly undeniable that Catholic bishops ardently believe in virtue and mention its importance in various letters and statements. However, the American bishops, as a group, have never formally addressed the subject of virtue in a statement to the public or to the clergy, religious or laity, of the Catholic Church.

If Catholics are to appreciate and understand the various Christian virtues, they must hear as much about them from bishops and clergy as they do about laws against abortion, social justice, human rights, Gospel "values," and compassion. This is true because as

E. J. Dionne said in *Why Americans Hate Politics*, "Over time, when people stop *saying* things publicly, they stop *believing* them privately and when they stop believing them, they will, over time, stop *acting* on them."[40]

One final note about the bishops. They could learn something from the success John F. Kennedy enjoyed in tapping latent American idealism. In his inaugural address, Kennedy summoned his fellow Americans to generosity: "Ask not what your country can do for you, but what you can do for your country." It is not impossible for religious leaders both to make demands on people for the sake of the common good and to inspire, in the spiritual realm, the kind of enthusiasm Kennedy did in the political.

Conclusion

Those finding this brief, incomplete review of Catholicism in America somewhat bleak can draw consolation from the fact that I did not try to describe the improper accommodation of Catholic moral theology to modernity, especially its embrace of historicism.

On the brighter side, there are signs of hope in the Catholic Church of the United States. But that is another story. Suffice it to say that the new catechism could prove to be an important source for overcoming religious ignorance and imprudent accommodation to the *Zeitgeist*. In my judgment, many Catholics would respond favorably—even eagerly—to informed and authoritative persuasion by their religious leaders.

Notes

1. Jane Austen, *Persuasion* (New York: Viking Penguin, 1986); Alessandro Manzoni, *The Betrothed* (*I Promessi Sposi*), (New York: Viking Penguin, 1987). All subsequent references to these books appear in the text.

2. Thomas Aquinas, *Summa Theologica*, II, ii (New York: Beniziger Brothers, Inc., 1947), II, ii, q. 47, a. 1, a. 4, pp. 1389–91.

3. Ibid., a. 8, pp. 1393–94.

4. Joseph Pieper, *The Four Cardinal Virtues* (Notre Dame, IN: University of Notre Dame Press, 1966), 10.

5. Aquinas, *Summa*, II, ii, q. 49, a. 1, pp. 1401–2.

6. Ibid., a. 3, p. 1403.

7. Ibid., a. 4, pp. 1403–4.

8. Ibid., a. 6, pp. 1404–5.

9. St. Gregory the Great, *Pastoral Care*, trans. Henry Davis, S.J. (New York: Paulist Press, 1950), Part III, ch. 9, p. 107.

10. Aquinas, *Summa*, II, ii, q. 136, a. 2, pp. 1750–51.

11. Quoted in Aquinas, *Summa*, II, ii, q. 136, a. 3, p. 1751.

12. St. Augustine, *De Moribus Ecclesiae Catholicae* (Washington, DC: The Catholic University of America Press, 1966), ch. 19–21, pp. 30–34.

13. St. Augustine, *The Confessions*, trans. John K. Ryan (New York: Doubleday Image Books, 1960), bk. 7, ch. 5, p. 162.

14. St. Augustine, *The Confessions*, bk. 8, ch. 5, p. 188.

15. Will Herberg, *Protestant, Catholic, Jew,* (Garden City, NY: Doubleday & Co., 1969), 3.

16. Ibid., 2.

17. Ibid., 263.

18. Ibid., 270.

19. Ibid.

20. Robert Wuthnow, *Acts of Compassion: Caring for Others and Helping Ourselves* (Princeton: Princeton University Press, 1991), 153. Remarks on Wuthnow are taken from a review of his book by J. Brian Benestad, *America* 168, no. 18 (1993): 20, 22.

21. Wuthnow, *Acts of Compassion*, 178.

22. Ibid., 182.

23. Ibid., 185.

24. Ibid., 115.

25. Ibid., 87–88.

26. E. J. Dionne, *Why Americans Hate Politics* (New York: Touchstone, Simon & Schuster, 1991), 221.

27. Ibid.

28. Leszek Kolakowski, *Modernity on Endless Trial* (Chicago: University of Chicago Press, 1990), 69.

29. Ibid., 84.

30. William Galston, *Liberal Purposes: Goods, Virtues, and Diversity in the Liberal State* (New York: Cambridge University Press, 1991), 292.

31. Plato, *The Republic* (New York: Basic Books, 1968), 485d, p. 165.

32. Christopher Lasch, "For Shame," *The New Republic* 207, no. 7 (1992): 29.

33. Plato, *The Laws* (New York: Basic Books, 1980), 647a, p. 27.

34. Lasch, "For Shame," 32.

35. Ibid., 34.

36. James D. Hunter, *Culture Wars: The struggle to define America* (New York: Basic Books, 1991), 44–45.

37. Alexis de Tocqueville, *Democracy in America*, vol. 2, bk. 1 (New York: Random House, Vintage Books, 1945), ch. 10, 48.

38. Hugh J. Nolan, ed., *Pastoral Letters of the United States Catholic Bishops*, vol. 1, *1792–1983*; vol. 2, *1792–1940*; vol. 3, *1962–1974*; vol. 4, *1975–1983* (Washington, DC: National Conference of Catholic Bishops, United States Catholic Conference, 1983, 1984). In composing the next few pages in the text I have drawn from my book review on Volume 3 and Volume 4 of the *Pastoral Letters*, published in the *Catholic Historical Review* 72, no. 4 (1986): 687–689.

39. James Malone, *Origins* 14, no. 11 (1984), 16.

40. Dionne, *Why Americans*, 20.

CHAPTER 11

The Screwtape Files: Sources and Conditions of Anti-Virtue

Jean Bethke Elshtain

The Newtape File

First Installment

As compiled by Jean Bethke Elshtain, she having discovered a mysterious virus in her computer one day as she worked on yet another piece on whither virtue. . . .

I

Dear Nephew, my little popinjay,

My mood is nearly jaunty. Please don't misunderstand. My dyspepsia and misanthropy are intact. But things have been going so well for us lately that I have decided I can take occasional hemlock breaks. I have quaffed a few this evening. This no doubt accounts for my jubilation—a word I don't much like, frankly, as it belongs to the Enemy's armamentarium far more than our own. I fear I shall disgust you, but you are no doubt familiar with the Enemy's notion of the kerygma or "good news," this good news being "That they might have life and might have it more abundantly." Their good news was terrible news for Our Father Below. Frankly, we were overwhelmed for many human centuries combating this idea.

Fortunately, we were able, through a good deal of terribly hard work of which you are the heir (and please do not forget it) to enlist some of the Enemy's own camp in our effort. I recall many of Cursed Memory who presented a wonderfully sour and pinched notion of what faith—a frisson seizes me whenever I must write that wretched word—required. So long as we could push the notion that the good news was really bad news of the most sour and nasty sort, we at least had a fighting chance.

We have succeeded most wonderfully. There is no precise turning point, but over time our legions managed to press the notion that Freedom and Faith were antinomies—yes, stark opposites!—and it seems our victory in this regard is secure, at least in that great republic in which you and I now make our temporary abode. Why, I have had two vacations in the past decade! You, of course, cannot afford to take one just yet because there are tough cases in that not-yet-accursed geographic region to which I have assigned you. Can you not do something with the Smith Family of Fremont, Nebraska? You did succeed, my precious pervertlet, in convincing them of the need for what is called cable TV. But the parents seem to have set strict hours for viewing and will not permit the five-year-old to watch MTV despite the fact that her best friend is well and truly "into it," as one of their slang expressions has it. Ah, but I didn't write to chide you. Not tonight. For I have had my own "good news." Our new computer system is working wonderfully. It is much easier to track our progress and progress it is: this calls for more hemlock!

Let me just summarize a few of our triumphs for I know you are a bit "down" about the wretched Smiths and other such hard cases. I have already noted the glorious equation of freedom with license and faith in The Enemy with servitude of the most life-denying sort. But there is much else to be thankful for as we enter those weeks of consumerist excess called The Holiday Season. Another triumph for us, by the way, for we have nearly effaced—at least in the media, more and more our faithful allies on many fronts—any serious and solid mention of The Enemy Savior, that "true Baby, with flesh, blood, hands, and legs," as our foe, Martin Luther, described Him. "Away in the Manger" and all that. If only we could get those hideous Christmas hymns banned! A bevy of our dedicated legal servants is working on this front, and I am confident of a victory in the first decade of the next millennium. Our strategy is to have all such reminders of that stubborn infant removed from public sight and sound. Yes, I know, the churches remain a visible redoubt, a reminder to those not yet solidly in the camp of Our Father Below. But who knows? So many wondrous things have fallen into our lap with but modest effort on our part. Perhaps we will one day see churches themselves stripped of outward insignia of the faith. Perhaps we can get them ensconced behind high walls, the architectural equivalent of what I believe is called a "brown paper bag." This "brown paper bag" was at one time a lingering sign of residual shame as our sort of viewing and reading matter was required to be covered up. Yes, I feel the bile rise at the triumphant thought: we have uncovered what was once shameful. Now we must push to cover what was once (and in some recalcitrant minds is yet) sacred. These reversals are what we seek.

It is nearly time for my soft-core "porn" film on a TV channel devoted exclusively to the purpose—and round-the-clock at that! Feature it: the lonely housewife, the agitated adolescent, the bored businessman, the gullible child, all can now be drawn, with a mere push on the button of their remotes, into a world of fleshly excess so at odds with the Enemy's eros. In this never-ending struggle for and over the body we have been required from the beginning to insinuate the view that faith and the body's needs and desires were at war with one another. This has been a very tricky fight, and you may be too young to understand it fully. We have worked ceaselessly to instill the notion that life and joy were reducible to momentary and passing pleasure of the most "instant" sort. We had to get people hooked, addicted to the fleshly, hence at war with their own bodies. But I exhaust myself to think of this effort. I will instruct you further in future letters. Let us just savor the moment.

Your affectionate uncle,

Newtape

II

Dear Nephew, my hellborn one,

Ah, how I delight in writing you as my esteemed Uncle Screwtape once instructed me, he of diabolical dishonor, now emeritus. He has well earned his current sojourn in a New York City establishment by the pithy name Sex. I fear, however, that Uncle may be nearly exhausted and well-nigh flummoxed; indeed, he may even be somewhat vexed. For the perverse pleasures of this cavern of delicious iniquity have outstripped even his imagination. (But, then, he is over 30.) I understand that our own Madonna of Manichean Delectations (oh, what a treasure she is, what a splendid job I have done, for she has been my special assignment, as you know) dictated the decor. And here, I confess, she has gone beyond even my instructions. For the decor is alive: human bodies poised and posed as if on the very brink of entry into the Kingdom Below. The weekly newsmagazines calmly report this as if it were mere reportage of normal everyday life in what the locals call The Big Apple. Think of it Beelzebubkin! The glorious free publicity, the "normalizing" (as in-vogue academic jargon of the standard inelegant sort would have it) of what was once extreme. I drooled profusely as I read the report, so much so that my bile count dropped precipitously. Indeed, I am being transfused as I dictate. I am all aquiver as I picture in my mind's fiendish eye the following: "Two guys hung from the ceiling in chains and black leather. A female on all fours held her hindquarters up to the cat-o'-nine-tails. Hard bodied couples struck the straining poses of simulated sex. On a giant video screen, the evening's star knelt to shave a man's pubic hair. All the while, dance music throbbed. The occasion? A New York book party, naturally."

This Madonna is a wonder, a prime candidate for Demonification, for induction into the cloven-footed Hall of Infamy. Her book, also called *Sex*, costs nearly fifty dollars and sold 150,000 copies on the first day. All the lonely people—bored and with money to spare. What is most delicious about all this is that it transpires under the word "Freedom." We have succeeded beyond our wildest imaginings in making tens of thousands believe they are engaging in strong and courageous action by buying, viewing, and—best yet—engaging in untrammeled lewd and licentious behavior. They are the prophets of progress. Theirs is the "philosophy of the future," as Uncle Screwtape once wrote. Our devilkin, Madonna, describes her mission as "opening people's minds." (Their pocketbooks, too, but mentioning that would no doubt be supererogatory.) She proclaims to adoring legions that she is a "revolutionary." She fights foes of "free expression." We are working hard not to allow her the merest glimmer of how ludicrous her position is—pushing on a wide-open door as if she were bursting through a ten-foot-thick cement wall en route to the glorious goal of Freedom. For our task has been to perversely (how else?) inculcate the notion that late 20th century moderns in the West live in a world that is constrained and embattled and beset by what we have got people to call "Victorianism." I must constrain myself—I am now braying with such hysterical delight I threaten to dislodge my bile tube.

Can you not see what we have accomplished, dear Nephew? Two citations may help to illustrate my central point, one you seem not quite to have mastered or you would be enjoying somewhat better success with those annoying Smiths. A 19th century writer, whose lightly-worn piety we were never able to dislodge, one Alexis de Tocqueville, proclaimed—I shudder to repeat it—"The soul has wants which must be satisfied." That pesky word "soul." It was an uphill battle for us until the happy day we dislodged that notion, confining it to the musty dustbin of pious memory or empty incantation. Savor the victory for Our Father Below embodied in the transformation of that wretched soul business into our Old Nickian ally Woody Allen's insistence that "The heart wants what it wants." I scripted this myself, murmuring it over and over as Allen prepared for his press announcement professing love for his (more or less) adopted daughter.

"More or less" is important, Nephew, please take note. For this locution speaks to our tremendous victories in dispelling any solidity or *gravitas*, as The Enemy might have it, to the notion of "family." Our Woody took advantage of it—we have worked hard to nurture his narcissism—and thus he could honestly—honestly!—claim that the teenager he had photographed nude and bedded was not only not a biological child, she was not properly an adopted child either—for he had never married his companion of 11 years although they have a bio-child together. He is merely sleeping with his ex-lover's daughter and, as he stressed in one of his many delicious interviews with the press, she is an "adopted daughter. . . . I could have met her at a party or something. . . . I was not a father to her adopted kids in any sense of the word. . . . The last thing I was interested in was the whole parcel of Mia's children." A chthonian wonder, is it not? Woody is "in love" and that's that.

That nuisance Miss Manners may pose a problem here, for she was overheard to jest that the incest taboo may be universal everywhere save in New York. This is the sort of humor we can do without—it may set people's minds to thinking. We need to keep them focused on Woody's words: "I don't find any moral dilemmas whatsoever. I didn't feel that just because she was Mia's daughter, there was any great dilemma." Fortunately, Our Madonna keeps coming through for us because she portrays her exhibitionism as a crusade. I am genuinely giddy at the way she mouths our platitudes and insistently eviscerates not only Freedom but Truth of any of The Enemy's meanings and designs. Perhaps, my serpentine one, you were too busy trying to disrupt Mother Smith's work at the local Hospice (the snide comments from her feckless "friend" that Mrs. Smith had been looking a bit worn and dowdy of late and should take more time "for herself" was a nice touch, good work!) to catch Our Madonna's film, "Truth or Dare." I was so deeply touched, indeed moved, by the simulated sex scenes played out against an altar-like backdrop, and by the writhing in a nun-like habit with a large cross flopping against Our Madonna's bosom, and—oh, splendid shiver of demonic delight—by the prayers led by Our Madonna herself before each exhibitionistic frenzy she calls "art." She actually invokes The Enemy, praying for success in trashing all He holds dear. You must watch this film on video, Nephew. It is elixir for the flagging spirit. "Truth," you see, is a confession of all one's "fantasies," and in this confession lies freedom. One dares to be free. One is brave. One is a freedom-fighter! Our North Americans love this kind of talk, especially when it taps that residue of anti-Catholicism we strove mightily—and still do—to promote.

One moment in the film I especially treasure. I "freeze" it whenever I screen it in my properly chilled loft. Our Madonna, her hair demurely covered by a scarf, her body demurely covered by a black dress, her eyes hidden behind dark glasses, reading her Freedom Sermon of an appropriate two minutes' length with the cameras clicking, the flashes popping, the videos whirring, the microphones humming. Oh, cursed image, how treasured: she was in Rome and fighting our foe, Pope John Paul II, for it seems the Vatican had issued a statement questioning Our Madonna's entertainment standards. Our Madonna responded automatically (this is how we must get all to respond, including those not-yet-damned Smiths) that she was the victim of repression and "as an American," she protested the Vatican's "censorship" in the name of the most fundamental of all freedoms, "freedom of expression." Oh, I could wax so eloquently on this juicy reduction of freedom to "express yourself." It is so cloven-footed! So demonolatric! Although you are not philosophically inclined, Nephew, just think for a moment. Express yourself. Here, tidily encapsulated, are gnostic moments of the most limpid sort.

Your affectionate uncle,

Newtape

III

Dear Nephew,

I trust it did not escape your notice that I have eliminated an affectionate diminutive in my greeting. I am just a bit annoyed that those undamned Smiths persist in tithing. You did succeed in staying Mr. Smith's hand briefly—he had pen in hand, checkbook before him, and you planted, in rapid succession, visions of a new car and a motorboat—but he pushed those seductive objects out of his mind and went ahead with his obnoxiously virtuous duty. May I suggest, Nephew, that perhaps your eagerness got the better of you. You should have remained with the vision of the car just a bit longer. By trotting out a second object Mr. Smith's heart "wants," you inadvertently triggered his concern about having too much when so many have too little. If you had fixed the car image a bit longer, allowed Mr. Smith to linger a while, things might have turned our way. But the word "selfish" came into his mind, then "excessive," then "I don't really need these things"—a sentence I hope to eradicate from the English language by the year 2020. At that point all was lost. You see, and I am annoyed that I must teach you what you ought by now to have learned, if he had construed his desire as reasonable, he might have found a way to shave off his givings to the church. Please remember that overeagerness in the pursuit of diabolism is no virtue, not when we have them more or less where we want them. The "cultural context," as certain of the smart set like to put it, is already temptation-friendly. We need not jump the gun.

Let me explain, for you seem to be in the grip of an unwarranted anxiety. You recall, I assume, our hero of the moment, Woody. I fear you may not understand the full extent of all he has taught. For his primary lesson is that guilt is everywhere; hence, it is nowhere. He has wonderfully trivialized guilt. He is guilty when he gets up in the morning. So, what difference does it make to add a little incest? By blurring any distinction between big and small things, he has helped to make our work easier.

The Enemy, as you were taught in The Infernal Day School, is an obsessive, distinction maker. He worked all too successfully to instil this noxious habit in those debased creatures he seems truly, as Uncle Screwtape pointed out, to love. The more the popular and elite cultures embraces the view that guilt is bad, the better for us. And if guilt applies to everything by definition, its trivialization is the next best thing to eliminating it altogether. I, for one, am so relieved that the pesky fellow Sigmund Freud has been misinterpreted in ways that more often than not support our cause. Freud was far too priggish and moral to be securely in the camp of Our Father. Undamnable fellow! He kept insisting on reflective ethical standards and the like. It was a close call for a while but we appear to have tilted things our way by promoting the view that guilt itself is bad, rather like a nasty, automatic tic to be demeaned and turned into a joking matter—à la Woody—or extirpated altogether. Because Freud is so pervasive a name, it was our lucky break to be able to associate his authority with our distinction-eroding work. You will recall—but please keep it to yourself, you are often far too blabby about our work—that Freud claimed the poor human race labored under too heavy a burden of guilt unattached to real infractions. Appropriate remorse for injuries actually inflicted is, for Freud, and I am sorry to report this, a "good" not a "bad" thing. To be sure, he made certain comments about The Enemy which have served us well. But he never left-off talking about the integrity of being Jewish and similar babbling that seemed to undercut his salutary atheism. Thankfully, this is behind us. What is left is the acidic residue—the all-pervasive moan and groan that guilt is bad or comic. A tremendous triumph for Our Father Below.

Keep your eye on the prize, Nephew. Try some distinction-erosion of your own. Those wretched Smiths, parochial rustics that they are, pay no attention to heavy metal and groups with demonic designer names: "Black Sabbath," "Judas Priest," and the like. Though even here things sometimes get tricky. For often such groups seem to be mocking rather than worshipping Our Father Below. Undamned human humor! Perhaps you could entice the teenage son into listening to the gloriously violent and marvelously misogynistic forms of "rap music." I'm thinking of lyrics my cloven-hoofed compatriot Demonica—as clever a deviltress as ever confounded human beings—helped to write. In your backwater you perhaps missed "Death Certificate," a song promoting salutary racism. Koreans are described as "Oriental one-penny countin' mother-f——s" and threatened with being burned "to a crisp." A second estimable lyric excoriates the "white Jew telling you what to do," and the remedy is breathtaking in its fiendish directness: a "bullet in his temple." One of my own favorites—Demonica played this for me the other evening when I was in a bit of a slump, having watched that horrible Bruce Springsteen spread the joys of parenthood and adult responsibility during a televised concert—is "Momma's Gonna Die Tonight," about murdering and dismembering his Mother shouted at fever pitch by an energetic recruit for Our Father Below, one Ice-T. (Demonica instructed me that his musical genre is "speed metal," not "rap," but I told her to stop making distinctions.)

I am performing a nasty little thought experiment even as I write, imagining the capaciously cruel possibilities of this move. Suppose young Bud began listening day and night, implanting lyrics of hatred of women and Jews and others in his budding (I am clever today!) mind. Suppose Mother Smith announces she must disallow this "immoral" stuff in her home. One of two strategies, both with the imprimatur of Our Father Below, should kick in immediately. Forewarned is forearmed, Nephew, and I will brook no flabby excuses from your corner should you fail.

I suggest this first Machiavellian maneuver—old Nicky, what a charming fellow—as it is less subtle. Young Bud must scream "Censorship!" in the face of his beleaguered Mother's protests. She is trying to censor him. He may accuse her of racism, too, but that would be rather ham-fisted as he knows her to be a leader in local interracial activities. She even taught him Martin Luther King's "I have a dream" speech at one point. I hope you found this as sickening as I have, by the way. But the censorship charge might stick. When she protests that she is censoring nothing, rather, she is being a responsible parent, the riposte out of young Bud's mouth should be something along the lines of this: "You are forcing me to self-censor. You are denying me my constitutional rights to free expression." Here, you see, we are on the ever-shifting sands of distinction erosion once again. For the charge of censorship is now so pervasive it is virtually meaningless. We have more work to do, but we are nearly there in our effort to denude censorship of any lingering weightiness. I chortle each time I think of a mother beseeching a child to avoid hate-mongering (in other words, our sort of love lyrics) and one of the late, and sorely missed, authoritarian regimes of central eastern Europe banning the works of a dissident. Because this reminds me that we have been successful beyond our wildest projections in covering both such moments under one word: "censorship." I implore you, Nephew, take advantage of the "cultural context."

A second strategy, more subtle and probably not for a neophyte nemesis such as yourself, is to push Mother Smith into a fearful anxiety about all of American popular culture. Her overreaction will serve our purposes well. If she becomes hysterical and insists that Bud must listen only to albums of the Mormon Tabernacle Choir or Percy Faith chorales or that icky Lawrence Welk fellow,

No doubt, my little fiend, this sounds mysterious to you. But it is really quite simple. Our Father Below's great demiurgic allies planted the Manichean notion eons ago that evil was its own autonomous principle, a great and gloriously destructive force. The saying "The Devil made me do it"—although turned and twisted by noxious humans into something of a joke—really expresses our sort of Truth. So long as we convince people that they are not responsible; so long as we encourage them to whine and moan and whimper over any slight; so long as we encourage them to disdain any distinction between a snub and slavery (each creates victims!), our side can breathe easier.

A second example. I know you will lap it up eagerly with that purple tongue of yours. Convince as many as you can that "family values" is whatever anybody says it is. What finer example of distinction riddance could we hope for? The media once again is enormously helpful. Although much of the data shows how "ordinary people" continue to daunt us somewhat, they are in the direct line of fire by our allies. For example, 49 percent of top television writers and executives believe adultery is wrong but "everybody else" finds it wrong by 85 percent. I say, look on the gloomy bright side. We are half there with the entertainment moguls. I find myself so cheered every day by the way statistical abuse plays into our hands my temperature drops by 10–15 degrees. Recently, for example, I read that only one in five families fits the Ozzie and Harriet model. When people read this they believe it means only one in five families consists of two parents with children. Not at all, my uncuddly one! Sleight of hand is a great thing. It means that only one in five families consists of a father who is the sole wage-earner, a mother who works for pay not-at-all, and two, precisely two, children. How delectable! And how the social scientists line up with us: we have so many recruits from sociology and political science we have had to add clerks to our Higher Education for Lower Purposes division. A wretched fellow named David Blankenhorn keeps trying to put out accurate information on this score, but I am determined that you not have precise information on what he calls "the truth" for fear you might inadvertently let the cat out of the bag that the vast majority of families consist of a mother and father with children. I read a definition of family the other day which would suit our purposes if we could strip it of all humor. Unfortunately, as written, the description evokes laughter and perhaps moments of recognition on the part of those not solidly in our camp. I include it here but please do not, I repeat, do not, under any circumstances, permit this to circulate in its present funny form. What we must do is get this or a similar definition accepted as solemn "truth."

> **family** (n.) A social unit involving a mother, a father, and children; a father, a father, and children; a mother, a mother, and children; a father and children; a mother and children; children and children; a social worker and children; a lawyer and a child; the Children's Defense Fund, lawyers, and a child; or any group of people who appear together on "Donahue."

I know we are making serious headway when the current superstar of country music, one obnoxiously nice chap named Garth Brooks, includes a song called "Freedom of Choice" on his most recent album. It is a marvel of distinction erosion and particularly effective coming, as it does, from such a decent fellow. Fortunately, for us, he is naive as he has swallowed wholesale our statistics and proclaims that those who proclaim traditional family values "believe family values are June and Walt and 2.3 children. To me it [family values] means laughing, being able to dream." Then he goes on to offer up in all seriousness the definition of family as any arrangement that makes people happy and healthy. This may—just may—disqualify a truly estimable story about family values as no values at all. I clipped it from print the other day. A pregnant singer named Courtney Love posed, large with child, for Vanity Fair with a smoldering cigarette between her fingers. She confesses to "her long love affair with the painkiller Percodan and with heroin, which she says she used during the first trimester." In fact, she and hubby, a punk/rocker named Kurt Cobain of a group called Nirvana (they thanked Satan for their MTV music-video award on the annual show, a real high point for me), used "a lot of drugs" and "copped dope" and decided to get pregnant because it was a "bad time" to do so and because she and hubby "need new friends." Need I add that Demonica, the *force majeure* behind this delicious debacle, was dishonored recently by Our Father Below with an Infernal Hall of Fame membership at our annual awards ritual. You have much to aspire to, and I want you to step up your efforts with young Bud Smith. He remains glum around his Mother, but he continues to accompany the family to church. This must stop.

Your affectionate uncle,

Newtape

V

Dear Nephew, my plutonic sprout,

I am pleased as punch (spiked with Demon Rum, of course) at your recent success in instilling in young Missy Smith the conviction that she is "fat" and must starve herself into conformity with the popular image of an attractive young woman as looking exactly like an attractive young man with small breasts attached. The androgyny craze works in our favor. Need I say why? Distinction destruction, of course! This torture of the body in the name of a mandated vision of the flesh is just what the Diabolical Doctor ordered. And it has the additional salutary effect of driving yet another wedge between mother and father, child and parent, in the name of power or freedom or choice or beauty. The more we "disempower" people from working out their own problems, the better. The more the outside intrudes in the form of culturally authoritative sanctions against legitimate authority the better. For, left to their own devices, ordinary folks might revert to a vocabulary damning—if I may take one of Our Father Below's words in vain— our best interests. Hope, Faith, and Charity—these must not abide! Terms of everyday ethics, as certain wretched humans call it, are very difficult to kill. Yet kill them we must, and a domestic war of all against all fueled by our propaganda is the most efficient method yet devised for undermining the ethical menace.

May I note a trend very much in our favor? I refer to a further debasement of language, this time in the direction of a salutary "abstractedness." The more people are "deeply concerned" about things far away, outside their purview of concrete responsibility, the better for us. You know that Our Father Below wants us to appear, as often as possible, in the form of an angel of light. Abstract benevolence and sentiment serve us, oh, so nicely. There are so many splendid examples! I have picked but three for your delectation.

The first is a story I overheard during a visit some years ago to a place in northwestern Massachusetts called "Happy Valley." Moviegoers were crowded into a small art film theater in a town called Northampton—sophisticated far beyond anything yet dreamed of in Fremont, Nebraska. One trendy couple described their recently concluded trip to Nicaragua, then under the happy control of the Sandinistas, and told of their virtuous labor shoveling manure on a state farm. They were helping the "peasants" to plant crops and fighting American imperialism. Those around the couple trembled with politically correct delight. This was, for me, a perfect moment. A trip to earn political kudos for oneself and to promote an abstraction ("the revolution"). For that very season had brought news of struggling farm families all over America, including some whose farms were being foreclosed in western Massachusetts. But no assistance from the abstractly benevolent went to them, for they were defined politically by an updated version of Marx's phrase—and he was a genial phrase-maker, was he not?—"rural idiots."

A second example I have ripped from past and present headlines. Think, dear Nephew, of all the prominent men who are what is called "progressives" on women's issues who treat real flesh and blood, concrete women before them, with contempt. And think, as well, of the pact with Our Father Below some women's groups make when they say working with a well-known sexual predator may make them "uncomfortable" but if he is "correct" on their issues (abortion, sexual harassment—if somebody else is doing it), then they must mute their ire and stem their scorn. I noticed that the most recent instance featured a "progressive" whose sexual misconduct was well-known to women's groups. But they held their fire until after he had been reelected because he was on "their side" on the "key issues." Now they are clamoring for an investigation because the thing has become too embarrassing. Our Father Below adores this sort of thing: projecting altruism outward toward the correct public policy, the globally benevolent, the politically correct, the theoretically grand, while suffocating virtue that might operate personally, in everyday life. I am particularly fond of grand theories of Justice that diminish by contrast the acts of everyday life called by The Enemy's camp "charity" or "decency" or some other such poisonous possibilities. One of The Enemy's allies, though himself an unbeliever, proclaimed that he should like to be able to "love my mother and also love justice." Thankfully, this nuisance, Albert Camus, was killed at an early age. He was a bone in my throat. He kept insisting that one had to tend to concrete matters concretely and that one could not leapfrog over particular ties in favor of abstract and by definition impossible ones, as our ally, Jean-Paul Sartre, argued so successfully for so many years.

Here is a third instance, of a similar sort. Another delicious item from my file, a love-letter in *The New York Times* under the title "A Man's Child-Care Crusade." This is the story of one Richard B. Stolley, editorial director of Time Inc. Magazine Company who heads something called Child Care Action Campaign. It seems that when Mr. Stolley was young he was an admirably inattentive father. His ex-wife stayed home with the children. "It was her problem," he says. "But this 63-year-old grandfather, an athletic-looking man who jogs regularly and wears Italian suits, has had a dramatic change of mind," so says *The Times*. I am so pleased their reporter did not catch on. For Mr. Stolley has not changed his mind at all. I confess: I was at first apprehensive when I began the piece. But I quickly got reassured for Mr. Stolley, who is "angry" and "outraged" at the child-care situation, still wants anybody but himself to care for children. You see, Mr. Stolley used to think child care was something that someone else should do so that it did not hamper him. Today, Mr. Stolley thinks child care is something someone else should do. But this can be treated as a marvelous change of heart because the "someone else" is no longer a wife but the government or the employer! *The New York Times* is our solid ally on this front. Too bad the reporter really couldn't decipher Mr. Stolley's line, "Everywhere you look in our society, if child care breaks down, everything else starts grinding to a halt." And what did he have in mind? Did he mean children grow up bereft of love and care, and this is bad for children? No, he means "work in this magazine company involves strange hours and depends on child-care arrangements." What's good for Time Inc. is good for America! I could not stop smirking for several moments at this giddy portrayal of Mr. Stolley as a transformed sort of guy. What a windfall for us and unplanned by anyone, just another delicious example of the "cultural context."

I fear I may have tired you, but these exemplary stories should give you renewed energy for the struggle with the Smiths, precious devilkin.

Your affectionate uncle,

Newtape

Compiler's note: This is the first installment only. Other letters are stuck in the machine. Newtape has only just begun. Clearly he is on a roll.

The Possibility of Civil Society

David Blankenhorn

As a social institution, the family is steadily weakening in almost all modern societies. Moreover, the communal ties and institutional supports which surround and help to sustain the family—the local social ecologies of family life—are also steadily weakening in modern societies. Taken together, these developments suggest a worldwide trend among the rich countries that we might term the decline of civil society.

What are the dimensions and consequences of this trend? How do opinion leaders in the United States understand and describe this trend? Most important, what are the public policy and cultural responses to this trend in modern societies? These are large, difficult questions. Guided largely by the scholars who have contributed essays to this volume, let me try, in a very preliminary way, to answer them.

The Decline of Civil Society

In his study of family change in Sweden, Switzerland, New Zealand, and the United States, David Popenoe concludes that "it is possible to postulate a single family trend involving movement away from the bourgeois family and even away from the nuclear family-kinship system." Popenoe describes this "general family trend" in advanced nations as "heading in the direction of a post-nuclear family system."[1]

This movement toward the post-nuclear family contains five measurable components. First, rising rates of divorce and unwed childbearing, which mean the steady disintegration of the married, mother-father childraising unit. Second, the growing inability of families to carry out their primary social functions: maintaining the population level, regulating sexual behavior, socializing children, and caring for family members. Third, the transfer of influence and authority from families to other institutions, such as schools, peer groups, the media, and the state. Fourth, smaller and more unstable family units. And fifth, the weakening of familism as a cultural value in relationship to other values, such as personal autonomy and egalitarianism.[2]

The weight of scholarly evidence strongly supports Popenoe's basic thesis. From 1970 to 1990, for example, the member countries of the OECD typically experienced a remarkable 30 to 50 percent increase in the number of one-parent families. Of course, the velocity of this phenomenon varied from country to country. At one extreme, rates of family fragmentation have been comparatively modest in Switzerland, New Zealand, France, and Japan, while at the other extreme, Sweden, the United States, Great Britain, and Australia are probably the countries with the modern world's weakest and most rapidly deteriorating family systems.[3]

In addition, in much of Europe, unwed childbearing, while increasing, currently accounts for only a small proportion of all one-parent homes. In the United States, by contrast, about 31 percent of all children are born to unwed mothers. Unwed childbearing has now reached a rough parity with divorce as a generator of father-absent homes in the United States.[4]

Despite these important variations, however, the widely respected family scholar Urie Bronfenbrenner points out that "the underlying dynamics and ultimate effects of family change are strikingly similar around the globe."[5] Similarly, in his study of worldwide changes in divorce patterns, William J. Goode summarizes: "If we consider decisions about marriage or fertility, relations between parents and children, cohabitation, living alone, divorce, women's work, or the ideology of egalitarianism within the family, the present trends are toward avoiding long-term emotional or economic investments in the family."[6] In sum, the core family dynamic across modern societies is clearly toward what might be termed deinstitutionalization, characterized primarily by the weakening of marriage, the decline of familistic cultural norms, and the splitting apart of the mother-father "nucleus" of the nuclear family.

Moreover, family decline in modern societies has apparently been accompanied by a parallel decline in much of the rest of civil society. By civil society, I mean not only the family, but also the larger group of what Peter Berger and Richard John Neuhaus call "mediating structures," or what Robert D. Putnam calls "norms and networks of civic engagement" that operate largely beyond the reach of both the laws of the state and the incentives of the market.[7] As Jean Bethke Elshtain reminds us, observers of democracy "have long recognized the vital importance of civil society," understood as

> the many forms of community and association that dot the landscape of a democratic culture, from families to churches to neighborhood groups to self-help movements to volunteer assistance to the needy. Historically, political parties, too, were a robust part of this picture.[8]

In the United States, the density and variety of the civil society has long been celebrated as a hallmark of American exceptionalism and a defining feature of the national character. In the 1830s, for example, Alexis de Tocqueville famously described the American habit of forming voluntary "associations." Tocqueville writes:

> Americans of all ages, all conditions, and all dispositions, constantly form associations. They have not only commercial and manufacturing companies, in which all take part, but associations of a thousand other kinds,—religious, moral, serious, futile, extensive or restricted, enormous or diminutive. The Americans make associations to give entertainments, to found establishments for education, to build inns, to construct churches, to diffuse books, to send missionaries to the antipodes; and in this manner they found hospitals, prisons, and schools. If it be proposed to advance some truth, or to foster some feeling by the encouragement of a great example, they form a society. Whereas, at the head of some new undertaking, you see the Govern-

ment in France, or a man of rank in England, in the United States you will be sure to find an association.[9]

Yet during the past three decades, these primary institutions of civic engagement, the seedbeds of American democracy, have undergone decline and decay. The political scientist Robert Putnam offers a small but striking example of this phenomenon. About 80 million Americans went bowling at least once during 1993, nearly a third more than voted in the 1994 congressional elections. But while the number of bowlers has jumped 10 percent since 1980, participation in bowling leagues has dropped 40 percent. More and more, Americans are bowling alone.[10]

In many ways, large and small, millions of Americans have been steadily disengaging from the civil society during the past three decades. For example, the number of people who report having "attended a public meeting on town or school affairs" has dropped by more than one-third since 1973. Voting has declined 25 percent since the early 1960s. Membership in parent-teacher associations has dropped from 12 million Americans in 1964 to 7 million in 1993. Participation in religious services and church-related groups, while still quite high compared to other societies, has declined by about one-sixth since the 1960s. Among nonagricultural workers, union membership has decreased by more than 50 percent since the 1950s. Virtually the entire panoply of major fraternal, women's, and service organizations—from the Red Cross to the Boy Scouts to the Jaycees to the League of Women Voters—has experienced a steady erosion of members and volunteers. To be sure, there are some complicating factors in this story, and even some countervailing facts. But the overall trendline is clearly toward the weakening of voluntary associations and the decline of civic engagement.[11]

These are the developments in the United States. I do not have trendline analyses regarding voluntary associations and civic involvement in other rich countries. But my hypothesis is that, in most societies, family decline will be inextricably linked to the decline of the other institutions of civil society. In addition to the evidence from the United States, there are two theoretical reasons for this hypothesis.

First, the profound societal changes that serve to weaken the family—principally, in my view, the increasingly individualistic cultural values which seem to blossom under conditions of affluence and modernity—are precisely the same forces that serve to erode the rest of the civil society. Second, the family is the first and by far the most important institution of civil society. In this sense, the family is the cradle of the civil society: the essential foundation upon which the rest of the civil society depends. Consequently, a weakening family system almost certainly signals a weakening civil society. In short, as the family goes, so (probably) goes the civil society.[12]

What is the importance of civil society in a modern democracy? Quite simply, it would be hard to overstate its importance. The Australian analyst Barry Maley describes the institutions of the civil society, from married couples to trade unions to sporting associations, as

> centers of moral instruction and forms of discipline and authority divorced from the state and encouraging their own kinds of behavior and characteristic virtues, such as service to others, duty, self-sacrifice and honesty. They are also the best safeguards of liberty, to the extent that their existence and flourishing protects against overwhelming concentration of power.

Maley sums it up with admirable brevity: the civil society consists of "those institutions which transform children into good citizens."[13]

This is the heart of the matter. Civil society turns children into good citizens. Government alone, no matter how well constituted, cannot achieve this goal. The incentives of a free-market economy, as valuable as they are, cannot achieve this goal. Only the family and the other associations of civil society can turn children into good citizens. As the title of this volume suggests, these institutions are our seedbeds of civic virtue—the foundational sources of competence, character, and citizenship in free societies. For this reason, Don E. Eberly calls the mediating structure of civil society "the most important structures for a free people to maintain."[14]

Yet these very structures seem to be decomposing before our

eyes, not despite our growing freedom and affluence, but in many ways because of it. Here we must confront the essential paradox—I would say essential crisis—of the modern liberal state. Put simply, the liberal state presupposes and depends upon social virtues that it cannot create or sustain. Philosophically, those virtues derive, in Europe and America, largely from the Judeo-Christian religious tradition and from traditions of civic republicanism. Institutionally, they reside in, and spring from, the associations of the civil society, especially the family. Liberal polities presuppose these virtues and depend upon these institutions in order to create the good citizens without which self-government is impossible. Yet the liberal polity, almost by definition, is indifferent and at times even hostile to these very virtues and institutions.

Let us be clear. The modern liberal state is probably mankind's greatest achievement of the past two centuries. But, as we seem increasingly to be realizing, it is a fragile and even perishable achievement. We frequently refer to America, probably the greatest exemplar of liberal society, as the "American experiment." Yet as Mary Ann Glendon, Jean Bethke Elshtain, and other contributors to this volume are reminding us, experiments can fail. If the American experiment fails, it will almost certainly be due to this harsh paradox: in a regime based on freedom, the decay of civil society erodes the virtues that make freedom possible.

The Family Debate in the United States

Since at least the early 1970s, policy makers and other opinion leaders in the United States have been engaged in a vigorous and often politically divisive debate over "the family" and "family values." Much of this debate, perhaps inevitably, has been inchoate and at times even silly, as when we have conducted the argument through references to popular television shows. (How do we feel about "Ozzie and Harriet" reruns? Do we approve of "Murphy Brown's" decision to have a baby on her own? Should we build orphanages like the one in the movie "Boys Town"?)

Moreover, too much of the debate, again perhaps inevitably, has been highjacked for narrow political purposes. As a result, in

Washington, D.C., "family policy" remains a term largely unburdened by specific meaning. During presidential election years, especially, "family values" tend to become little more than rhetorical weapons with which candidates seek to bludgeon their opponents.

Yet despite these considerable handicaps, a genuine debate has indeed occurred. Much of the serious debate has revolved around two questions. First, is child well-being declining in the United States? And second, is the family getting weaker or is it just "changing"? At bottom, then, the debate has centered on this central issue: What are the dimensions and consequences of contemporary family change in the United States?

I want to suggest that this debate, so central to U.S. public discourse from the early 1970s through the early 1990s, is now largely over. Or more precisely, I believe that the debate has now entered a new stage, focussing on a fundamentally new question.

The old debate is over because one side won. Especially over the past three or four years, an impressive and growing consensus has emerged among scholars, policy makers, and other opinion leaders from across the political spectrum. Child well-being is declining. The family is weakening. Case closed. More importantly, with a degree of unanimity that would have seemed highly unlikely only a few years ago, opinion leaders now concur that the principal cause of declining child well-being in the U.S. is family fragmentation, or the steady break-up of the mother-father child-raising unit.[15]

The old debate focussed on describing the problem. Is it really a problem? How big is the problem? What caused it? The new debate, now being born, will focus on describing the solution. We know the problem. What are we prepared to do about it? This is the new question that I believe will, or at least ought to, define increasingly the U.S. family debate in the months and years ahead.

On this new question—what is to be done?—I detect almost no consensus among U.S. opinion leaders. Indeed, with important but rare exceptions, I detect very little discussion. We seem to be engaged in a bout of bipartisan hand-wringing over the problem, without, at least yet, devoting much effort at all to proposing serious solutions. But if this prediction is accurate, we may yet have the opportunity for an interesting conversation in the United

States, and perhaps in other nations as well, during the closing years of this century. That conversation will be about the possibility of restoring the civil society.

The Civil Society Strategy

In most of the rich countries, any movement in the coming years to strengthen the civil society must adopt one of three strategies. The first is the welfare state strategy. Although Sweden and the other societies of Scandinavia are probably the best exemplars of this strategy, all of the rich countries have adopted at least some important components of the welfare state model. The basic premise of this strategy is to use the instruments of government to meet human needs, primarily by market place regulations and other public policies aimed at increasing economic security and reducing economic inequality.

As Elshtain puts it: "For most of us in the modern West, the welfare state emerged from a set of ethical concerns and passions that grew as civil society began to succumb to market forces."[16] Her point is important. In many ways, welfare state policies are designed to do, in a much more centralized and forceful manner, precisely what the civil society has historically done and still seeks to do—to limit and at times even to counteract the logic and influence of the free market economy.

A second possible approach to strengthening civil society is the laissez faire strategy. This strategy, of course, is the exact opposite of the welfare state strategy. The welfare state approach seeks to curb the imperialism of the market; laissez faire seeks to curb the imperialism of the state. Where the welfare state model views government as the solution, including the solution to the weakening of civil society, the laissez faire model views government as the problem, including the problem of the weakening of civil society.

From this perspective, the welfare state itself, not the market, is primarily responsible for the weakening of the civil society. By claiming for itself ever more authority over people's lives— authority that otherwise would reside in families and other community associations—the welfare state "crowds out" the civil society, taking away its functions, weakening its structures, and draining its resources, thus gradually turning free citizens into clients of the state.

In the United States, the 1994 congressional elections produced a remarkable, perhaps even historic, victory for the Republican Party. To the degree that the victorious Republicans have offered a policy agenda for the civil society, I believe it is fair to say that their current agenda—aimed largely at cutting taxes and reducing the size of the federal government—reflects an almost unqualified endorsement of this anti-welfare state or laissez faire approach.

Let me state my own preference by suggesting, in a very brief and speculative way, a third possible strategy for invigorating the civil society. Unlike the first two strategies, this third strategy has not yet gained many adherents or even been well articulated. For lack of a better name, let us call it the civil society strategy.

This strategy insists upon the important failures of the welfare state approach. Put simply, whatever its other merits—and there are some important ones—the modern welfare state, as it exists today in most of the rich countries, does very little to sustain, and occasionally a lot to threaten and undermine, the seedbed institutions of the civil society. Moreover, the welfare state simply cannot perform the functions of the civil society. Again, whatever its other merits, the welfare state cannot turn children into good citizens. On this point, the evidence seems clear and decisive.[17]

Yet while limited government is a necessary condition for civil society, it is almost certainly not a sufficient condition. If the welfare state will not turn children into good citizens, it seems equally clear that reducing or even dismantling the welfare state will not, by itself, turn children into good citizens.

Consider the United States. The story of America is the story of freedom—the story of a "sweet land of liberty." Compared to the other rich countries, the U.S. stands out clearly as a lightly governed, lightly regulated society. Yet the U.S. has what is almost certainly the modern world's weakest and most rapidly declining family system. Its larger civil society has been weakening for at least the past three decades. Precisely due to this decay of the civil society, the U.S. is now several decades into a chronic social recession.

If the laissez faire model were sufficient to insure the success of the civil society, the United States would be a very different nation than the nation it is today. Looking to the future in the U.S., will more freedom—less government, lower taxes, fewer regulations, more prosperity—generate a revival of American civil society? I wish that it could. But I do not think that it will. Freedom is very good. But for civil society, freedom is not enough.

My argument, then, is for a third way. Not a strategy based on the programs of the welfare state. Nor a strategy based solely on the incentives of the free market. But instead, a strategy based explicitly on restoring the institutions of the civil society. I cannot offer the blueprint for such a strategy. But I can suggest five principles to shape such a strategy:

1. A primary goal of public policy and private initiative in the coming generation should be to protect and strengthen the civil society.

2. The centerpiece goal of a civil society strategy should be to strengthen marriage as a social institution—to increase the proportion of children who grow up with their two married parents and decrease the proportion who do not.

3. A second goal of a civil society strategy should be to increase the proportion of children who grow up in safe, supportive communities—"natural" communities in which stable families, linked by communal institutions based on shared values, maintain a common life.

4. Regarding any public policy proposal, the first question to ask should be: Will this policy strengthen or weaken the institutions of civil society?

5. Regarding any major societal goal, the first question to ask should be: Can this goal be achieved by utilizing and empowering the institutions of civil society?

Reviving and recreating the civil society is the great challenge for the coming generation of leaders in the modern democracies. Government can play an important role in such a strategy, but much of that role will be limited and indirect. Ultimately, restoring the seedbeds of virtue is not the task of government institutions any more than it is the task of economic institutions. It is a task for a free people who want to become a good society.

Notes

1. David Popenoe, *Disturbing the Nest: Family Change and Decline in Modern Societies* (New York: Aldine de Gruyter, 1988), 295.

2. Ibid., 295–306. See also, Popenoe, "American Family Decline, 1960–1990: A Review and Appraisal," *Journal of Marriage and the Family* 55, no. 3 (August 1993): 527–55.

3. Elizabeth Duskin, "Overview," in *Lone-Parent Families* (Paris: Organization for Economic Cooperation and Development, 1990), 9; Constance Sorrentino, "The changing family in international perspective," *Monthly Labor Review* 113, no. 3 (March 1990): 41–56.

4. David Blankenhorn, *Fatherless America: Confronting Our Most Urgent Social Problem* (New York: Basic Books, 1995), 132, 285n18.

5. Urie Bronfenbrenner, "Discovering What Families Do," in David Blankenhorn, Steven Bayme, and Jean Bethke Elshtain (eds.), *Rebuilding the Nest: A New Commitment to the American Family* (Milwaukee: Family Service America, 1990), 27.

6. William J. Goode, *World Changes in Divorce Patterns* (New Haven: Yale University Press, 1993), 9. Goode describes the "general pattern" of rising divorce rates in Europe as rooted in a "long-term tendency for individuals to seek their own interests and happiness rather than to stay married for the sake of their children or the interests of 'the family' " (p. 25).

7. Peter L. Berger and Richard John Neuhaus, *To Empower People: The Role of Mediating Structures in Public Policy* (Washington, D.C.: AEI Press, 1977); Robert D. Putnam, "Bowling Alone: America's Declining Social Capital," *Journal of Democracy* 6, no. 1 (January 1995): 66.

8. Jean Bethke Elshtain, *Democracy on Trial* (New York: Basic Books, 1995), 5–6.

9. Alexis de Tocqueville, *Democracy in America*, Vol. II (New York: Schocken Books, 1961), 128–29.

10. Putnam, "Bowling Alone," 70.

11. Ibid., 67–73.

12. Numerous analysts in the U.S. have proposed that we look to "community networks" to address problems stemming from family fragmentation. From this perspective, we need not worry much about the spread of one-parent homes, for example, since single mothers and their

children can (at least theoretically) find the "support systems" they need from the surrounding community.

But this analysis simply ducks the issue. A viable community presupposes, and depends upon, a viable family system. Only wishful thinking permits us to suppose that we can watch the family unit decline while simultaneously keeping and even strengthening the rest of the civil society.

13. Barry Maley, "Morals and Modernity," in David Popenoe, Andrew Norton, and Barry Maley, *Shaping the Social Virtues* (St. Leonards, Australia: Center for Independent Studies, 1994), 96, 105.

14. Don E. Eberly, *Restoring the Good Society: A New Vision for Politics and Culture* (Grand Rapids, MI: Baker Books, 1994), 103.

15. I admit that my colleagues and I have been participants in this debate at least as much as observers of it. So perhaps my judgement is clouded. Yet my assessment of the debate—and especially my view of who won and who lost what I am calling the old debate—is widely shared even by those who "lost" and who therefore do not agree with me about much of anything else. For example, see Judith Stacey, "Scents, Scholars, and Stigma: The Revisionist Campaign for Family Values," *Social Text* 12, no. 3 (Fall 1994): 51–75; Arlene Skolnick and Stacey Rosencrantz, "The New Crusade for the Old Family," *American Prospect*, no. 18 (Summer 1994): 59–65; and Ellen Willis, "Why I'm Not 'Pro-Family,' " *Glamour* (October 1994): 150–53. For an assessment of this subject from President Clinton's Deputy Assistant for Domestic Public Policy, see William A. Galston, "Beyond the Murphy Brown Debate" (New York: Institute for American Values, December 1993).

16. Elshtain, *Democracy on Trial*, 17.

17. More broadly, across the world, highly centralized, relatively inflexible bureaucratic structures—whether administered by elected governments, communist parties, or multinational corporations—are facing increasing pressure to either reform themselves or become extinct.

Index

Contributors

J. Brian Benestad is Professor of Theology at the University of Scranton, the Jesuit university of Northeastern Pennsylvania. He recently contributed an article to *Liberalism at the Crossroads,* entitled "William Galston's Defense of Liberalism: Forging Unity Amid Diversity." He is also editing a three-volume collection of articles written by Professor Ernest Fortin of Boston College.

David Blankenhorn is president of the Institute for American Values, a private, nonpartisan organization in New York City devoted to research, publication, and public education on issues of family well-being and the civil society. He is the author of *Fatherless America: Confronting Our Most Urgent Social Problem* and the chief editor of *Rebuilding the Nest: A New Commitment to the American Family.*

Don S. Browning is the Alexander Campbell Professor of Religious Ethics and the Social Sciences at the Divinity School of the University of Chicago and director of the Religion, Culture, and Family Project, funded by the Lilly Endowment, Inc. He is the author most recently of the books *Religious Thought and the Modern Psychologies* and *A Fundamental Practical Theology.*

Jean Bethke Elshtain is the Laura Spelman Rockefeller Professor of Social and Political Ethics at the University of Chicago and the author of numerous books and essays on women, politics, and the family. She was a Guggenheim Fellow in 1991–1992. Her books include *Public Man, Private Woman, Women and War,* and *Democracy on Trial.*

William A. Galston is Professor at the School of Public Affairs, University of Maryland at College Park, and Senior Research Scholar at the University's Institute for Philosophy and Public Policy. From January 1993 until May 1995 he served as Deputy Assistant to the President for Domestic Policy. Professor Galston is the author of five books and numerous articles on American politics, public policy, political theory, and family issues in the United States, most recently *Liberal Purposes* and *Virtue*.

Mary Ann Glendon is Learned Hand Professor of Law at Harvard University Law School and one of the nation's leading scholars in the field of comparative law. Profiled in Bill Moyers' "World of Ideas" television series, Professor Glendon is the author of *Abortion and Divorce in Western Law*, *The Transformation of Family Law*, *Rights Talk: The Impoverishment of Political Discourse*, and *A Nation Under Lawyers*.

Stanley Hauerwas is Gilbert T. Rowe Professor of Theological Ethics at the Divinity School, Duke University. His most recent book is *Dispatches from the Front: Theological Engagements with the Secular*.

Thomas C. Kohler is Professor of Law at Boston College Law School and has also taught at Columbia University's Graduate School of Business as a visiting member of its faculty. He is a well-known scholar in the field of labor and employment law. He also has written extensively on issues in comparative law, social theory, and mediating groups and their treatment in American law. At present (1995–96), he is a Fulbright Lecturer and a German Marshall Fund Research Fellow at the Institut für Arbeitsrecht, Johann Wolfgang Goethe Universität, in Frankfurt, Germany.

Judith Martin, also known as Miss Manners, writes a nationally syndicated column and books on etiquette, including *Miss Manners' Guide for the Turn-of-the-Millennium*.

David Popenoe is Professor of Sociology and Associate Dean of the Faculty of Arts and Sciences at Rutgers University. Co-Chair of the Council on Families in America, his most recent book is *Life Without Father: Compelling New Evidence that Fatherhood and Marriage Are Indispensable for the Good of Children and Society*.

William M. Sullivan is Professor of Philosophy at LaSalle University. He is author, most recently, of *Work and Integrity: The Crisis and Promise of Professionalism in America* and co-author of *Habits of the Heart* and *The Good Society*.

James Q. Wilson is the Collins Professor of Management and Public Policy at UCLA. Previously, he was Shattuck Professor of Government at Harvard University. He is the author of *The Moral Sense, Crime and Human Nature* (with Richard J. Herrnstein), and *On Character*.

Alan Wolfe is University Professor and Professor of Sociology and Political Science at Boston University. He is the author of numerous books, among them *The Human Difference: Animals, Computers, and the Necessity of Social Science* and *Whose Keeper?: Social Science and Moral Obligation*. Besides his scholarly writings, his essays and reviews appear regularly in *The New Republic*, *The Wilson Quarterly*, *Harper's*, *The Washington Post*, and the *New York Times*. He is currently writing a book about middle class morality.